Rita Mei-Wah Choy

Read And Write Chinese

A Simplified Guide To The Chinese Characters

With
Cantonese and Mandarin Pronunciation
Yale and Pinyin Romanization

12-03-10

Read And Write Chinese
by Rita Mei-Wah Choy

Fifth Edition
Copyright © 1990 by
Rita Choy Hirschberg

Published by China West Books
P. O. Box 2804
San Francisco, California 94126

Printed in the United States of America

ISBN 0-941340-11-2

Other Books by the Author:
Understanding Chinese
Chinese Conversation
Practical Mandarin
The Citizenship Manual

To Paul, Jonathan and Toviah

ACKNOWLEDGEMENT

I am indebted to a number of people for their generous assistance in preparing this book.

Thanks go to my husband, Paul, for his assistance in preparing the introductory material and editing the English translations; to my father, John H.F. Choy, for consultations on the characters; and to my brothers Johnston and Kingston Choy, for their wizardry with the computer.

TABLE OF CONTENTS

INTRODUCTION

This book originated from a course we were giving in Chinese characters. The students, after mastering their first characters, soon found a need for a Chinese dictionary so that they could determine the meaning and pronunciation of new words they were encountering on signs and in newspapers. However, to their dismay they found that Chinese dictionaries are difficult to use. There is too much information for the beginning and intermediate student; words are difficult to locate; pronunciations are not usually given in Cantonese; and often the English definitions are not necessarily correct or appropriate.

To illustrate how cumbersome a Chinese dictionary is for a student, consider that a good one contains 7,000 or more characters, whereas only about 2,400 are commonly used. In a study done by Chen Hegin, it was found that if you were to learn the 800 characters that appear the most frequently in Chinese publications, you would know about 86% of all the characters you will see. Doubling your vocabulary to 1,600 would take you to 95% recognition. Doubling again to 3,200 gives about 99%. The remaining 4,000 characters provide only 1% more comprehension. This excessive number of characters in the dictionary makes it difficult to find the desired character.

The purpose of this book is to provide a handy, easy to use reference that lists the 3,200 most useful characters and gives the English definitions, Mandarin pronunciation in Pinyin romanization, Cantonese pronunciation in Yale romanization, and the writing stroke order for each. In this, the fifth edition, we have added 270 characters so that all of the characters on the official list for adult education in China are included. We have also added three more cross-reference indexes: Chinese by number of strokes, Mandarin romanization and Cantonese romanization, to make it easier to locate the word that you want. And, as an aid to self study, we have indicated the relative importance of each character so that you can prioritize your learning.

The book is laid out in the following manner: first, an explanation of the listings and how to use the book; then, a section of background information on Chinese characters; followed by a pronunciation guide; then the table of radicals; the main text; then finally, the four cross-reference indexes.

HOW TO USE THIS BOOK

Explanation of Character Listings

For each character the following information is given:

Num. Freq.	Char.	Stroke Order for Writing	English Definition
			Cant. Roman. *Mand. Roman.*

Number is a character number used to aid in cross-reference indexing.

Frequency is an indicator of the relative frequency of occurance of the character in printed matter, and therefore an indicator of the character's importance:

    *** - Very important. The 300 most frequently used characters. These make up 65% of printed materials.

    ** - Important. 700 additional characters which together with the first group account for 88% of the characters in printed materials.

    * - For reference. 2,210 additional characters which account for 99%.

At the back of the book there is a complete listing of the *** and ** characters.

Character is the common printed script form of the character.

Stroke Order provides the proper order of the strokes which should be followed to write the character correctly.

English Definitions provides the most common definitions for the character. A comma separates definitions of the same part of speech; a semi-colon separates definitions of different parts of speech. Verbs are given in the infinitive form unless following another verb (separated by a comma). Nouns omit the article (a).

Cantonese Pronunciation is the Cantonese pronunciation using the Yale Romanization system. Refer to the pronunciation section of this book for more information.

Mandarin Pronunciation is the Mandarin pronunciation using the Pinyin Romanization system. A comparison chart between Pinyin and other romanization systems is given in the pronunciation section.

In the case of multiple definitions and/or pronunciations, superscript numbers denote the corresponding definitions and pronunciations.

How To Find A Character

The characters are listed by radical. Within each radical section, the characters are listed by number of strokes (not including the radical). Thus, to locate a word, first determine the radical as discussed in the section on radicals. Then, refer to the radical index on P. 31 to find the location of that radical's section. Then, count the number of remaining strokes. The top of each page shows the radical section and the range of number of strokes of the words on that page.

There are other ways to locate words. There are four cross-reference indexes: by Chinese character, English definition, Cantonese romanization and Mandarin romanization. The Chinese Character Index lists all the characters by total number of strokes, which is useful when the radical is difficult to determine. Next to each character is a character number. The characters are listed sequentially by character number throughout the book.

Suggestions For Study

If you are a beginning student and would like to teach yourself a few useful characters, concentrate on the ones with three stars (***). We suggest learning no more than 10 new characters per day. Each day, write out your new characters several times. Review the characters you learned in the previous days. Pronounce the words out loud in the dialect of your choice.

After you have some familiarity with a large number of characters it will become important that you notice how each character is used in combination with others. As described in the section "Notes on Character Meanings", how characters are used in combinations can profoundly affect their meaning. A good book to obtain to help you understand combinations is Understanding Chinese, by the same author and publisher. This book gives definitions and pronunciation of the most useful combinations made from 800 most commonly used characters. It also contains a section on simplified Chinese grammar as well as lists of useful short phrases and words by subject area.

Your understanding of Chinese characters will also be greatly enhanced

by taking a course in Mandarin. Having a general idea of sentence struct-
ure will make it easier to interpret the printed materials that you encounter.

To aid in learning the correct pronunciation of the characters, audio cassette tapes are available which contain the pronunciation of the characters in
this book in both Mandarin and Cantonese. The tapes are available from
China West Books at the address on page 2.

ABOUT CHINESE CHARACTERS

Development of the Characters

Unlike Western languages, Chinese does not have an alphabet, per se.
Each character, while pronounced as a single syllable, generally represents
a whole word. Often two or three characters are combined to express non-
basic words. Actually, each character is really a picture; many can be traced
back to early picture forms. The shapes of these characters have evolved
over a long period of time, to some extent due to developments in writing
implements. The early picture forms were drawings of objects, animals, or
nature. Here are some examples:

Modern Form	Meaning	Early Form
目	eye	～
日	sun	☉
水	water	川
山	hill	⩜
門	door	ⴹⴺ
車	car	ⵟ
月	moon	ⅅ

Most characters, however, do not directly descend from the pictures of
their meanings; they are composed of a combination of basic pictures that
may or may not have any apparent relationship to their meaning. Sometimes they contain one of the basic pictures simply because the character
sounds like the sound of that picture's character.

The Chinese language has over forty thousand characters. Many of these are formal, literary words that are found only in operas, poems and old books, and are seldom encountered in daily use. A reasonably educated person in China will have a vocabulary of about 5,000; typewriters carry about 7,000, and dictionaries between 7,000-10,000. Fortunately, you need to learn only the 800 most common ones to understand about 85% of what you will encounter. The 3,200 in this book will give you 99% comprehension.

Radicals - The Elements of Chinese Characters

Although there is no alphabet in Chinese, learning characters is not as difficult as requiring memorization of up to 20 random strokes. Rather, a character is made up of one or more basic elements, known as radicals. A radical is a group of strokes that generally descends from a basic word and appears in many other words. For example,

the Word	is Composed of	
好 good	女 female	子 son, male
明 clear	日 sun	月 moon

Strictly speaking, there is only one radical per character, which is the element that is most prominent and the one by which the word is listed in the dictionary. However, as you become familiar with Chinese you will notice that characters are generally composed of 2-4 of these elements.

Here is another example:

the Word	is Composed of		
想 to think	木 wood	目 eye	心 heart

The character is listed under the heart radical. Other words with the heart radical will generally have something to do with the heart, for example:

忌	fear	恩	kindness
恕	to excuse	怒	angry

Similarly, words having the radical 亻 , which is man, will have something to do with people; characters with 木 , which is wood, will be related to wood, etc. Sometimes a radical will be present in a word only for its sound; that is, the pronunciation of the character may be similar to that of the radical but the meaning has no relationship.

As you look through the section of the book with the characters having the heart radical, you will notice that some of the characters do not contain 心 but rather 忄 . This is because some radicals take on different forms when in different positions in the character. The heart radical is written 心 when at the bottom of a character but as 忄 when on the left side. A number of other radicals change form, for example:

	At top, bottom	At side
man	人	亻
water	水	氵
fire	灬	火
wood	木	木

The radical index (p. 31) shows all of the alternate forms of radicals. The size of the radical will also change according to its position in the character in order to fit its shape.

Determining the Primary Radical of a Character

Recognition of radicals is important for two reasons. First, it is much easier to learn characters by thinking "man + bird + mouth" than by memorizing 15 strokes. And second, most dictionaries list entries by their primary radical. However, it is often not obvious which is the radical of a character. Here are some tips which will help you determine it, in most cases:

First, break up the character into its elements:

(1) 想 → 品	(2) 但 → 唱
(3) 姐 → 川	(4) 台 → 吕

In case (1), the larger portion, the bottom half, is the radical.

In case (2), the larger portion, the left half, will be the radical.

In case (3), if there are equal size parts, the one on the left will be the radical.

In case (4), the one which is the most common will be the radical.

Certain very common elements, when present in a character, will almost always be the radical. These are:

Thus, the radical of 台 is 口 ; the radical of 划 is 刂 ; the radical of 這 is 辶 , etc.

Using a Dictionary

The most common method for arranging characters in a dictionary is by radical. To use such a dictionary, as well as this book, use the following procedure:

1. Determine the radical of the character that you are looking for.

2. Count the number of strokes in the radical.

3. Look in the radical table (index by radical) under that number of strokes and find your radical.

4. All of the characters having that radical will be grouped in the same section of the dictionary. Count the number of remaining strokes in the desired character.

5. Look at the tops of the pages in that section of the dictionary for the number of remaining strokes to locate the character.

Some dictionaries provide a glossary to help you determine which is the radical. Others use alternative systems for organizing the characters, such as the "Bing" System. With the Bing System you must determine which is the first stroke used in writing the character. You turn to this section, then determine which is the second writing stroke. After turning to that subsection, you count the remaining number of strokes and the words are arranged by ascending number of strokes. The reason it is called Bing is that the character "Bing" has one of each type of stroke:

the Character "Bing"	Stroke no.	Name of Stroke	Stroke
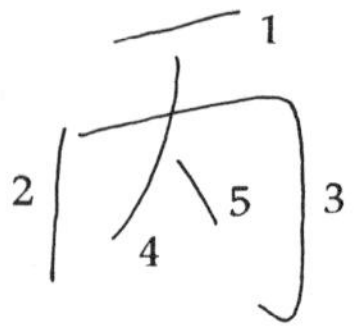	1	horizontal	一
	2	vertical	丨
	3	corner	㇇ ㇆
	4	diagonal	丿
	5	dot	丶

This system has the advantage that it is often easier to determine the first stroke than the radical.

There is a Chinese Phonetic Alphabet that is used in many dictionaries to show the user how to pronounce the word (in Mandarin). In this book there is an explanation of this phonetic alphabet, CNPA, in the Mandarin pronunciation tables.

Alternate Forms of the Characters

Mainland China has been developing a set of simplified characters in an attempt to improve literacy. Many characters have a simplified form already in common use. An example is the word for "side":

Long Form	邊
Simplifed Form	边

A complete list of the simplified forms is beyond the scope of this book; entire dictionaries are devoted to the subject. The simplified forms are not used in Taiwan and are only occasionally used in Hong Kong and the United States.

There are also variations in the printed forms of the characters. Each character has six different forms according to the style of printing:

張	Square
張	Printed Script
张	Handwritten Script
张	Grass
張	Banner
張	Seal

The first is the printed "Square", also known as Sun dynasty form. It is found in telephone books, newspapers, and books. The second is Printed Script, which is the type style used in this book. The third, Handwritten Script, is how characters are hand written in correspondence. The fourth, Grass, is a free-flowing, artistic style which is not as easily readable, and is found on paintings. The fifth, Banner, is used on large banners. The sixth, Seal, is used in making seals with a person's name.

Sometimes there will be a variation between printed forms of characters. For example, the word for "for" can be found as either 為 or 為 . Both are correct.

Calligraphy

Calligraphy, or beautiful writing, is very important in Chinese. No matter how simple or complex the character may look, there is a pattern that should be followed in order to write the character correctly. Chinese stresses beauty and balance. If the character's strokes are not written in the proper sequence, the character will look lopsided.

Characters should be written from top to bottom and from left to right. For example:

If any strokes are to be enclosed in a box they should be written before the box is closed:

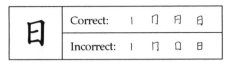

When a character has several horizontal strokes which are pierced by a long vertical stroke, the vertical stroke is written last:

The radical ⻌ , although appearing on the left side of characters, is written last as it encloses the other strokes on two sides:

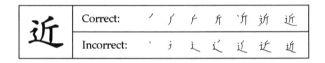

There are eight basic strokes in writing characters. These are:

Stroke	丶	一	丨	亅	-	/	ノ	乀
Example	永	大	中	永	永	永	永	永

When writing with a brush, the calligrapher will put emphasis on certain parts of the stroke:

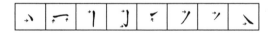

Similarly, there are places in each stroke where thin, sharp points should be left:

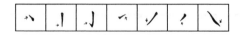

This varying of pressure on the brush is the way that the calligrapher expresses himself and adds to the beauty of Chinese characters. Of course, good calligraphy requires practice. School children use "nine-square-box" paper to imitate samples of good calligraphy and to practice balance:

Layout of Printed Material

Chinese text is usually laid out vertically from top to bottom, with lines progressing from right to left:

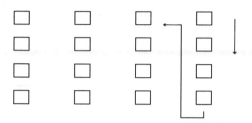

Chinese books are therefore read, from the Western point of view, from back to front. However, Chinese is often written horizontally, for example on signs and in materials published in Western countries. In such a case the characters are written from left to right.

Chinese Dialects

Throughout history, poor communications and lack of good transportation in China, along with its rugged, far flung terrain resulted in many areas of China being isolated from each other. The spoken language in the various areas developed and maintained significant differences which we now call dialects. The differences between the dialects are great enough that speakers of different dialects often cannot understand each other. Fortunately, the written language is generally the same everywhere and is thus the unifying means of communication throughout China. The two most important dialects today are Mandarin and Cantonese. Mandarin originated in Northern China while Cantonese originated in the south.

In order to solve the problem of many dialects impairing oral communication, the government of mainland China declared Mandarin as the official dialect of China and required everyone to learn it. Mandarin is also spoken in Taiwan. Cantonese is still spoken in the Canton province of China, and is the dialect of Hong Kong, Singapore, and Macau. Cantonese is also spoken by the vast majority of Chinese people that have emigrated from

China to the U.S., Great Britain, Canada, and Southeast Asia. Within Cantonese there are sub-dialects such as Toih Saan, Sun Wuih and Hoi Peng. Other important Chinese dialects include Shanghai, Fukkein, Mongolian and Junshai. In this book we provide pronunciations for all words in Mandarin and Cantonese.

Notes on Character Meanings

The written language is patterned after the Mandarin dialect. There are some words in Cantonese for which there are no formal characters. As a result, characters have been created to enable these words to be written. Here are some examples:

Word	Cantonese	Definition
咗	*jó*	past tense
冇	*móuh*	none
係	*haih*	is
嘅	*ge*	possessive "s"
唔	*m̀h*	not
哋	*deih*	plural
啱	*ngàam*	correct
咁	*gám*	so
乜	*màt*	what
嘢	*yéh*	thing

In Chinese, the way characters are used in combination critically affects their meaning. For example, when a noun character is repeated it means "all of":

人	person	人人	everybody
次	time	次次	every time

When opposites are put together, the result is:

大 big	大小 size
小 small	
快 fast	快慢 speed
慢 slow	

When an adjective character is repeated, it means "very":

好	good	好好	very good
快	fast	快快	very fast

Many words are formed by two or more characters. Examples are:

Character	Definition
已經	already
所以	therefore
除非	unless
生意	business
出世	to be born
打理	look after

The subject of character combinations is very important and is treated in detail in <u>Understanding Chinese</u>, by the same author.

Guide to Pronunciation

In an effort to convey the correct pronunciation of Chinese, several romanization systems have been developed, each with its own merits. For Mandarin we have used the Pinyin system, which is the official romanization system of Mainland China. For the benefit of those familiar with other systems, we have included a chart that converts Pinyin into the Yale, Wade-Giles and the Chinese phonetic alphabet (CNPA) systems. For Cantonese this book uses the Yale system, which is the most universally used system. Of critical importance in Chinese are the tones with which the words are pronounced. Chinese words are mono-syllables, and many of the English consonants do not exist in Chinese. Due to the limited possibilities for making words, each word is spoken in a specific tone, or vocal inflection. If the word is pronounced with the wrong tone, it will be heard as a different word. This section includes tone tables for each of the dialects. It will be very beneficial to practice speaking the tones out loud, and to always pronounce words with the correct tone.

The following charts are presented to aid your understanding of Chinese pronunciation:

1. For Cantonese:

    a. Yale romanization and English equivalents
    b. Tone chart

2. For Mandarin:

    a. Pinyin romanization and English equivalents, compared with Yale romanization and Chinese Phonetic Alphabet, for the individual sound-elements

    b. Comparison of Pinyin, Yale, and CNPA for all possible word sounds

    c. Tone chart

1. Cantonese

Yale to English

Initials	As in English
b	b
ch	ch
d	d
f	f
g	g
h	h
j	j
k	k
l	l
m	m
n	n
p	p
s	s
t	t
w	w
y	y
gw	g + w
kw	qu in squat
ng	ng in king

Finals		As in English	
Short	Long		
a		a	in father
ai	*aai*	ai	in eye
ak	*aak*	ock	in lock
am	*aam*	om	in bomb
an	*aan*	on	in gone
ang	*aang*	ong	in gong
ap	*aap*	op	in operate
at	*aat*	ot	in cot
au	*aau*	ow	in how
e		ea	in measure
ei		ay	in bay
ek		eck	in neck
eng		eng	in bengal
eu		ork	in work - rk
eui		o	in work + e in seen
euk		ork	in work - r
eun		o	in work + n

Finals	As in English
eung	o in work + ng in king
eut	o in work + t
i	ee in see
ik	ick in lick
im	eem in seem
in	een in seen
ing	ing in king
ip	eep in weep
it	eat
iu	ew in few
o	aw in crawl
oi	oy in boy
ok	alk in talk
on	awn in lawn
ong	ong in long
ot	ought
ou	o in two
u	oo in zoo
ui	ooey in phooey
uk	uke in duke
un	une in tune
ung	oon in soon + g
ut	oot in boot
yu	you
yun	y + une in tune
yut	you + it

Tone Chart

The system presented in this book is a "modified-Yale" system. It uses six tones, instead of Yale's seven, combining the high level tone with the high falling, as these are virtually indistinguishable. An *h* after the last vowel in a Final denotes the lower tones. Although Yale does not use the *h* for words beginning with *m*, *n*, or *ng*, for simplicity this book will use the *h* with all initials.

Name of Tone	Symbol	*Pitch Diagram	Example
High Falling	`	5 4 3 2 1	分 *fàn*
High Rising	´	5 4 3 2 1	粉 *fán*
Middle Level	none	5 4 3 2 1	訓 *fan*
Low Falling	h̀	5 4 3 2 1	焚 *fàhn*
Low Rising	h́	5 4 3 2 1	憤 *fáhn*
Low Level	h	5 4 3 2 1	份 *fahn*

* 5 - highest pitch

2. Mandarin

Comparison of Romanizations

The following two tables give a comprehensive list of all of the possible word-sounds that exist in Mandarin. For each word-sound, the tables compare the two most popular Mandarin romanization systems, Pinyin and Yale, the Chinese National Phonetic Alphabet (CNPA), and the English pronunciation. Table (A) lists the elements used in building words; Table (B) lists all of the combinations of these elements, in effect all the word sounds, of Mandarin. For words with two syllables, the accent is on the last one. The lists are keyed to Pinyin, which is the romanization used in this book.

Table A

Pinyin	Yale	CNPA	As in English
b	b	ㄅ	b
c	ts	ㄘ	ts in its
ch	ch	ㄔ	ch
d	d	ㄉ	d
f	f	ㄈ	f
g	g	ㄍ	g
h	h	ㄏ	h
j	j (ji/jy)	ㄐ	j
k	k	ㄎ	k
l	l	ㄌ	l
m	m	ㄇ	m
n	n	ㄋ	n
p	p	ㄆ	p
q	ch (chi/chy)	ㄑ	ch
r	r	ㄖ	r
s	s	ㄙ	s
sh	sh	ㄕ	sh
t	t	ㄊ	t
w	w	ㄨ	w
x	sy	ㄒ	sh + y
yh	y	ㄧ	y
z	dz	ㄗ	d + z
zh	j	ㄓ	j

Pinyin	Yale	CNPA	As in English
a	a	ㄚ	a in father·
ai	ai	ㄞ	i in rise
an	an	ㄢ	on in honest
ang	ang	ㄤ	ong in gong
ao	au	ㄠ	ow in cow
ê (ie)	e (ye)	ㄝ	ea in pleasure
e	e	ㄜ	a in affection
ei	ei	ㄟ	ay in pay
en	en	ㄣ	un in fun
eng	eng	ㄥ	ung in lung
er	er	ㄦ	er in mother
i	i	ㄧ	ea in tea
ia	ya	ㄧㄚ	ea in tea + a in father
ian	yan	ㄧㄢ	ea in tea + en in fence
iang	yang	ㄧㄤ	ea in tea + ong in gong
iao	yau	ㄧㄠ	ea in tea + ow in cow
ie	ye	ㄧㄝ	ea in pleasure
in	in	ㄧㄣ	ean in bean
ing	ing	ㄧㄥ	ing in king
iong	yung	ㄩㄥ	ea in tea + own + g
iu	you	ㄧㄡ	ea in tea + you
o	o	ㄛ	o in coffee
ong	ung	ㄨㄥ	own + g
ou	ou	ㄡ	o in go
u	u	ㄨ	oo in cool
ü	yu	ㄩ	you + e in she
ua	wa	ㄨㄚ	oo in cool + a in father
uai	wai	ㄨㄞ	oo in cool + i in rise
uan	wan	ㄨㄢ	oo in cool + on in honest
üan	ywan	ㄩㄢ	you + e in she + en in fence
uang	wang	ㄨㄤ	oo in cool + ong in gong
üe	ywe	ㄩㄝ	you + e in she + ea in pleasure
ui	wei	ㄨㄟ	oo in cool + ay in pay
un	wun	ㄨㄣ	oo in cool + oon in moon
ün	yun	ㄩㄣ	you + e in she + ean in bean
uo	wo	ㄨㄛ	oo in cool + o in coffee

Table B

Pinyin	Yale	CNPA
a	a	ㄚ
ai	ai	ㄞ
an	an	ㄢ
ang	ang	ㄤ
ao	au	ㄠ
ba	ba	ㄅㄚ
bai	bai	ㄅㄞ
ban	ban	ㄅㄢ
bang	bang	ㄅㄤ
bao	bau	ㄅㄠ
bei	bei	ㄅㄟ
ben	ben	ㄅㄣ
beng	beng	ㄅㄥ
bi	bi	ㄅㄧ
bian	byan	ㄅㄧㄢ
biao	byau	ㄅㄧㄠ
bie	bye	ㄅㄧㄝ
bin	bin	ㄅㄧㄣ
bing	bing	ㄅㄧㄥ
bo	bo	ㄅㄛ
bu	bu	ㄅㄨ
ca	tsa	ㄘㄚ
cai	tsai	ㄘㄞ
can	tsan	ㄘㄢ
cang	tsang	ㄘㄤ
cao	tsau	ㄘㄠ
ce	tse	ㄘㄜ
cen	tsen	ㄘㄣ
ceng	tseng	ㄘㄥ
cha	cha	ㄔㄚ
chai	chai	ㄔㄞ
chan	chan	ㄔㄢ
chang	chang	ㄔㄤ
chao	chau	ㄔㄠ
che	che	ㄔㄜ
chen	chen	ㄔㄣ
cheng	cheng	ㄔㄥ
chi	chr	ㄔ
chong	chung	ㄔㄨㄥ
chou	chou	ㄔㄡ
chu	chu	ㄔㄨ
chua	chwa	ㄔㄨㄚ
chuai	chwai	ㄔㄨㄞ
chuan	chwan	ㄔㄨㄢ
chuang	chwang	ㄔㄨㄤ
chui	chwei	ㄔㄨㄟ
chun	chwun	ㄔㄨㄣ
chuo	chwo	ㄔㄨㄛ
ci	tse	ㄘ
cong	tsung	ㄘㄨㄥ
cou	tsou	ㄘㄡ
cu	tsu	ㄘㄨ
cuan	tswan	ㄘㄨㄢ
cui	tswei	ㄘㄨㄟ
cun	tswun	ㄘㄨㄣ
cuo	tswo	ㄘㄨㄛ
da	da	ㄉㄚ
dai	dai	ㄉㄞ
dan	dan	ㄉㄢ
dang	dang	ㄉㄤ
dao	dau	ㄉㄠ
de	de	ㄉㄜ
dei	dei	ㄉㄟ
den	den	ㄉㄣ
deng	deng	ㄉㄥ
di	di	ㄉㄧ
dian	dyan	ㄉㄧㄢ
diao	dyau	ㄉㄧㄠ
die	dye	ㄉㄧㄝ
ding	ding	ㄉㄧㄥ
diu	dyou	ㄉㄧㄡ
dong	dung	ㄉㄨㄥ
dou	dou	ㄉㄡ
du	du	ㄉㄨ
duan	dwan	ㄉㄨㄢ
dui	dwei	ㄉㄨㄟ
dun	dwun	ㄉㄨㄣ
duo	dwo	ㄉㄨㄛ
e	e	ㄜ
ei	ei	ㄟ
en	en	ㄣ
er	er	ㄦ
fa	fa	ㄈㄚ
fan	fan	ㄈㄢ
fang	fang	ㄈㄤ
fei	fei	ㄈㄟ
fen	fen	ㄈㄣ
feng	feng	ㄈㄥ
fo	fo	ㄈㄛ
fou	fou	ㄈㄡ
fu	fu	ㄈㄨ
ga	ga	ㄍㄚ
gai	gai	ㄍㄞ
gan	gan	ㄍㄢ

Pinyin	Yale	CNPA
gang	gang	ㄍㄤ
gao	gau	ㄍㄠ
ge	ge	ㄍㄜ
gei	gei	ㄍㄟ
gen	gen	ㄍㄣ
geng	geng	ㄍㄥ
gong	gung	ㄍㄨㄥ
gou	gou	ㄍㄡ
gu	gu	ㄍㄨ
gua	gwa	ㄍㄨㄚ
guai	gwai	ㄍㄨㄞ
guan	gwan	ㄍㄨㄢ
guang	gwang	ㄍㄨㄤ
gui	gwei	ㄍㄨㄟ
gun	gwun	ㄍㄨㄣ
guo	gwo	ㄍㄨㄛ
ha	ha	ㄏㄚ
hai	hai	ㄏㄞ
han	han	ㄏㄢ
hang	hang	ㄏㄤ
hao	hau	ㄏㄠ
he	he	ㄏㄜ
hei	hei	ㄏㄟ
hen	hen	ㄏㄣ
heng	heng	ㄏㄥ
hong	hung	ㄏㄨㄥ
hou	hou	ㄏㄡ
hu	hu	ㄏㄨ
hua	hwa	ㄏㄨㄚ
huai	hwai	ㄏㄨㄞ
huan	hwan	ㄏㄨㄢ
huang	hwang	ㄏㄨㄤ
hui	hwei	ㄏㄨㄟ
hun	hwun	ㄏㄨㄣ
huo	hwo	ㄏㄨㄛ
ji	ji	ㄐㄧ
jia	jya	ㄐㄧㄚ
jian	jyan	ㄐㄧㄢ
jiang	jyang	ㄐㄧㄤ
jiao	jyau	ㄐㄧㄠ
jie	jye	ㄐㄧㄝ
jin	jin	ㄐㄧㄣ
jing	jing	ㄐㄧㄥ
jiong	jyung	ㄐㄩㄥ
jiu	jyou	ㄐㄧㄡ
ju	jyu	ㄐㄩ
juan	jywan	ㄐㄩㄢ
jue	jywe	ㄐㄩㄝ
jun	jyun	ㄐㄩㄣ
ka	ka	ㄎㄚ
kai	kai	ㄎㄞ
kan	kan	ㄎㄢ
kang	kang	ㄎㄤ
kao	kau	ㄎㄠ
ke	ke	ㄎㄜ
ken	ken	ㄎㄣ
keng	keng	ㄎㄥ
kong	kung	ㄎㄨㄥ
kou	kou	ㄎㄡ
ku	ku	ㄎㄨ
kua	kwa	ㄎㄨㄚ
kuai	kwai	ㄎㄨㄞ
kuan	kwan	ㄎㄨㄢ
kuang	kwang	ㄎㄨㄤ
kui	kwei	ㄎㄨㄟ
kun	kwun	ㄎㄨㄣ
kuo	kwo	ㄎㄨㄛ
la	la	ㄌㄚ
lai	lai	ㄌㄞ
lan	lan	ㄌㄢ
lang	lang	ㄌㄤ
lao	lau	ㄌㄠ
le	le	ㄌㄜ
lei	lei	ㄌㄟ
leng	leng	ㄌㄥ
li	li	ㄌㄧ
lia	lya	ㄌㄧㄚ
lian	lyan	ㄌㄧㄢ
liang	lyang	ㄌㄧㄤ
liao	lyau	ㄌㄧㄠ
lie	lye	ㄌㄧㄝ
lin	lin	ㄌㄧㄣ
ling	ling	ㄌㄧㄥ
liu	lyou	ㄌㄧㄡ
long	lung	ㄌㄨㄥ
lou	lou	ㄌㄡ
lu	lu	ㄌㄨ
lü	lyu	ㄌㄩ
luan	lwan	ㄌㄨㄢ
lüan	lywan	ㄌㄩㄢ
lüe	lywe	ㄌㄩㄝ
lun	lwun	ㄌㄨㄣ
lün	lyun	ㄌㄩㄣ
luo	lwo	ㄌㄨㄛ
ma	ma	ㄇㄚ
mai	mai	ㄇㄞ
man	man	ㄇㄢ
mang	mang	ㄇㄤ
mao	mau	ㄇㄠ
me	me	ㄇㄜ

Pinyin	Yale	CNPA
mei	mei	ㄇㄟˋ
men	men	ㄇㄣˊ
meng	meng	ㄇㄥˊ
mi	mi	ㄇㄧ
mian	myan	ㄇㄧㄢ
miao	myau	ㄇㄧㄠ
mie	mye	ㄇㄧㄝ
min	min	ㄇㄧㄣ
ming	ming	ㄇㄧㄥ
miu	myou	ㄇㄧㄡ
mo	mo	ㄇㄛ
mou	mou	ㄇㄡ
mu	mu	ㄇㄨ
na	na	ㄋㄚ
nai	nai	ㄋㄞ
nan	nan	ㄋㄢ
nang	nang	ㄋㄤ
nao	nau	ㄋㄠ
ne	ne	ㄋㄜ
nei	nei	ㄋㄟ
nen	nen	ㄋㄣ
neng	neng	ㄋㄥ
ni	ni	ㄋㄧ
nian	nyan	ㄋㄧㄢ
niang	nyang	ㄋㄧㄤ
niao	nyau	ㄋㄧㄠ
nie	nye	ㄋㄧㄝ
nin	nin	ㄋㄧㄣ
ning	ning	ㄋㄧㄥ
niu	nyou	ㄋㄧㄡ
nong	nung	ㄋㄨㄥ
nou	nou	ㄋㄡ
nu	nu	ㄋㄨ
nü	nyu	ㄋㄩ
nuan	nwan	ㄋㄨㄢ
nüe	nywe	ㄋㄩㄝ
nun	nwun	ㄋㄨㄣ
nuo	nwo	ㄋㄨㄛ
ou	ou	ㄡ
pa	pa	ㄆㄚ
pai	pai	ㄆㄞ
pan	pan	ㄆㄢ
pang	pang	ㄆㄤ
pao	pau	ㄆㄠ
pei	pei	ㄆㄟ
pen	pen	ㄆㄣ
peng	peng	ㄆㄥ
pi	pi	ㄆㄧ
pian	pyan	ㄆㄧㄢ
piao	pyau	ㄆㄧㄠ
pie	pye	ㄆㄧㄝ
pin	pin	ㄆㄧㄣ
ping	ping	ㄆㄧㄥ
po	po	ㄆㄛ
pou	pou	ㄆㄡ
pu	pu	ㄆㄨ
qi	chi	ㄑㄧ
qia	chya	ㄑㄧㄚ
qian	chyan	ㄑㄧㄢ
qiang	chyang	ㄑㄧㄤ
qiao	chyau	ㄑㄧㄠ
qie	chye	ㄑㄧㄝ
qin	chin	ㄑㄧㄣ
qing	ching	ㄑㄧㄥ
qiong	chyung	ㄑㄩㄥ
qiu	chyou	ㄑㄧㄡ
qu	chyu	ㄑㄩ
quan	chywan	ㄑㄩㄢ
que	chywe	ㄑㄩㄝ
qun	chyun	ㄑㄩㄣ
ran	ran	ㄖㄢ
rang	rang	ㄖㄤ
rao	rau	ㄖㄠ
re	re	ㄖㄜ
ren	ren	ㄖㄣ
reng	reng	ㄖㄥ
ri	r	ㄖ
rong	rung	ㄖㄨㄥ
rou	rou	ㄖㄡ
ru	ru	ㄖㄨ
rua	rwa	ㄖㄨㄚ
ruan	rwan	ㄖㄨㄢ
rui	rwei	ㄖㄨㄟ
run	rwun	ㄖㄨㄣ
ruo	rwo	ㄖㄨㄛ
sa	sa	ㄙㄚ
sai	sai	ㄙㄞ
san	san	ㄙㄢ
sang	sang	ㄙㄤ
sao	sau	ㄙㄠ
se	se	ㄙㄜ
sei	sei	ㄙㄟˋ
sen	sen	ㄙㄣ
seng	seng	ㄙㄥ
sha	sha	ㄕㄚ
shai	shai	ㄕㄞ
shan	shan	ㄕㄢ
shang	shang	ㄕㄤ
shao	shau	ㄕㄠ
she	she	ㄕㄜ

Pinyin	Yale	CNPA	Pinyin	Yale	CNPA
shei	shei	ㄕㄟ	xia	sya	ㄒㄧㄚ
shen	shen	ㄕㄣ	xian	syan	ㄒㄧㄢ
sheng	sheng	ㄕㄥ	xiang	syang	ㄒㄧㄤ
shi	shr	ㄕ	xiao	syau	ㄒㄧㄠ
shou	shou	ㄕㄡ	xie	sye	ㄒㄧㄝ
shu	shu	ㄕㄨ	xin	syin	ㄒㄧㄣ
shua	shwa	ㄕㄨㄚ	xing	sying	ㄒㄧㄥ
shuai	shwai	ㄕㄨㄞ	xiong	syung	ㄒㄩㄥ
shuan	shwan	ㄕㄨㄢ	xiu	syou	ㄒㄧㄡ
shuang	shwang	ㄕㄨㄤ	xu	syu	ㄒㄩ
shui	shwei	ㄕㄨㄟ	xuan	sywan	ㄒㄩㄢ
shun	shwun	ㄕㄨㄣ	xue	sywe	ㄒㄩㄝ
shuo	shwo	ㄕㄨㄛ	xun	syun	ㄒㄩㄣ
si	sz	ㄙ	ya	ya	ㄧㄚ
song	sung	ㄙㄨㄥ	yan	yan	ㄧㄢ
sou	sou	ㄙㄡ	yang	yang	ㄧㄤ
su	su	ㄙㄨ	yao	yau	ㄧㄠ
suan	swan	ㄙㄨㄢ	yê	ye	ㄧㄝ
sui	swei	ㄙㄨㄟ	yi	yi	ㄧ
sun	swun	ㄙㄨㄣ	yin	yin	ㄧㄣ
suo	swo	ㄙㄨㄛ	ying	ying	ㄧㄥ
ta	ta	ㄊㄚ	yo	yo	ㄧㄛ
tai	tai	ㄊㄞ	yong	yung	ㄧㄨㄥ
tan	tan	ㄊㄢ	you	you	ㄧㄡ
tang	tang	ㄊㄤ	yu	yu	ㄩ
tao	tau	ㄊㄠ	yuan	ywan	ㄩㄢ
te	te	ㄊㄜ	yue	ywe	ㄩㄝ
teng	teng	ㄊㄥ	yun	yun	ㄩㄣ
ti	ti	ㄊㄧ	za	dza	ㄗㄚ
tian	tyan	ㄊㄧㄢ	zai	dzai	ㄗㄞ
tiao	tyau	ㄊㄧㄠ	zan	dzan	ㄗㄢ
tie	tye	ㄊㄧㄝ	zang	dzang	ㄗㄤ
ting	ting	ㄊㄧㄥ	zao	dzau	ㄗㄠ
tong	tung	ㄊㄨㄥ	ze	dze	ㄗㄜ
tou	tou	ㄊㄡ	zei	dzei	ㄗㄟ
tu	tu	ㄊㄨ	zen	dzen	ㄗㄣ
tuan	twan	ㄊㄨㄢ	zeng	dzeng	ㄗㄥ
tui	twei	ㄊㄨㄟ	zha	ja	ㄓㄚ
tun	twun	ㄊㄨㄣ	zhai	jai	ㄓㄞ
tuo	two	ㄊㄨㄛ	zhan	jan	ㄓㄢ
wa	wa	ㄨㄚ	zhang	jang	ㄓㄤ
wai	wai	ㄨㄞ	zhao	jau	ㄓㄠ
wan	wan	ㄨㄢ	zhe	je	ㄓㄜ
wang	wang	ㄨㄤ	zhei	jei	ㄓㄟ
wei	wei	ㄨㄟ	zhen	jen	ㄓㄣ
wen	wen	ㄨㄣ	zheng	jeng	ㄓㄥ
weng	weng	ㄨㄥ	zhi	jr	ㄓ
wo	wo	ㄨㄛ	zhong	jung	ㄓㄨㄥ
wu	wu	ㄨ	zhou	jou	ㄓㄡ
xi	syi	ㄒㄧ	zhu	ju	ㄓㄨ

Pinyin	Yale	CNPA
zhua	jwa	ㄓㄨㄚ
zhuai	jwai	ㄓㄨㄞ
zhuan	jwan	ㄓㄨㄢ
zhuang	jwang	ㄓㄨㄤ
zhui	jwei	ㄓㄨㄟ
zhun	jwun	ㄓㄨㄣ
zhuo	jwo	ㄓㄨㄛ
zi	dz	ㄗ

Pinyin	Yale	CNPA
zong	dzung	ㄗㄨㄥ
zou	dzou	ㄗㄡ
zu	dzu	ㄗㄨ
zuan	dzwan	ㄗㄨㄢ
zui	dzwei	ㄗㄨㄟ
zun	dzwun	ㄗㄨㄣ
zuo	dzwo	ㄗㄨㄛ

Tone Chart

There are four tones in Mandarin, plus a neutral tone used in ending words. Yale and Pinyin have the same tone markings.

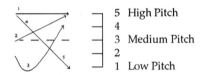

5 High Pitch
4
3 Medium Pitch
2
1 Low Pitch

Name of Tone	Symbol	Number on Pitch Chart	Example
Upper Level	−	1	搭 dā
Upper Rising	／	2	答 dá
Lower Rising	˅	3	打 dǎ
Upper Falling	`	4	大 dà
Neutral	none	5	快快 kwài kwai

Radical Index

Number	Radical	Meaning	Page
One Stroke			
1	一	horizontal	38
2	｜	vertical	39
3	丶	dot	39
4	ノ	diagonal	39
5	乙	second	40
6	亅	hook	41
Two Strokes			
7	二	two	41
8	亠	cap	42
9	* 人 亻	man	42
10	儿	long legs	53
11	入	enter	54
12	八	eight	55
13	冂	borders	56
14	冖	crown	56
15	冫	ice	56
16	几	table	57
17	凵	can	58
18	* 刀 刂	knife	58
19	* 力	strength	61
20	勹	wrap	63
21	匕	spoon	64
22	匚	basket	64
23	匸	box	64
24	十	ten	65
25	卜	foretell	66
26	卩 卪	seal	66
27	厂	cliff	67
28	厶	go	67
29	又	also	67
Three Strokes			
30	* 口	mouth	68
31	* 囗	fence	79
32	* 土 扌	earth	80
33	士	soldier	85
34	夂	summer	86
35	夕	evening	86
36	* 大	big	86
37	* 女	woman	88
38	子	son	93
39	* 宀	roof	94
40	寸	inch	98

Number	Radical	Meaning	Page
41	小	small	98
42	尢	lame	99
43	尸	foot	99
44	屮	sprout	101
45	* 山	mountain	101
46	巛 川	stream	103
47	工	work	103
48	己	self	103
49	* 巾	napkin	104
50	干	interfere	106
51	幺	fine	106
52	* 广	shelter	107
53	廴	court	109
54	廾	play	109
55	弋	shoot	109
56	弓	bow	110
57	彐 彑	broom	111
58	彡	shape	111
59	* 彳	double man	112

Four Strokes

Number	Radical	Meaning	Page
60	* 心 忄	heart	114
61	戈	sword	123
62	戶 户	family	124
63	* 手 扌	hand	125
64	支	support	140
65	攴 攵	tap	140
66	* 文	literature	142
67	斗	measure	142
68	斤	catty	143
69	方	square	143
70	无 旡	since	144
71	* 日	sun	144
72	曰	say	148
73	月	moon	149
74	* 木	wood	150
75	欠	owe	162
76	止	stop	163
77	歹	bad	164
78	殳	kill	164
79	毋	do not	165
80	比	compare	165
81	毛	hair	166
82	氏	clan	166
83	气	air	166
84	* 水 氵	water	167
85	* 火 灬	fire	179
86	爪 爫	claw	184
87	父	father	184

Number	Radical		Meaning	Page
88	爻		two x's	185
89	爿		bed	185
90	片		slice	185
91	牙		tooth	186
92	* 牛	牛	ox	186
93	* 犬	犭	dog	187

Five Strokes				
94	玄	亠	deep	188
95	* 玉	王	jade	189
96	瓜		melon	190
97	瓦		tile	190
98	甘		sweet	191
99	生		live	191
100	用		use	191
101	* 田		field	191
102	疋		cloth	193
103	* 疒		sickness	193
104	癶		climb	195
105	白		white	196
106	皮		skin	196
107	皿		vessel	196
108	* 目	罒	eye	198
109	矛		lance	200
110	矢		arrow	200
111	* 石	石	stone	201
112	示	礻	show	202
113	禸		track	204
114	* 禾		grain	204
115	穴		cave	206
116	立		stand	208

Six Strokes				
117	* 竹	⺮	bamboo	208
118	* 米		rice	211
119	* 糸	糹	silk	213
120	缶		pottery	218
121	网		net	219
122	羊		sheep	220
123	羽	羽	feather	220
124	老	耂	old	221
125	而		yet	221
126	耒		plough	222
127	耳		ear	222
128	聿		learn	223
129	* 肉	月	meat	224
130	臣		officer	228
131	自		from	229

Number	Radical		Meaning	Page
132	至		reach	229
133	臼		uncle	229
134	舌		tongue	230
135	舛		dance	230
136	舟		beat	230
137	艮		good	231
138	色		color	231
139	* 艸	艹	grass	231
140	虍		tiger	238
141	* 虫		insect	238
142	血		blood	242
143	行		walk	242
144	* 衣	衤	clothes	242
145	西		west	245

<table>
<tr><td colspan="5" align="center">Seven Strokes</td></tr>
</table>

Number	Radical		Meaning	Page
146	見		see	245
147	角		horn	246
148	* 言		speech	246
149	谷		valley	253
150	豆		bean	253
151	豕		pig	254
152	豸		leopard	254
153	* 貝		shell	255
154	赤		red	258
155	走	赱	run	258
156	* 足	𧾷	leg	259
157	身		body	261
158	* 車		vehicle	262
159	辛		difficult	264
160	辰		time	264
161	* 辵	辶	travel	264
162	* 邑	阝	county	269
163	酉		chief	270
164	釆		free	272
165	里		mile	272

<table>
<tr><td colspan="5" align="center">Eight Strokes</td></tr>
</table>

Number	Radical		Meaning	Page
166	* 金	釒	gold	273
167	長		long	278
168	* 門		door	278
169	* 阜	阝	mound	279
170	隶		secondary	282
171	隹		single	282
172	* 雨	雨	rain	283
173	青		green	284
174	非		not	284

Number	Radical	Meaning	Page
Nine Strokes			
175	面	face	284
176	革	revolution	284
177	韋	leather	285
178	音	sound	285
179	* 頁	page	286
180	風	wind	289
181	飛	fly	289
182	* 食 食	eat	289
183	首	head	291
184	香	fragrant	291
Ten Strokes			
185	* 馬	horse	291
186	骨	bone	293
187	高	tail	293
188	髟	whisker	293
189	鬥	fight	294
190	鬯	wine	294
191	鬼	ghost	294
Eleven Strokes			
192	* 魚	fish	295
193	* 鳥	bird	296
194	鹵	salt	297
195	鹿	deer	297
196	麥	wheat	298
197	麻	hemp	298
Twelve Strokes			
198	黃	yellow	298
199	黍	millet	298
200	黑	black	298
Thirteen Strokes			
201	鼎	tripod	299
202	鼓	drum	299
203	鼠	rat	299
Fourteen Strokes			
204	鼻	nose	299
205	齊	even	300

Number	Radical	Meaning	Page
Fifteen Strokes			
206	齒	front tooth	300
Sixteen Strokes			
207	龍	dragon	300
Seventeen Strokes			
208	龜	turtle	300
209	龠	flute	300

CHARACTER LISTINGS

		一　Section

1 *** 一	一	one yàt　　　　　　　　yī
2 ** 丁	一 丁	person, servant dìng　　　　　　　dīng
3 *** 七	一 七	seven chàt　　　　　　　qī
4 *** 三	一 二 三	three saàm　　　　　　　sān
5 ** 丈	一 ナ 丈	husband, 10 Chinese feet (measurement) jeuhng　　　　　　zhàng
6 *** 上	丨 卜 上	[1] to ascend; [2] up, [2] above [1] séuhng; [2] seuhng　　[1] [2] shàng
7 *** 下	一 丁 下	to descend; down, below, low hah　　　　　　　xià
8 *** 不	一 ア オ 不	no; not bàt　　　　　　　bù
9 * 丐	一 丁 丅 丐	beggar koi　　　　　　　gài
10 * 丑	フ 刀 丑 丑	clown cháu　　　　　　　chǒu
11 ** 且	丨 冂 月 月 且	besides, moreover ché　　　　　　　qiě
12 ** 世	一 十 廿 世 世	generation, world sai　　　　　　　shì

13 *	丘	ノ イ ﾄ 斤 丘	small hill yàu　　　　　qiū
14 *	丙	一 ｢ 冂 丙 丙	the third of the ten stems bíng　　　　bǐng
15 *	丢	ノ ⌐ 牛 壬 丢　丢	to throw, lose diù　　　　　diū
16 **	並	丶 丷 丷 丷 并 前 並 並	side by side; also, moreover bihng　　　bìng

| | ｜ | Section |

| 17 *** | 中 | 丶 ⼝ ⼝ 中 | middle, center, China; Chinese
jùng　　　　zhōng |
| 18 * | 串 | ⼝ 吕 串 | string, chain, row
chyun　　　chùan |

| | 丶 | Section |

19 *	丸	ノ 九 丸	pill yún　　　　　wán
20 *	丹	ノ 几 丹 丹	red; pill dàan　　　　dān
21 ***	主	丶 ⼆ 丅 ﾃ 主	God, master, host, owner jyú　　　　　zhǔ

| | ／ | Section |

| 22 * | 乃 | ㇋ 乃 | is, then
náaih　　　nǎi |

23 **	久	ノ ク 久	long time gáu	jiǔ
24 **	之	丶 亠 ラ 之	of jì	zhī
25 *	乎	丿 丶 丷 丛 乎	exclamation word in ancient writing fùh	hū
26 *	乍	丿 丨 个 乍 乍	suddenly ja	zhà
27 *	乏	丿 ㇏ 厶 乡 乏	to lack faht	fá
28 *	乖	丿 亠 千 升 乖 乖 乖 乖	obedient gwàai	guāi
29 *	乘	丿 亠 千 升 乖 乖 乖 乖 乖 乘	to multiply, ride in a vehicle sìhng	chéng

<table>
<tr><td colspan="5" align="center">乙　　　Section</td></tr>
</table>

30 *	乙	乙	the second of the ten stems yuht	yǐ
31 ***	九	丿 九	nine gáu	jiǔ
32 *	乞	丿 ㇒ 乞	to beg hàt	qǐ
33 ***	也	㇇ ㇜ 也	also, still yáh	yě
34 *	乳	丿 ㇐ ㇔ ㇛ 孚 孚 孚 乳	milk, breast yúh	rǔ

35 *	乾	一 十 十 古 古 宙 直 卓 乾 乾 乾	dry; heaven
			gòn; kìhn　　　　*gān; qián*
36 **	亂	ノ 爫 爫 爫 爫 爲 爲 爲 雋 雋 亂 亂	disorder
			lyuhn　　　　*lùan*

↓　Section

37 ***	了	⁊ 了	[1] to finish, [1] understand; [2] ending word to show past tense
			[1] *liúh*; [2] *lak*　　[1] *liǎo*; [2] *le*
38 *	予	⁊ ⁓ 予 予	to give
			yúh　　　　*yǔ*
39 ***	事	一 丆 亓 亓 亐 亨 亨 事	affair, matter
			sih　　　　*shì*

二　Section

40 ***	二	一 二	two
			yih　　　　*èr*
41 *	云	二 云 云	to say
			wàhn　　　　*yún*
42 **	互	一 丆 万 互	each other
			wuh　　　　*hù*
43 ***	五	一 丁 五 五	five
			ńgh　　　　*wǔ*
44 **	井	二 丰 井	a well
			jéng　　　　*jǐng*
45 ***	些	丨 卜 止 止 此 此 些	few
			sè　　　　*xiē*

No.	Character	Stroke order	Meaning	Cantonese	Mandarin
46 *	亞	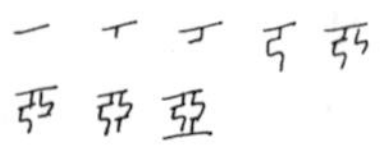	second	a	yà
		亠 Section			
47 *	亡		to die, lose	mòhng	wáng
48 **	交		to hand over; trade, friend	gàau	jiāo
49 *	亦		also, likewise	yihk	yì
50 *	享	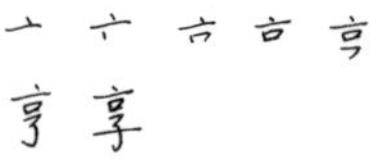	to enjoy	héung	xiǎng
51 **	京	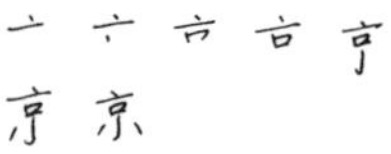	capital	gìng	jīng
52 *	亭		pavilion	tìhng	tíng
53 **	亮	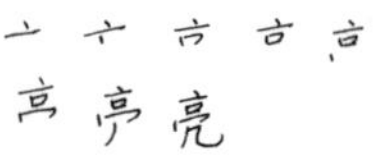	bright	leuhng	liàng
		人 Section			
54 ***	人		man, people	yàhn	rén
55 *	什	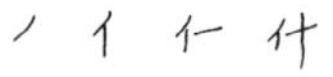	[1] what; [2] miscellaneous	[1] sahm; [2] jaahp	[1] shén; [2] shí
56 *	仁	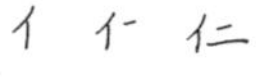	benevolent	yàhn	rén

57 **	仇	イ 仆 仇	to hate; hatred, enemy
			sàuh chóu
58 *	仆	イ 仆 仆	to fall forward
			fuh pū
59 ***	今	ノ 人 △ 今	at present
			gàm jīn
60 ***	介	人 介 介	to introduce, lie between
			gaai jiè
61 *	仍	イ 仍 仍	still
			yìhng réng
62 *	仔	イ 仔 仔 仔	[1] child, [1] son; [2] meticulous
			[1] jái; [2] jí [1] zǎi; [2] zǐ
63 *	仕	イ 仁 仕 仕	gentleman, scholar
			sih shì
64 ***	他	イ 他 仳 他	he; other
			tà tā
65 *	仗	イ 仁 仕 仗	[1] to rely on; [2] battle
			[1] jeuhng; [2] jeung [1][2] zhàng
66 **	付	イ 仁 付 付	to pay, give
			fuh fù
67 *	仙	イ 仆 仙 仙	immortal; angel, cent
			sìn xiān
68 ***	代	イ 仁 代 代	to represent, substitute; generation, dynasty
			doih dài
69 **	令	人 △ 令 令	to cause, command; law; your
			lihng lìng

70 ***	以	丨 𠄌 凵 㠯 以	by, with	
			yíh	yǐ
71 *	仰	亻 亻 仁 仰 仰	to respect, raise head	
			yéuhng	yǎng
72 *	仲	亻 仆 仂 仲 仲	the middle one	
			juhng	zhòng
73 **	件	亻 亻 化 仁 件	item, piece; document	
			gihn	jiàn
74 **	任	亻 亻 仁 任 任	duty, task; to undertake	
			yahm	rèn
75 *	企	丿 人 个 슌 企 企	to stand	
			kéih	qǐ
76 *	伉	亻 亻 仁 仿 伉	married couple	
			kong	kàng
77 *	伊	亻 亻 伊 伊 伊	he, she, that one	
			yì	yī
78 *	伍	亻 仁 仃 伍 伍	five; a company of soldiers	
			ńgh	wǔ
79 *	仿	亻 亻 仁 仿 仿	imitate	
			fóng	fǎng
80 *	伏	亻 亻 付 伏 伏	to hide, lie prostrate	
			fuhk	fú
81 *	伐	亻 亻 代 伐 伐	to attack, cut, chop	
			faht	fá
82 **	休	亻 仁 什 休 休	to rest, stop	
			yàu	xiū

83 *	伙	亻 亻 亻 伙 伙	partner, fellow *fó* *huǒ*
84 *	份	亻 亻 仏 份 份	part, portion, share *fahn* *fèn*
85 **	伯	亻 亻 亻 佰 佰 伯	[1] father's older brother, [1] uncle; [2] husband's older brother [1][2] *baak* [1] *bó;* [2] *bǎi*
86 *	估	亻 亻 什 估 估 估	to estimate, guess *gú* *gū*
87 *	伴	亻 亻 亻 亻 伴 伴	to accompany; companion *buhn* *bàn*
88 *	伶	亻 亻 伙 伙 伶 伶	actor, actress; lonely, clever *lìhng* *líng*
89 **	伸	亻 亻 伂 佃 但 伸	to stretch, extend *sàn* *shēn*
90 **	何	亻 亻 仁 佰 佰 何	which, what *hòh* *hé*
91 *	似	亻 亻 亻 似 似 似	to resemble; similar, like *chíh* *sì*
92 ***	但	亻 亻 佃 佃 但 但	but, however *daahn* *dàn*
93 *	佈	亻 亻 亻 佑 佑 佈	to spread, inform *bou* *bù*
94 **	位	亻 亻 亻 位 位 位	[1] seat, [1] position; [2] polite measure for people [1] *wai;* [2] *wái* [1][2] *wèi*
95 **	低	亻 亻 亻 任 低 低	low *dài* *dī*

#	Char	Strokes	Meaning / Pronunciation
96 **	住	亻 亻` 亻二 亻丨 住 住	to reside, stop *jyuh*　　　　*zhù*
97 *	佐	亻 亻一 亻土 佐 佐 佐	to assist; assistant *jó*　　　　*zuǒ*
98 **	佔	亻 亻卜 亻卜 亻占 佔 佔	to seize by force *jim*　　　　*zhàn*
99 ***	你	亻 亻 亻尔 亻尔 你 你	you *néih*　　　　*nǐ*
100 *	伺	亻 亻𠃌 亻司 伺 伺 伺	¹ to detect, ¹ watch, ² wait on someone ¹ *jih*; ² *sih*　　¹ *sì*; ² *cì*
101 *	佃	亻 亻 亻田 佃 佃 佃	to farm, hunt *dihn, tìhn*　　*diàn, tián*
102 *	佛	亻 亻 亻弓 佛 佛 佛	Buddha *faht*　　　　*fó*
103 ***	作	亻 亻 亻乍 作 作 作	to make, do, compose *jok*　　　　*zuò*
104 *	佣	亻 亻 亻用 佣 佣 佣	commission *yúng*　　　　*yōng*
105 *	佩	亻 亻 亻凡 佩 佩 佩	to respect, admire, wear; pendant *pui*　　　　*pèi*
106 *	佳	亻 亻二 亻土 佳 佳 佳	fine *gàai*　　　　*jiā*
107 *	佻	亻 亻 亻兆 佻 佻 佻	frivolous *tiù*　　　　*tiāo*
108 **	使	亻 亻一 亻口 佢 使 使	¹ to use, ¹ cause, ¹ command; ² messenger ¹ *sí*; ² *si*　　¹ ² *shǐ*

109 ***	來	一 厂 厂 厂 來 來 來	to come
			lòih　　　　　lái
110 *	侈	亻 亻 伊 伊 侈	extravagant
			chí　　　　　chǐ
111 **	例	亻 亻 亻 伤 仍 例 例	regulation, example
			laih　　　　　lì
112 *	侍	亻 亻 仕 仕 仕 侍 侍	to wait upon, serve
			sih　　　　　shì
113 *	侏	亻 亻 仁 仹 侏 侏 侏	dwarf
			jyù　　　　　zhū
114 **	供	亻 亻 亻 仕 仕 供 供	[1] to confess, [1] supply, [1] provide, [2] offer
			[1] gùng; [2] gung　　　[1] gōng; [2] gòng
115 **	依	亻 亻 伫 伫 依 依 依	to rely on, obey; according to
			yì　　　　　yī
116 *	侮	亻 亻 化 化 侮 侮 侮 侮	to insult, humiliate
			móuh　　　　　wǔ
117 *	侯	亻 亻 亻 伫 伫 伕 侯 侯	Marquis
			hàuh　　　　　hóu
118 **	侵	亻 亻 亻 伊 伊 侵 侵 侵	to invade, intrude
			chàm　　　　　qīn
119 *	侶	亻 亻 伊 伊 伊 伊 侶 侶	companion
			léuih　　　　　lǚ
120 *	侷	亻 亻 伊 侷 侷 侷 侷	cramped, uneasy
			guhk　　　　　jú
121 ***	便	亻 亻 仃 佰 佰 佰 便 便	[1] convenient, [2] inexpensive; [1] then, [1] to go to bathroom
			[1] bihn; [2] pìhn　　　[1] biàn; [2] pián

122 **	係	亻亻′亻″亻系亻系亻糸 亻糸 係	to be; relation
			haih xì
123 *	促	亻亻′亻″亻口亻尸 亻尸 促 促	to urge; hurried
			chùk cù
124 *	俊	亻亻″亻″亻″亻″ 亻夋 亻夋 俊	handsome
			jeun jùn
125 *	俏	亻亻′亻″亻″亻″ 俏 俏 俏	pretty, elegant
			chiu qiào
126 **	俗	亻亻′亻″亻″亻″ 俗 俗 俗	custom; common
			juhk sú
127 *	俘	亻亻′亻″亻孚 亻孚 俘	captive, war prisoner
			fù fú
128 **	保	亻亻′亻口亻口 亻口 俘 俘 保	to protect, guarantee
			bóu bǎo
129 *	俟	亻亻″亻″亻″亻″ 亻矣 俟 俟	to wait
			jih sì
130 *	俠	亻亻′亻亻亻亻 俠 俠	hero
			hahp xiá
131 **	信	亻亻′亻″亻信亻信 信 信 信	to believe, trust; letter, message; confidence
			seun xìn
132 *	俄	亻亻′亻″亻″亻″ 俄 俄 俄	moment, Russia
			ngòh é
133 **	修	亻亻′亻″亻″亻″ 攸 修 修 修	to repair, modify, study
			sàu xiū
134 *	俯	亻亻′亻″亻广亻府 俯 俯 俯	to bend down
			fú fǔ

135 *	俱	亻 亻 亻 佴 佴 佴 佴 倶 俱 俱	all, entirely keùi ju
136 *	倆	亻 亻 亻 佰 佰 倆 倆 倆	both leúhng liǎng
137 *	併	(併) 亻 亻 亻 併 併	to combine ping bìng
138 *	倉	人 人 今 今 今 今 倉 倉 倉	warehouse chòng cāng
139 **	倍	亻 亻 亻 亻 亻 佇 佇 倍 倍	to double, increase (e.g. triple, quadruple) púih bèi
140 ***	們	亻 亻 亻 們 們 們 們 們 們	word denoting plural mùhn men
141 **	倒	亻 亻 亻 任 任 佳 佳 倒 倒	[1] to fall over, [1] pour; [2] inverted [1] dóu; [2] dou [1] dǎo; [2] dào
142 ***	候	亻 亻 亻 忰 忰 忰 忰 候 候	to wait hauh hòu
143 *	倚	亻 亻 忄 忕 佐 佐 倚 倚 倚	to lean towards, rely on yí yǐ
144 ***	借	亻 亻 亻 供 供 借 借 借 借	to borrow, lend je jiè
145 *	倡	亻 亻 亻 亻 倡 倡	to originate cheùng chàng
146 *	倫	亻 亻 伀 伀 伀 俭 倫 倫	relationship leùhn lún
147 *	值	亻 亻 亻 佰 佰 值 值 值	price, worth; on duty jihk zhí

148 *	倘	亻 亻 亻 亻 亻 亻 亻 倘 倘	if, suppose tóng	tǎng
149 *	倔	亻 亻 亻 亻 伍 伍 倔 倔	stubborn, rude gwaht	jué
150 ***	個	亻 亻 们 們 們 們 們 個 個	measure word for objects and people go	gè
151 *	俾	亻 亻 亻 亻 伯 伯 伸 俾 俾	to enable, allow béi	bǐ
152 **	假	亻 亻 亻 作 作 作 作 作 假 假	[1] to pretend; [1] false, [1] fake; [2] holiday [1] gá; [2] ga	[1] jiǎ; [2] jià
153 *	倦	亻 亻 亻 亻 亻 侠 侠 倦 倦	tired, weary guhn	juàn
154 *	偏	亻 亻 亻 伫 伫 伫 偏 偏 偏	inclined pìn	piān
155 **	偉	亻 亻 亻 件 件 佛 信 借 偉 偉	great wáih	wěi
156 *	偕	亻 亻 亻 仳 仳 俏 俏 偕 偕 偕	to accompany gàai	xié
157 ***	做	亻 亻 什 什 估 佔 佔 做 做 做	to do, make jouh	zuò
158 *	健	亻 亻 亻 亻 亻 信 律 律 健 健	strong, healthy gihn	jiàn
159 *	側	亻 亻 们 们 但 但 伺 倶 側 側	side of; inclined jàk	cè
160 **	停	亻 亻 亻 亻 信 信 信 停 停 停	to stop tìhng	tíng

161 *	偵	亻 亻' 亻" 亻宀 亻尸 侦 侦 侦 偵 偵	to spy; detective jing　　　　　zhēn
162 *	偶	亻 亻 亻" 亻 亻 亻 但 偶 偶 偶 偶	idol, mate; accidental ngáuh　　　　ǒu
163 *	偷	亻 亻 亻 亽 亻 亻 亻肖 亻肖 偷 偷	to steal tāu　　　　　tōu
164 *	傢	亻 亻' 亻' 亻宀 亻宀 亻方 亻方 傢 傢 傢	furniture gà　　　　　jiā
165 *	傅	亻 亻宀 亻十 亻什 亻甫 亻甫 亻甫 亻甫 傅 傅 傅	teacher, coach fuh　　　　fù
166 *	傑	亻 亻' 亻' 亻夕 亻夕 傑 傑 傑 傑 傑	hero, distinguished person giht　　　　jié
167 *	傘	人 亽 众 夳 夳 夳 傘	umbrella saan　　　　sǎn
168 **	備	亻 亻' 亻宀 亻什 亻什 伊 伊 佛 備 備	to prepare, get ready beih　　　　bèi
169 *	傲	亻 亻宀 亻什 亻宀 亻宀 亻宀 亻宀 傲 傲 傲 傲	to be proud, haughty ngouh　　　ào
170 *	催	亻 亻' 亻宀 亻宀 亻宀 伴 伴 伴 催 催 催	to urge, hasten chēui　　　cuī
171 *	傭	亻 亻' 亻宀 亻宀 亻宀 亻宀 傭 傭 傭 傭 傭	servant yùhng　　　yōng
172 **	傳	亻 亻宀 亻宀 亻向 亻向 傳 傳 傳 傳 傳	[1] to transmit, [1] spread, [1] infect; [2] biography [1] chyùhn; [2] jyuhn　　[1] chuán; [2] zhuàn
173 *	債	亻 亻宀 亻什 亻住 亻住 佳 債 債 債 債	debt jaai　　　　zhài

174 **	傷	亻 亻' 亻' 伫 佇 佈 佤 伤 傷 傷	to injure, hurt; wound seùng　　shāng
175 *	傾	亻 亻化 亻化 亻化 亻何 亻何 亻何 傾 傾 傾 傾 傾	inclined; to confide, tumble down kìng　　qīng
176 *	僅	亻 亻' 亻' 亻' 佳 佳 佳 借 借 傳 傳 僅	only, barely gán　　jǐn
177 *	僕	亻 亻'' 亻'' 亻'' 亻'' 亻'' 伴 伴 僕 僕 僕 僕	servant buhk　　pú
178 **	僱	亻 亻' 亻' 亻' 伊 伊 傛 俸 俸 倛 倛 僱	to hire, employ gu　　gù
179 *	僚	亻 亻' 仹 伏 伏 依 依 俙 俙 俙 僚 僚	colleague liùh　　liáo
180 *	僥	亻 亻' 亻' 佳 佳 佳 佳 僥 僥 僥	by luck, by chance hiù　　jiǎo
181 *	僧	亻 亻' 亻' 亻' 佛 佛 佛 佃 倌 倌 僧 僧 僧	Buddhist monk jàng　　sēng
182 *	僑	亻 亻' 亻化 亻化 伏 依 僑 俙 俙 僑 僑	to emigrate; emigrant kiùh　　qiáo
183 *	僞	(僞) 亻 亻' 亻' 伊 伊 傷 僞 僞	hypocritical, fake ngaih　　wěi
184 **	像	亻 亻' 亻' 亻' 佰 佈 佣 俦 傷 像	figure, image, portrait; to resemble; like jeuhng　　xiàng
185 *	傻	亻 亻化 仙 仙 伆 伆 仮 仮 傻 傻 傻	foolish, silly sòh　　shǎ
186 ***	價	亻 亻' 亻' 亻' 佰 佃 佃 價 價 僧 價 價 價	price, value ga　　jià

187 *	億	亻亻亻亻亻亻亻 倍倍倍倍億億	hundred million
			yik — yì
188 *	儉	亻亻亻亻亻亻 价价儉	thrifty
			gihm — jiǎn
189 *	儀	亻亻亻亻亻亻佯 佯佯佯儀儀儀	manner, instrument, ceremony
			yìh — yí
190 *	僻	亻亻仁伊伊侷侶 侶侶僻僻僻僻	depraved, secluded, eccentric
			pik — pì
191 *	儒	亻亻亻伫师师 伈僵僵僵僖儒	scholar, dwarf
			yùh — rú
192 *	儘	亻亻伫伫伫伸佳傔 傔傔傔傔儘	utmost, extreme
			jeuhn — jǐn
193 *	償	亻亻亻亻亻佟佟佟 佟佟償償償償	to pay back, repay
			seùhng — cháng
194 *	優	亻亻亻亻伃伃伃 俱傴傴傴優優優	excellent, distinguished
			yàu — yōu
195 *	儲	亻亻亻亻信信信信 信信儲儲儲儲儲	to store, save
			chyúh — chǔ
196 *	儷	亻亻亻仴佰佃佃佃 佃傮僲儷儷儷儷	married couple
			laih — lì

儿 Section

197 *	允	ㄥ ㄙ ㄠ 允	to promise, allow
			wáhn — yǔn
198 ***	元	一 二 元	the chief, the first, dollar
			yùhn — yuán

199 *	兄	丶 冂 口 兄	older brother *hìng*　　　　*xiōng*
200 **	充	丶 一 ㄊ 云 充	full; to fill, serve as, pretend *chùng*　　　　*chōng*
201 *	兆	丿 丿 丬 兆 兆 兆	omen, million *siuh*　　　　*zhào*
202 *	兇	ㄴ ㄩ ㄩ 凶 兇	fierce, cruel *hùng*　　　　*xiōng*
203 ***	先	丿 丿 丷 生 先	before, first; ancestor; former *sìn*　　　　*xiān*
204 **	光	㇑ 丬 丬 业 光	bright; light, empty *gwòng*　　　　*guāng*
205 *	克	一 十 古 古 古 克	to overcome; gram *hàk*　　　　*kè*
206 *	兑	丶 丷 丷 兯 兑 兑	to exchange *deui*　　　　*dùi*
207 **	免	㇆ ㇆ 冎 呙 冎 免 免	free of charge, free; to avoid *mìhn*　　　　*miǎn*
208 ***	兒	丿 ㇑ ㇒ 臼 臼 臼 兒	son, child *yìh*　　　　*ér*
209 *	兔	㇆ ㇆ 冎 呙 冎 免 兔 兔	rabbit *tou*　　　　*tú*
210 *	兜	丶 丬 丬 丬 佝 佝 佝 佝 佝 兜	to round up, wrap, solicit; sack *dàu*　　　　*dōu*

入　　Section

211 **	入	ノ 入	to enter
			yahp　　　　　rù
212 ***	内	l 冂 内	inside, within
			noih　　　　　nèi
213 **	全	入 亽 仐 全 全	complete, entire
			chyùhn　　　　quán
214 ***	兩	一 宀 币 币 雨 兩	two, a few; ounce
			leúhng　　　　liǎng

八　Section

215 ***	八	ノ 八	eight
			baat　　　　　bā
216 **	公	八 公 公	fair, public; old man, husband's father, father-in-law
			gùng　　　　　gōng
217 ***	六	` 亠 六	six
			luhk　　　　　liù
218 ***	共	l 十 艹 共 共	together, total
			guhng　　　　gòng
219 **	兵	ノ ㇒ ㇒ 丘 丘 兵	soldier
			bìng　　　　　bīng
220 **	其	l 十 廿 甘 其 其	possessive pronoun
			kèih　　　　　qí
221 **	具	l 冂 目 且 具	tool
			geuih　　　　jù
222 ***	典	` 冂 曰 曲 曲 典 典	dictionary, ceremony
			dín　　　　　diǎn

| 223 * | 兼 | `丶 丷 二 屮 兰 ⺶ 羊 兼 兼 兼` | in addition

gìm   *jiān* |
| 224 * | 冀 | `ⅰ ⅱ 丬 北 北 北 背 背 背 背 莆 冀 冀` | to hope

kei   *jì* |

<table>
<tr><td colspan="4" align="center">冂   Section</td></tr>
</table>

225 *	册	`丨 冂 冊 冊`	volume of a book *chaak* *cè*
226 ***	再	`一 冂 再 再 再`	again *joi* *zài*
227 *	冒	`冂 冂 日 門 冐 冒 冒`	to risk, offend, feign *mouh* *mào*
228 *	冕	`冂 冂 日 門 冐 冒 昌 昂 晃 冕`	crown *mìhn* *miǎn*

<table>
<tr><td colspan="4" align="center">冖   Section</td></tr>
</table>

| 229 * | 冗 | `丶 冖 宀 冗` | wordy

yúng   *rǒng* |
| 230 * | 冠 | `冖 冖 宇 完 冠 冠 冠` | [1] hat; [2] premiere

[1] *gùn;* [2] *gun*   [1] *guān;* [2] *guàn* |

<table>
<tr><td colspan="4" align="center">冫   Section</td></tr>
</table>

| 231 ** | 冬 | `丿 夂 夂 冬` | winter

dùng   *dōng* |
| 232 * | 冱 | `丶 冫 冫 江 沍 沍 冱` | icy

wuh   *hù* |

233 **	冰	ﾑ ﾑｲ ﾑｲ 冰 冰	ice	
			bīng	*bīng*
234 *	冶	ﾑ ﾑ' ｼ 冶 冶 冶	to smelt, melt	
			yéh	*yě*
235 **	冷	ﾑ ﾑ' ｼ 冷 冷 冷	cold, indifferent	
			láahng	*lěng*
236 **	准	ﾑ ﾑ' ｲ 冴 冴 准 准 准 准	to permit, approve	
			jéun	*zhǔn*
237 *	凋	ﾑ ﾑ' 冈 冈 冈 凋 凋 凋 凋	to wither, fade	
			diu	*diāo*
238 *	凍	ﾑ ﾑ' 冴 冴 冴 冴 凍 凍 凍	to freeze; cold	
			dung	*dòng*
239 *	凜	ﾑ ﾑ' 冴 冴 冴 冴 冴 冴 冴 冴 凜	shivering	
			láhm	*lǐn*
240 *	凝	ﾑ ﾑ' 冴 冴 冴 冴 冴 冴 冴 冴 冴 冴 冴 凝	to coagulate, freeze	
			yìhng	*níng*

几　Section

241 *	几	ﾉ 几	small table	
			gèi	*jī*
242 *	凡	几 凡	common, every	
			fàahn	*fán*
243 *	凰	几 几 凡 凤 凤 凤 凤 凤 凰 凰	female phoenix	
			wòhng	*huáng*
244 *	凱	｜ 屮 屮 屮 豈 豈 豈 豈 凱	victory	
			hói	*kǎi*

| 245 * | 凳 | ㄱ ㄲ ㄲ' 水 水 水 丞 丞 丞 丞 丞 凳 | stool, bench

dang   *dèng* |

凵 Section

246 *	凶	ㄴ 凵 凶 凶	evil, dangerous *hùng* *xiōng*
247 *	凸	ㅣ ㅣ 十 卢 凸 凸	to protrude; convex *daht* *tū*
248 ***	出	凵 屮 出	to go out *chèut* *chū*
249 *	凹	ㅣ 冂 凵 凹 凹 凹	to indent; concave *nàp* *āo*
250 *	函	一 丁 丂 丐 丞 丞 函	letter, note *haàhm* *hán*

刀 Section

251 ***	刀	ㄱ 刀	knife, sword *dōu* *dāo*
252 *	刁	ㄱ 刁	sneaky *dìu* *diāo*
253 *	刃	刀 刃	edge of a sword *yahn* *rèn*
254 ***	分	ノ 八 分	[1] to divide, [1] depart; [1] minute; [1] cent, [2] portion [1] *fàn;* [2] *fahn* [1] *fēn;* [2] *fèn*
255 **	切	一 七 切	[1] pressing; [2] to cut; [3] all [1][2] *chit;* [3] *chai* [1][3] *qiè;* [2] *qiē*

256 *	刊	ノ ニ チ 升 刊	to publish; publication
			hón　　　　kǎn
257 *	划	一 ヽ 戈 戈 划	to row a boat
			wà　　　　huá
258 **	列	一 丁 歹 歹 列	to list, display; row
			liht　　　　liè
259 *	刑	一 二 于 开 刑	punishment
			yìhng　　　　xíng
260 *	删	ノ 刀 册 册 删	to eliminate, delete
			saàn　　　　shān
261 ***	初	ヽ ラ ネ ネ 初	beginning, at first
			chò　　　　chū
262 *	判	ヽ ソ ソ 半 半 判	to judge; decision
			pun　　　　pàn
263 ***	别	ヽ 口 尸 另 别	to distinguish, separate; do not; other
			biht　　　　bié
264 **	利	ノ 二 千 禾 禾 利	to benefit; profit, benefit, interest; sharp
			leih　　　　lì
265 *	刨	ノ 勹 匂 勺 包 刨	to dig
			paàuh　　　　páo
266 *	刮	ノ 二 千 千 舌 舌 刮	to scrape, shave
			gwaat　　　　guā
267 ***	到	一 エ 互 至 至 到	to arrive, go, attain
			dou　　　　dào
268 **	制	ノ 亻 二 午 告 制	to regulate, ration, restrain
			jai　　　　zhì

269 **	刷	フ ⁊ 尸 尸 吊 吊 刷	to brush, scrub; brush *chaat*　　　*shuā*
270 *	券	丶 ⸝ 丷 半 关 券	bond, ticket, coupon *hyun*　　　*quàn*
271 **	刻	丶 一 亠 亥 亥 亥 刻	to engrave, carve, treat harshly; quarter hour, moment *hàk*　　　*kè*
272 *	刺	一 厂 冂 朿 束 束 刺	[1] to stab, [1] sting, [2] assassinate; [1] thorn [1] *chi;* [2] *chik*　　　[1] *cì;* [2] *qì*
273 *	剎	ノ メ 乄 乊 羊 羊 杀 剎	Buddhist monastery; moment *saat*　　　*chà*
274 *	剃	丶 丷 ⻀ 岁 弟 弟 剃	to shave *tai*　　　*tì*
275 *	則	l 冂 冃 目 貝 貝 則	rule, law; then *jàk*　　　*zé*
276 *	削	丶 丷 ⺌ 屮 肖 肖 削	to sharpen *seuk*　　　*xuē*
277 ***	前	丷 丷 亠 丷 艹 首 前	in front of, before; earlier, previous, former *chìhn*　　　*qián*
278 *	剗	一 弋 戈 戈 戔 剗	to trim, spade *cháan*　　　*chǎn*
279 *	剖	丶 亠 ⸜ 立 辛 音 音 剖	to dissect *fáu*　　　*pōu*
280 **	剛	l 冂 冂 冈 用 冈 岡 剛	strong; recently; to have just... *gòng*　　　*gāng*
281 *	剝	⺄ 彑 彑 圼 录 录 剝	[1] to strip, [1] deprive, [2] peel [1] [2] *mòk*　　　[1] *bō;* [2] *bāo*

282 *	副	一 亅 而 币 乬 晶 晶 畐 副	assistant; to assist; second *fu* *fù*
283 *	剪	丷 兰 产 芀 肯 前 剪	to cut with scissors; scissors *jín* *jiǎn*
284 *	割	丶 丷 宀 宀 宔 宝 害 害 割	to cut *got* *gē*
285 **	剩	丿 二 千 千 禾 乖 乖 乘 剩	to leave over; left over *sihng* *shèng*
286 **	創	丿 人 人 今 今 今 户 侴 倉 倉 創	[1] to create, [1] start; [2] wound [1] *chong*; [2] *chòng* [1] *chuàng*; [2] *chuāng*
287 **	劃	一 一 一 聿 聿 書 書 書 書 書 書 劃	uniform, plan; to plan, divide *waahk* *huà; huá*
288 *	劉	丶 ⺊ 幻 切 圳 卯 丣 罘 翠 鉍 劉	to slaughter *làuh* *liú*
289 *	劇	丨 ⺊ 卢 广 户 卢 虍 虏 虏 虏 豦 豦 劇	opera; extremely *kehk* *jù*
290 *	劈	一 ⺆ 尸 尸 启 后 启 启 昍 辟 辟 劈	to chop, split open *pek* *pī; pǐ*
291 *	劍	丿 人 人 仝 合 合 合 僉 僉 僉 劍	sword *gim* *jiàn*
	力 Section		
292 ***	力	刁 力	strength, energy, force, power *lihk* *lì*
293 **	功	一 丅 工 功	merit, achievement *gùng* *gōng*

No.	Character	Stroke order	Meaning	Cantonese	Mandarin
294 ***	加	フ 力 力 加 加	to add, increase, join; Canada	*gà*	*jiā*
295 *	劣	亅 小 小 少 劣	bad, inferior	*lyut*	*liè*
296 **	助	丨 冂 月 且 助	to assist	*joh*	*zhù*
297 **	努	ㄑ 女 女 女フ 奴 努	to strive	*nóuh*	*nǔ*
298 *	劫	一 十 土 去 去 劫	to rob	*gip*	*jié*
299 *	勁	一 ㄑ 巛 巛 巠 巠 巠 勁	^{1} strength; ^{2} powerful	^{1} *gìng;* ^{2} *gihng*	^{1} *jìn;* ^{2} *jìng*
300 *	勃	一 十 十 𠫓 孛 孛 孛 勃	flourishing; suddenly	*buht*	*bó*
301 **	勇	フ マ マ 甬 甬 甬 甬 勇	brave, courageous	*yúhng*	*yǒng*
302 *	勉	ノ ク ク 各 各 免 免 免 勉	to encourage	*míhn*	*miǎn*
303 **	動	ノ 二 千 台 台 台 重 重 重 動	to move; motion	*duhng*	*dòng*
304 *	勒	丶 十 廿 廿 廿 苫 苫 革 革 勒	to bridle, curb, tie up	*lahk*	*lè; lēi*
305 **	務	フ マ 子 予 矛 矛 矛 矜 矜 務	duty, responsibility	*mouh*	*wù*
306 **	勝	ノ 几 月 月' 月' 朕 朕 勝	^{1} to win, ^{1} conquer, ^{2} be able to	^{1} *sing;* ^{2} *sìng*	^{1} *shèng;* ^{2} *shēng*

307 **	勞	`丶 丶 ⺊ ⺊ 炏 炏` 炏 勞	to work hard; labor	
			lòuh	*láo*
308 *	募	`丶 丶 ⺋ 艹 艹 莒` 莒 莒 莫 莫 募	to enlist, raise funds	
			mouh	*mù*
309 *	勦	`巛 巛 巛 勾 쓥 쓪` 甹 筆 彙 勦	to suppress	
			jíu	*jiǎo*
310 **	勢	`一 十 土 ⺦ 夫 坴` 刲 执 执 勢	power, strength, opportunity, situation, gestures	
			sai	*shi`*
311 **	勤	`丶 十 艹 艹 艻 芇` 莒 莒 芇 革 董 勤	diligent	
			kàhn	*qín*
312 *	勳	`丿 ⺅ ⺆ 台 台 血 軎` 重 熏 勳	merit	
			fàn	*xūn*
313 *	勵	`厂 厂 厂 严 严 屏 屏` 屏 屛 厲 厲 厲 厲 勵	to encourage	
			laih	*li`*
314 **	勸	`丶 十 艹 艹 艻 艻 苗 莪` 菂 荤 莪 莪 菅 藿 勸	to advise, persuade	
			hyun	*quàn*

勹　　Section

315 *	勻	`丿 勹 勾 勻`	equally, evenly	
			wàhn	*yún*
316 *	勾	`勹 勾 勾`	[1] to hook, [1] cancel, [1] entice, [2] collude	
			[1][2] *ngàu*	[1] *góu;* [2] *gòu*
317 *	勿	`勹 勿`	do not	
			maht	*wù*
318 **	包	`勹 勹 句 包`	to wrap, include; package	
			bàau	*bāo*

319 *	匆	ㄅ 勿 匆	hurried
			chùng　　　　cōng
320 *	匈	ㄅ 勹 匂 匈 匈	tumultuous
			hùng　　　　xiōng

ㄴ　Section

321 **	化	ノ イ 个 化	to transform
			fa　　　　huà
322 ***	北	丨 ㅓ 才 北 北	north
			bàk　　　　běi
323 *	匙	丨 冂 月 日 旦 早 早 界 是 匙	¹ spoon, ² key
			¹ chìh; ² sìh　　　　¹ chí; ² shi

匚　Section

324 *	匠	一 匚 匸 匞 匞 匠	workman, craftsman
			jeuhng　　　　jiàng
325 *	匣	匚 匸 匝 匣 匣 匣	box
			hahp　　　　xiá
326 *	匪	匚 匚 匪 匪 匪 匪	robber, thief
			féi　　　　féi

匸　Section

327 *	匹	一 匚 匹 匹	measure word for fabric or horses
			pàt　　　　pǐ
328 *	匿	匚 匚 匞 匞 匞 匿 匿 匿 匿	to hide, conceal; anonymous
			nìk　　　　nì

329 **	區	匸 匚 匝 匝 區 區	district keùi qū

		十　Section	

330 ***	十	一 十	ten sahp shí
331 ***	千	ノ 千	thousand, many chìn qiān
332 *	廿	十 廿 廿	twenty yeh niàn
333 **	升	ノ ニ チ 升	to rise, ascend, promote sìng shēng
334 *	卅	一 ナ 廾 卅	thirty sà sà
335 **	午	ノ ト ヒ 午	noon, midday ńgh wǔ
336 ***	半	丶 丷 半 半	half bun bàn
337 *	卒	丶 一 宀 立 卒 卒	soldier; to finish, die jyùt zú
338 *	卓	丨 ト 上 占 卓 卓 卓	distinguished, lofty cheuk zhūo
339 **	協	十 圵 協 協 協	to assist hihp xié
340 *	卑	ノ 亻 白 白 卑 卑	inferior, humble bèi bēi

341 ***	南	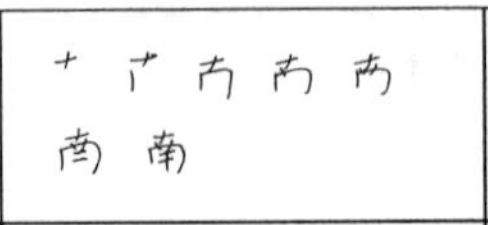	south	
			naahm	*nán*
342 *	博	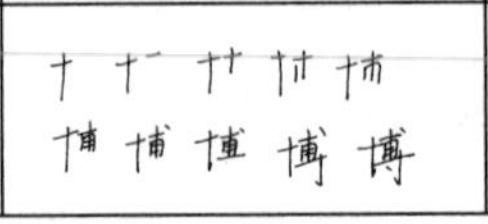	to gamble; wide	
			bok	*bó*
		卜 Section		
343 *	卜	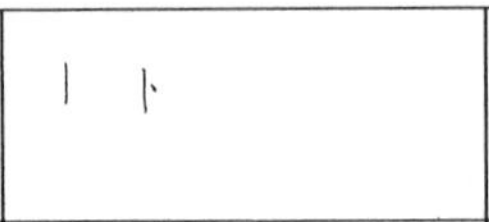	to foretell	
			bùk	*bǔ*
344 *	卡	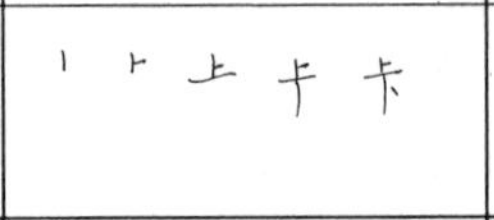	[1] card; [2] caught between	
			[1] *kàat;* [2] *káat*	[1] *kǎ;* [2] *qiǎ*
345 *	占		to foretell	
			jìm	*zhān*
346 *	卦	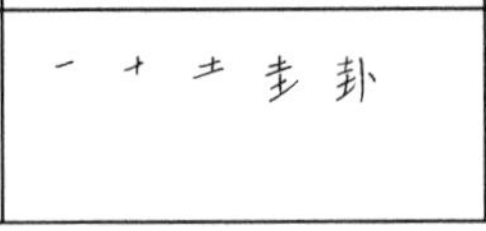	a stick for fortune telling	
			gwa	*guà*
		卩 Section		
347 **	印	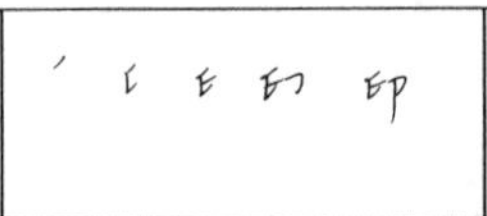	to print; seal, print	
			yan	*yìn*
348 **	危	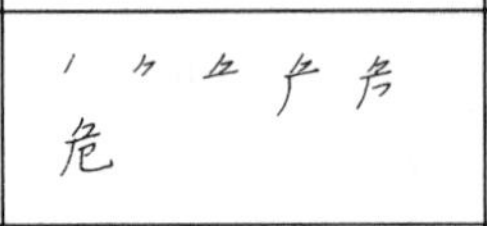	dangerous	
			ngàih	*wēi*
349 *	却	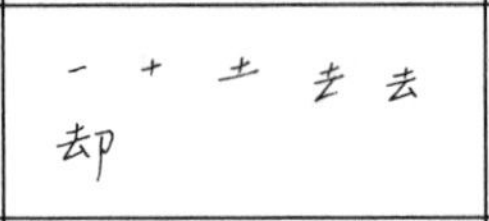	to refuse; but, nevertheless	
			keuk	*què*
350 *	卵	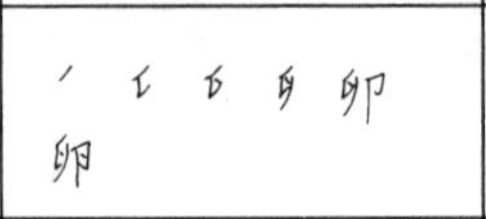	egg, ovum	
			léun	*luǎn*
351 *	卷	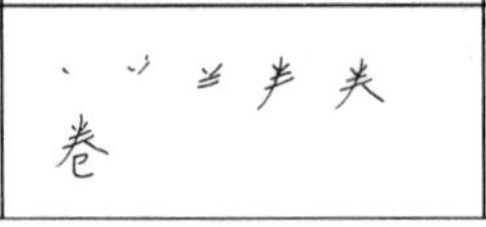	roll, volume of a book, examination paper	
			gyún	*juàn*

352 *	卽	(即) ¬ ¬ ¬ ∃ ᄐ ᄐ 卽	immediately; that is, then *jik*	*jí*
353 *	卸	ノ ト ← 午 午 缶 缶 卸	to unload, discharge *se*	*xiè*

厂 Section

354 **	厚	一 厂 厂 厈 厈 戶 厚 厚 厚	thick, generous *háuh*	*hòu*
355 ***	原	厂 厂 厃 所 厭 庐 庐 原 原	a plain; origin; originally *yùhn*	*yuán*
356 *	厭	厂 厃 厃 厅 厅 厈 屒 厝 屑 屑 厭 厭	to dislike, disgust *yim*	*yàn*
357 *	厲	厂 厂 厃 所 所 所 屇 厲 厲 厲 厲 厲 厲	strict, harsh, severe *laih*	*lì*

厶 Section

358 ***	去	一 十 土 去 去	to go; previous *heui*	*qù*
359 *	叄	厶 厶 厽 夅 矣 矣 叅 叄	three *saàm*	*sān*
360 **	參	厶 広 厽 乡 矣 參	[1] to join, [1] attend, [1] participate; [2] ginseng; [3] disorder; [3] uneven [1] [3] *chàam*; [2] *sàm* [1] *cān*; [2] *shēn*; [3] *cēn*

又 Section

361 ***	又	¬ 又	again, also *yauh*	*yòu*

362 *	叉	又 叉	fork chà chā
363 **	及	フ 及 及	to reach; and; about kahp jí
364 **	反	ノ 厂 反	to turn over, oppose, rebel; opposite faán fǎn
365 ***	友	一 ナ 友	friend, companion yáuh yǒu
366 **	取	一 丁 Π 耳 耳 取	to take; get chéui qǔ
367 *	叔	丨 卜 上 卡 ホ ホ 叔	uncle, father's younger brother sùk shū
368 ***	受	ノ 爫 爫 爫 受	to accept, receive, to be.... sauh shòu
369 *	叛	᠈ ᠈ 半 半 叛 叛	to rebel, revolt buhn pàn
370 *	叢	丨丨 业 业 业 业 芈 芈 芈 芈 芈 芈 叢	crowded, thick, dense chùhng cóng
		口 Section	
371 ***	口	丨 冂 口	mouth, opening háu kǒu
372 ***	古	一 十 古	ancient, old, primitive gú gǔ
373 **	句	ノ 勹 句	sentence, clause, phrase geui jù

No.	Character	Stroke Order	Meaning / Readings
374 **	另	口 号 另	other, another *lihng* *lìng*
375 ***	只	口 只	only, simply *jí* *zhǐ*
376 ***	可	一 亓 可	to be willing, fit, be able; how; but *hó* *kě*
377 ***	叫	口 叫 叫	to call, shout, name *giu* *jiào*
378 **	史	口 史 史	history; historical *sí* *shǐ*
379 *	叮	口 叮 叮	to sting, reiterate *ding* *dīng*
380 *	召	刀 刀 召	to call, summon *jiuh* *zhào*
381 **	司	丁 刁 司	to manage *sì* *sī*
382 *	叭	口 叭 叭	trumpet, "ba" sound *ba* *bā*
383 **	台	ㄥ ㄙ 台	stage, platform *tòih* *tái*
384 **	右	一 ナ 右	the right side *yauh* *yòu*
385 ***	吃	口 叱 吃 吃	to eat, have *hek* *chī*
386 **	各	丿 夂 夂 各	every, each *gok* *gè*

387 ***	名	′ ク タ 名	name, title, fame *mìhng* 　　　　*míng*
388 *	吋	口 口′ 吋 吋	inch *chyun* 　　　　*cùn*
389 *	吆	口 口′ 吆 吆	shout *jiu* 　　　　*yāo*
390 *	吉	一 十 士 吉	lucky; good luck *gàt* 　　　　*jí*
391 **	合	′ 人 人 合	to close, gather, combine; fit *hahp* 　　　　*hé*
392 **	同	丨 冂 冃 同	identical; and, with; together *tùhng* 　　　　*tóng*
393 *	后	′ 厂 斤 后	queen *hauh* 　　　　*hòu*
394 ***	向	′ 亻 冋 向	towards; direction *heung* 　　　　*xiàng*
395 *	吏	一 厂 戸 吏 步 吏	government official *leih* 　　　　*lì*
396 *	吐	口 口一 吐 吐	[1] to spit, [2] vomit [1] [2] *tou* 　　　[1] *tǔ*; [2] *tù*
397 *	含	′ 人 人 今 含	to hold in the mouth, include, hold *hàhm* 　　　　*hán*
398 *	呎	口 口′ 叮 呎 呎	foot (measurement) *chek* 　　　　*chǐ*
399 *	吵	口 口丿 呰 吵 吵	noisy; to disturb, quarrel *cháau* 　　　　*chǎo*

400 *	吟		to moan, recite a poem *yàhm* *yín*
401 ***	告	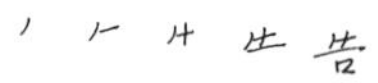	to tell, announce, impeach *gou* *gào*
402 *	吝		miserly *leuhn* *lìn*
403 *	吠	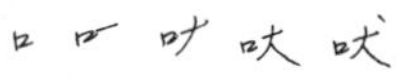	to bark (dog); barking *faih* *fèi*
404 **	吹	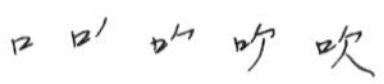	to blow, brag, boast; "kaput", ruined *cheùi* *chūi*
405 *	吼	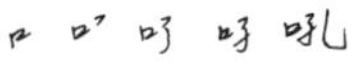	the cry of a beast; to roar *haàu* *hǒu*
406 **	呀	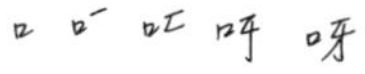	[1] oh! [1] ah! [2] a final article (exclamation point) [1] *a;* [2] *ah* [1] *yā;* [2] *ya*
407 *	君	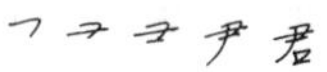	king, gentleman; sir, Mr. *gwàn* *jūn*
408 *	否		not *faú* *fǒu*
409 *	吞		to swallow *tàn* *tūn*
410 **	吧		[1] "ba" sound; [2] a final article indicating decisiveness [1] *bà;* [2] *bah* [1] *bā;* [2] *ba*
411 *	吾	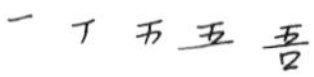	I, me, my *ǹgh* *wú*
412 **	吸	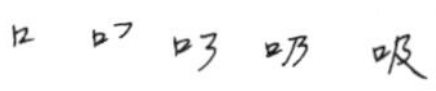	to inhale, suck *kàp* *xī*

413 *	呈	口 口 모 묘 呈	to offer, present
			chìhng chéng
414 *	吻	口 미 吻 吻	to kiss
			máhn wěn
415 *	呆	口 모 무 무 呆	dull
			ngòih ái
416 *	呵	口 口 哈 呵	[1] to scold, [1] exhale; [1] laughing sound; [2] exclamation of surprise [1] hò; [2] òu [1] hē; [2] ō
417 *	咐	口 미 미 吖 吩 咐	to direct
			fu fù
418 *	呪	口 口 呾 呪	to curse, swear
			jau zhòu
419 **	周	丿 冂 冂 用 周 周	environment; complete
			jàu zhōu
420 ***	呢	口 미 미 呢 呢 呢	[1] woolen; [2] a final article (! or ?) [1] lèih; [2] lè [1] ní; [2] ne
421 **	味	口 미二 咊 咊 味	flavor, taste, smell
			meih wèi
422 **	命	丿 人 ヘ 合 命	to order, name; order, destiny, fate, life
			mihng mìng
423 **	和	丿 二 千 禾 禾 和	[1] peace, [1] harmony; [2] and, [2] with [1] [2] wòh [1] hé; [2] hàn
424 *	呻	口 미 미 미 呻	to groan
			sàn shēn
425 *	咎	丿 夕 処 処 咎	fault, blame
			gau jiù

No.	Character	Strokes	Meaning	Cantonese	Mandarin
426 *	咀	口 叮 叭 咀 咀	[1] to chew; [2] mouth	[1][2] *jeúi*	[1] *jǔ*; [2] *zhǔ*
427 **	呼	口 口' 吖' 吟 呼	to exhale, call, greet	*fù*	*hū*
428 *	咱	口 口' 叩 叩 咱 咱	[1] we, [1] us, [2] I, [2] me	[1][2] *jà*	[1] *zán*; [2] *zá*
429 *	哈	口 叭 吟 吟 哈	laughing sound; exclamation of joy	*hà*	*hā*
430 **	品	口 吕 品	rank, article, quality, personality	*bán*	*pǐn*
431 *	咳	口 口' 吐 吃 咳 咳 咳	[1] to cough; [1] cough, [2] exclamation	[1] *kàt*; [2] *hài*	[1] *ké*; [2] *hài*
432 *	咬	口 口' 吐 吽 咔 咹 咬	to bite	*ngaáuh*	*yǎo*
433 *	哄	口 叮 叶 哄 哄 哄	[1] people bursting into laughter; [2] to cheat	[1] *hùng*; [2] *hung*	[1] *hōng*; [2] *hǒng*
434 *	哇	口 口' 吐 吐 哇	[1] baby talk, [1] sound of baby crying, [2] exclamation	[1][2] *wà*	[1] *wā*; [2] *wa*
435 *	咸	一 厂 厂 咸 咸 咸 咸	also	*haàhm*	*xián*
436 *	哉	一 十 士 吉 吉 吉 哉 哉 哉	exclamation	*jòi*	*zāi*
437 *	哀	丶 亠 一 声 声 亩 哀	sorrow	*òi*	*āi*
438 *	咽	口 叮 叩 叩 咽 咽 咽	throat	*yìn*	*yān*

439 *	哨	口 口' 口ㄴ 叭 哨 哨	to guard; outpost, whistle	
			saau	*shào*
440 *	哺	口 口一 叶 叶 叶 哺 哺	to feed	
			bouh	*bǔ*
441 ***	員	口 尸 吊 吊 昌 員	member of a profession	
			yùhn	*yuán*
442 *	唐	、 ㄧ 广 广 广 庐 庐 唐	Chinese; the Tang Dynasty	
			tòhng	*táng*
443 **	哥	一 丌 可 可 哥 、 哥	older brother	
			gò	*gē*
444 **	哭	口 吅 吅 哭 哭	to cry	
			hùk	*kū*
445 *	哮	口 口一 口± 哮 哮 哮 哮 哮	to roar, howl; asthma	
			haàu	*xiāo*
446 *	唉	口 口ㄴ 吣 吣 唉 唉 唉	oh! eh! (an exclamation)	
			aài	*āi*
447 *	唇	ㄧ 二 三 戶 戶 辰 辰 唇	lip	
			sèuhn	*chún*
448 *	哲	一 十 才 扌 扩 折 折 哲	wisdom, philosophy	
			jit	*zhé*
449 *	哪	口 叮 叨 唧 哪	[1] where, [1] which; [2] final article; [3] that one	
			[1][3] *náh*; [2] *ne*	[1] *nǎ*; [2] *na*; [3] *něi*
450 *	啥	口 口ノ 吣 哈 哈 啥	what	
			sá	*shà*
451 *	唬	口 口ʾ 叶 吽 吽 吽 唬 唬 唬	intimidate	
			fú	*hǔ*

452 ***	問	丨 冂 冂 冂 冃 冃 冃 門 問	to ask, inquire
			mahn　　　wèn
453 *	售	ノ 亻 亻 亻 什 佳 住 佳 售	to sell
			sauh　　　shòu
454 *	唯	口 唯	¹ sole, ¹ only; ² to answer quickly
			¹ wàih; ² wái　　¹ wéi; ² wěi
455 **	唱	口 口 口 口 唱 唱	to sing
			cheung　　chàng
456 *	唾	口 口 口 吐 吐 唾 唾 唾	to spit; saliva
			tou　　　tuò
457 **	商	丶 二 立 产 产 产 商 商	to consult; trade, merchant
			sèung　　shāng
458 *	啓	丶 ヲ 彐 户 户 户 彭 啓 啓	to open, start, describe; memo
			kái　　　qǐ
459 *	啞	口 口 吖 吖 吓 吓 啞 啞 啞	dumb, mute
			ngá　　　yǎ
460 **	啦	口 口 吓 吋 吵 吶 吶 啦	"la" sound; a final article (exclamation point)
			là; le　　　lā; la
461 **	啊	口 吖 吖 吲 呵 呵 啊	ah! ¹ (frightened), ² (surprised), ³ (doubting), ⁴ (realizing)
			¹ à; ² àh; ³ ǎ; ⁴ a　　¹ ā; ² á; ³ ǎ; ⁴ à
462 *	喚	口 口 吣 吣 吣 唤 唤 唤 喚 喚	to call
			wuhn　　huàn
463 **	善	ソ ゾ ギ 芊 羊 羊 善 善 善	good, kind; skillful, familiar; easily
			sihn　　shàn
464 ***	單	口 吅 吅 严 閃 閃 單 單	single; a bill
			daan　　dān

465 ***	喜	一 十 士 吉 吉 吉 喜 喜 喜	joy, happiness; to like	
			héi	xǐ
466 *	喉	口 口´ 叮 叮 叽 叽 唉 唉 喉	throat	
			hàuh	hóu
467 *	喻	口 口´ 吩 吩 吟 哈 哈 喻 喻	to tell, understand; sample	
			yuh	yù
468 *	哟	口 口´ 吩 吩 吩 哟 哟 哟	o!; a final article (exclamation point)	
			yò	yō
469 *	喘	口 口̀ 口¹ 叫 叫 呿 呿 喘 喘	to gasp	
			chyún	chuǎn
470 **	喊	口 口´ 吖 吖 咸 喊 喊 喊	to shout	
			haam	hǎn
471 *	喪	一 十 寸 寸 西 亜 車 喪 喪	[1] mourning, [1] funeral; [2] to lose	
			[1] sòng; [2] song	[1] sāng; [2] sàng
472 *	啼	口 口´ 口̀ 吖 吟 哈 哈 啼 啼	to cry, crow (rooster)	
			tàih	tí
473 *	喂	口 口´ 吅 吅 哭 哭 喂 喂	hello	
			waih	wèi
474 *	喧	口 口´ 吖 吖 咕 咕 唷 喧 喧	to clamor; noisy	
			hyùn	xuān
475 ***	喝	口 口´ 叩 叩 唱 唱 喝 喝 喝 喝	[1] to drink, [2] cheer	
			[1][2] hot	[1] hē; [2] hè
476 *	嗜	口 口´ 吐 吐 哄 嗟 嗟 嗜 嗜 嗜	to be fond of; hobby	
			si	shì
477 *	嗓	口 口´ 口̀ 唼 唼 嗓 嗓 嗓	throat, voice	
			sòng	sǎng

478 *	嗟	口 ロ˙ ロˊ 叮 咩 咩 咩 嗟 嗟 嗟	to sigh, mourn
			jè *jiē*
479 *	嗅	口 口ˊ 叮 叴 咱 咱 嗊 嗅 嗅	to smell
			chau *xiù*
480 *	嗚	口 叮 叮 呼 咛 咛 嗚 嗚	"wu" sound; expression for a sigh
			wù *wū*
481 *	嗆	口 口 叭 吣 吟 吟 吟 唅 唥	[1] choked from drinking, [2] choked from smoke
			[1][2] *chòng* [1] *qiāng;* [2] *qiàng*
482 *	嗦	口 口ˋ 叮 叶 咇 咇 唪 唪 嗦 嗦	to suck (e.g. baby with finger), shiver
			sò *suō*
483 ***	嗎	口 口ˊ 叮 吓 叱 吒 嗎 嗎	question mark
			mà *ma*
484 *	嘔	口 口ˊ 叹 呕 呕 嘔	to vomit
			ngáu *ǒu*
485 *	嘉	一 十 士 吉 声 壴 喜 嘉 嘉 嘉	fine; to praise
			gà *jiā*
486 *	嘜	口 口ˊ 吐 吐 吐 呋 咔 嗒 嘜 嘜	trademark
			màk *mà*
487 *	嗽	口 口ˊ 咘 咘 咻 咻 嗽 嗽 嗽	to cough, clear the throat
			sau *sòu*
488 *	嘗	⺊ ⺊ ⺊ ⺶ 峃 峃 峃 嘗 嘗 嘗 嘗 嘗	to try, taste
			seùhng *cháng*
489 *	嘆	口 口ˊ 叶 叶 哇 哇 嘆 嘆 嘆	to sigh
			taan *tàn*
490 *	嘿	口 口ˊ 叮 呷 哩 哩 嘿 嘿 嘿	hey!
			hàk *hēi*

491 *	噴	口 口 口 口⁺ 吐 呟 呟 噴 噴 噴 噴 噴	¹ to squirt, ¹ eject, ¹ spray; ² fragrant ¹ ² pan ¹ pēn; ² pèn
492 *	噤	口 口 口⁺ 吽 味 咻 咻 噤 噤 噤 噤	to refrain from speaking, shiver gam jìn
493 **	嘴	口 此 此 此 此 此 此 嘴 嘴 嘴 嘴	mouth jéui zǔi
494 **	器	口 口 吅 吅 哭 哭 哭 哭 器	vessel hei qì
495 *	噸	口 口 吓 吒 吨 吨 吨 噸 噸 噸 噸 噸	a ton deùn dūn
496 *	噬	口 口 吔 吓 咝 咝 吟 咝 嗞 噬	to bite saih shì
497 *	嚏	口 口⁺ 呌 呠 呠 嗒 嗒 嚏 嚏 嚏 嚏 嚏 嚏 嚏	to sneeze tai tì
498 *	嚇	口 口⁺ 口⁺ 吐 吁 哧 哧 味 嚇	¹ to threaten, ² frighten ¹ ² haak ¹ hè; ² xià
499 *	嚮	⠀ ⠀ ⠀ 乡 乡 乡 乡 娘 娘 娘 鄉 鄉 嚮 嚮 嚮 嚮	to long for heung xiàng
500 *	嚥	口 口 吐 吐 吐 吐 嗼 嗼 嗼 嗼 嚥 嚥	to swallow yin yàn
501 *	嚨	口 口 口 吣 吣 吣 唶 唶 嗌 嗌 嚨 嚨	throat lùhng lóng
502 *	嚼	口 口 吣 吣 吣 嗝 嗝 嘴 嘴 嘴 嚼 嚼	to chew jeuk jiáo
503 **	嚴	口 口 严 严 严 严 严 严 严 严 严 严 严 嚴 嚴	strict, severe yìhm yán

504 *	嚷	口 叮 啃 嗬 嗬 嗬 嗬 嗥 嗥 嚷 嚷 嚷	[1] to shout, [2] clamor
			[1] [2] *yeuhng* [1] *rǎng;* [2] *rāng*
505 *	嚻	口 叭 旪 呷 咢 咢 咢 咢 咢 嚻	clamor
			hiù *xiāo*
506 *	囊	云 市 串 串 串 嘉 嘉 嘉 嘉 囊 囊 囊 囊	bag, sack
			nòhng *náng*
507 *	囉	口 叨 唧 嗶 嗶 嗶 嗶 嗶 嗶 嗶 囉	[1] clamor; [2] to nag
			[1] *lòh;* [2] *lò* [1] *luó;* [2] *luō*
508 *	囑	口 口 吓 吓 呀 喂 喂 喂 喂 喂 喂 囑 囑 囑 囑	to direct, entrust
			jùk *zhǔ*

囗 Section

509 ***	四	丨 冂 四 四 四	four
			sei *sì*
510 *	囚	冂 冂 冈 囚	prisoner
			chàuh *qiú*
511 ***	回	冂 回 回	to return, reply, turn about; a round (boxing)
			wùih *húi*
512 ***	因	冂 冂 用 因 因	because; reason
			yàn *yīn*
513 *	囤	冂 冂 冈 囤 囤 囤	[1] storage bin; [2] to hoard
			[1] *deuhn;* [2] *tyùhn* [1] *dùn;* [2] *tún*
514 **	困	冂 冂 困 困 困 困	difficult, exhausted, fatigued; surrounded
			kwan *kùn*
515 *	固	冂 冂 冈 固 固	strong, firm, stubborn
			gu *gù*

516 *	圈	冂 冂 同 罔 罔 圂 圏 圈	[1] circle, [3] place to raise animals; [1] to circle, [2] keep
			[1] [2] hyùn; [3] gyuhn　　[1] quān; [2] juān; [3] juàn
517 ***	國	冂 冂 同 同 國 國 國 國	country, empire
			gwok　　　　　　guó
518 **	圍	冂 冂 冃 冃 冑 圉 圍 圍 圍	to surround; enclosure
			wàih　　　　　wéi
519 *	圓	冂 冂 冑 冐 冐 圓 圓	round, complete; a dollar
			yùhn　　　　　yuán
520 **	園	冂 冂 冏 冐 冑 冑 冑 冑 園 園	park, yard, garden
			yùhn　　　　　yuán
521 ***	圖	冂 冂 冃 冑 圉 圖 圖 圖	picture, illustration, pattern
			tòuh　　　　　tú
522 ***	團	冂 冂 冏 同 冐 冐 冑 圑 圑 圑 圑 團 團	lump, mass, group
			tyùhn　　　　　tuán

土　Section

523 ***	土	一 十 土	earth, soil, ground
			tóu　　　　　tǔ
524 ***	在	一 ナ 才 在	at, in, on; to exist
			joih　　　　　zài
525 ***	地	扌 切 地 地	place, land, ground
			deih　　　　　dì
526 *	址	扌 圵 圵 址 址	place, address
			jí　　　　　zhǐ
527 **	均	土 圠 均 均	to equalize; equal
			gwàn　　　　　jūn

528 ***	坐	ノ　人　从　坐　坐　坐	to sit, ride	
			joh	zuò
529 *	坑	土　圤　圹　圹　坑	ditch, pit	
			haàng	kēng
530 *	坊	土　圤　圹　坊　坊	[1] lane, [1] street, [2] workshop	
			[1] [2] fòng	[1] fāng; [2] fáng
531 *	坦	土　圤　坦　坦　坦　坦	level and smooth, frank	
			táan	tǎn
532 *	垂	ノ　一　二　午　乒　垂　垂	to hang, drop; reaching	
			sèuih	chúi
533 *	垃	土　圤　圹　圹　圹　垃	garbage	
			laahp	lā
534 *	坡	土　圤　圹　圵　圵　坡	slope	
			bò	pō
535 *	坪	土　圤　圹　圷　坪	level ground	
			pìhng	píng
536 *	坤	土　圤　圹　圳　坤　坤	the earth; female	
			kwàn	kūn
537 *	垣	土　圤　圹　圻　垣　垣　垣	wall, town	
			wùhn	yuán
538 *	垮	土　圤　圹　圵　垮　垮	to collapse	
			kwà	kuǎ
539 ***	城	土　圤　圵　坊　城　城　城	city	
			sìhng	chéng
540 *	型	二　开　刑　刑　型	mold, model	
			yìhng	xíng

No.	Char	Stroke order	Meaning / Reading
541 *	埋	土 圹 圹 坍 坍 坤 埋 埋	¹ to bury, ¹ hide, ² grumble ¹ ² *maaih*　　¹ *mái*; ² *mán*
542 *	堆	土 圹 圹 圹 圹 圹 堆	pile, group; to accumulate *deui*　　*dūi*
543 **	堂	丨 丷 丷 丷 丷 尚 尚 堂	hall, court *tòhng*　　*táng*
544 *	培	土 圹 圹 圹 垃 垃 培 培	to cultivate, nourish *pùih*　　*péi*
545 *	執	土 圭 圭 丯 幸 幸 刲 軌 執	to hold, grasp *jàp*　　*zhí*
546 *	域	土 圹 圢 圢 垣 垣 域 域 域	region, district *wihk*　　*yù*
547 **	堅	一 丁 工 王 工 臣 臤 臤 堅	strong, firm, durable *gìn*　　*jiān*
548 **	基	丨 十 廿 甘 其 其 其 基	foundation, base *gèi*　　*jī*
549 *	埠	土 圹 圹 圹 坨 坨 埠 埠	port, wharf *fauh*　　*bù*
550 *	堵	土 圤 圤 堵 堵 堵 堵 堵	to obstruct *dóu*　　*dǔ*
551 ***	報	土 圭 圭 幸 幸 郣 郣 報	to reciprocate, inform; newspaper *bou*　　*bào*
552 *	堪	土 圤 圤 圤 堪 堪 堪 堪	able, capable; to endure *hàm*　　*kān*
553 **	場	土 圹 圹 圹 坥 坥 坥 埸 場 場	yard, field *chèuhng*　　*cháng, chǎng*

554 *	堡	イ イ' イ゛ イ゛ イ゛ イ゛ イ゛ 保 保 堡	fort *bóu*　　　　　*baǒ*
555 *	堤	圡 圹 圩 圷 坥 坥 垾 垾 堤 堤	embankment, barrier *tàih*　　　　*dī*
556 *	堰	土 圵 圮 圮 圮 圮 圮 坥 堰 堰	embankment, barrier *yím*　　　　*yàn*
557 *	塗	氵 氵 氵 氵 沴 泠 涂 涂 塗	to smear, dab *tòuh*　　　　*tú*
558 *	塘	土 圵 圹 圹 圹 圹 塘 塘 塘 塘 塘	pond, embankment *tòhng*　　　*táng*
559 *	塞	丶 宀 宀 宀 宀 宇 审 宭 寒 塞	[1] to block; [1] cork, [2] frontier [1] *sàk;* [2] *choi*　　[1] *sāi;* [2] *sài*
560 *	填	土 圵 圵 圵 圴 垍 垍 埴 填 填	to fill up, fill in (a form); stuff *tìhn*　　　　*tián*
561 *	塌	土 圵 圫 圹 坰 垎 垇 塌	to collapse *taap*　　　　*tā*
562 *	塢	土 圵 圵 圵 圵 圬 垰 塢	dock *ou*　　　　*wù*
563 ***	塊	土 圵 圵 圹 圴 圴 垉 埍 塊 塊 塊	a piece, lump *faai*　　　　*kuài*
564 *	塔	土 圵 圵 圵 圵 圵 坽 塔 塔 塔 塔	pagoda, tower *taap*　　　　*tǎ*
565 *	境	土 圵 圵 圵 圹 垃 垃 垃 埞 堷 境 境	region, boundary, condition *gíng*　　　*jìng*
566 *	墊	土 圭 圭 幸 幸 執 執 墊	to place under, pay for another; cushion *dihn*　　　*diàn*

567 *	墓	丨 十 卄 艹 艻 苩 苩　莒 荁 莫 墓	grave	mouh　　　mù
568 *	塾	丶 亠 亠 古 古 亨 享　享 孰 孰 塾	old style family school	suhk　　　shú
569 *	墅	丨 口 曰 日 甲 里 野　野 野 野 墅	a house in the country	seuih　　　shù
570 *	塵	丶 一 广 广 户 鹿 鹿　鹿 鹿 鹿 塵	dust, dirt	chàhn　　　chén
571 *	墒	土 圠 圹 圻 圹 圬 塙　塙 塙 墒 墒	the moisture in the soil	sèung　　　shāng
572 *	墜	一 了 卩 阝 阼 阼 阽 阽　阽 陜 墜	to fall, sink	jeuih　　　zhuì
573 *	墮	一 了 卩 阝 阼 阼 阼 陊　陊 隋 隋 墮	to fall, degenerate, sink	doh　　　duò
574 **	增	土 圢 圴 圴 圴 埒 墙　墹 增 增 增 增	to increase, add to	jàng　　　zēng
575 *	墟	土 圠 圠 圠 圫 圫 圬　圬 圬 塷 塷 墟 墟	market, wasteland, ruined place	heui　　　xū
576 *	墳	土 圠 圫 圫 圫 圬 圬　圬 堉 墳 墳 墳	grave	fàhn　　　fén
577 **	墨	丨 口 四 四 甲 里 黑　墨	Chinese ink; dark	mahk　　　mò
578 *	壁	一 コ 尸 吊 启 启 启 启　辟 辟 壁	wall	bìk　　　bì
579 *	墾	丿 丬 夕 夕 豸 豸 豸　豹 豹 豤 豤 墾	to plow land, cultivate	hán　　　kěn

580 *	壇	士 圹 圹 圹 圹 壩 壇 壇 壇 壇 壇 壇 壇	altar
			tàahn　　　　　　tán
581 *	壕	士 圹 圹 圹 圹 圹 圹 壕 壕 壕 壕 壕 壕	trench
			hòuh　　　　　　háo
582 **	壓	一 厂 厂 厂 厂 厂 厂 厂 厭 厭 厭 厭 壓	to crush, oppress, repress, suppress
			ngaat　　　　　　yá
583 *	壘	丶 冂 冂 田 田 畾 畾 畾 壘	rampart
			leúih　　　　　　leǐ
584 **	壞	士 圹 圹 圹 圹 壞 壞 坤 坤 壊 壊 壊 壊 壞 壞	to ruin; bad, ruined, out of order
			waaih　　　　　　huài
585 *	壟	士 圹 圹 圹 圹 圹 圹 堵 堵 堵 堵 堵 堵 壟 壟	to monopolize
			lúhng　　　　　　lǒng
586 *	壤	士 圹 圹 圹 圹 圹 圹 圹 堭 堭 壤 壤 壤 壤 壤	soil, earth
			yeuhng　　　　　　ràng

士　　Section

587 *	士	一 十 士	scholar, officer, soldier
			sih　　　　　　shì
588 **	壯	㇄ 丬 丬 丬 壯	strong, healthy; to strengthen
			jong　　　　　　zhuàng
589 *	壹	士 圭 圭 吉 壴 壴 壴 壹 壹 壹	one
			yàt　　　　　　yī
590 *	壺	士 圭 吉 吉 吉 壴 壴 壺 壺 壺 壺	kettle
			wùh　　　　　　hú
591 *	壻	士 圹 圹 圻 圻 埕 埕 堰 塔 壻	son-in-law, husband
			sai　　　　　　xù

| 592 * | 壽 | 十 士 吉 吉 吉 壴 壴 壹 壹 壽 壽 壽 壽 | longevity, age *sauh*   *shòu* |

夂 Section

| 593 ** | 夏 | 一 丆 了 丆 百 百 頁 頁 夏 夏 | summer *hah*   *xià* |

夕 Section

594 *	夕	丿 勹 夕	evening, sunset *jihk* *xī*
595 ***	外	夕 夘 外	outside, exterior, foreign *ngoih* *wài*
596 ***	多	夕 多	many, much *dò* *duō*
597 **	夜	丶 亠 亣 亣 疒 夜	night *yeh* *yè*
598 **	夠	夕 多 多 夠 夠 夠 夠 夠	enough *gau* *gòu*
599 *	夢	丶 十 艹 芢 芢 莳 茐 苗 苗 莴 夢	to dream; dream *muhng* *mèng*
600 *	夥	丶 冂 口 日 旦 早 畀 果 果 夥 夥	many; group of people, companion *fó* *huǒ*

大 Section

| 601 *** | 大 | 一 ナ 大 | [1] big, [1] older, [1] grown up; [2] doctor [1] [2] *daaih*   [1] *dà*; [2] *dài* |

602 ***	天	一 天	sky, heaven, day
			tìn 　　　　　　*tiān*
603 ***	太	大 太	extreme, very; Mrs.
			taai 　　　　　　*tài*
604 ***	夫	一 夫	man, husband
			fù 　　　　　　*fū*
605 *	夭	丿 夭	[1] fresh-looking, [1] delicate; [2] to die young
			[1] *yiù*; [2] *yiú* 　　[1] *yāo*; [2] *yǎo*
606 **	失	丿 丿 失	to miss, lose; mistake
			sàt 　　　　　　*shī*
607 **	央	丶 冂 央	to beg; center
			yèung 　　　　*yāng*
608 *	夷	一 二 三 弓 夷 夷	even, level; to kill
			yìh 　　　　　　*yí*
609 *	夾	一 ナ 才 才 夾 夾	[1] to clip; [1] clip, [2] layer
			[1][2] *gaap* 　　[1] *jiā*; [2] *jiá*
610 **	奇	大 太 杏 杏 杏 奇	[1] remarkable, [1] strange, [1] curious, [2] odd (numbers)
			[1] *kèih*; [2] *gèi* 　[1] *qí*; [2] *jī*
611 *	奈	大 杰 杢 夽 奈	way to deal with a situation
			noih 　　　　　*nài*
612 *	奉	一 三 丰 夹 奉 奉	to offer
			fuhng 　　　　*fèng*
613 *	奔	大 太 本 夵 夰 奔	to run
			bàn 　　　　　*bēn*
614 *	奏	三 丰 夫 表 奏	to play music
			jau 　　　　　*zòu*

615 *	契	三 丰 刧 刧 契	contract, deed
			kai *qì*
616 **	套	大 太 本 杏 查 查 套 套	set, cover, series
			tou *tào*
617 *	奢	大 太 本 杏 夸 奔 奔 奢 奢 奢	extravagant, luxurious
			chè *shē*
618 *	奧	ノ イ 冖 冋 冋 向 用 胃 奧	mysterious, profound
			ou *aò*
619 **	奪	大 太 本 杏 本 奔 奎 奮 奪 奪	to take by force, seize
			deuht *dúo*
620 **	獎	㇏ 丬 爿 爿 爿 爿 爿 牂 將 將 獎	to praise, reward; prize
			jéung *jiǎng*
621 **	奮	大 夵 木 杏 杏 奔 奞 奞 奞 奞 奮 奮	to strive, struggle
			fáhn *fèn*

女   Section

622 ***	女	ㄑ ㄠ 女	female, daughter, girl, woman
			néuih *nǚ*
623 *	奴	女 奴	slave
			nòuh *nú*
624 *	奶	女 奶 奶	milk, breast
			náaih *nǎi*
625 *	妃	女 女 奻 妃	an imperial concubine
			fèi *fēi*
626 *	妄	丶 亠 亡 妄	foolishly
			móhng *wàng*

#	Character	Stroke order	Meaning / Pronunciation
627 *	奸	女 女二 奸	wicked, crafty, corrupt gàan — jiān
628 *	她	女 女㇀ 她 她	she, her tà — tā
629 ***	好	女 女' 奵 好	[1] good, [1] fine, [1] very; [2] to be fond of [1] hóu; [2] hou — [1] hǎo; [2] hào
630 ***	如	女 女 如 如	like, as; if yùh — rú
631 *	妙	女 女' 妙 妙	wonderful, splendid miuh — miào
632 *	妖	女 女' 妖 妖 妖	phantom yíu — yāo
633 *	妨	女 女 妨 妨 妨	to hinder fòhng — fáng
634 *	妥	' ㇉ 妥	sound, secure tóh — tuǒ
635 *	姈	女 女' 妗 妗 姈	sister-in-law, wife's sister kàhm — jìn
636 *	妒	女 女' 妒 妒 妒	to envy, be jealous douh — dù
637 *	妓	女 女 妓 妓 妓	prostitute geih — jì
638 **	妻	一 ㇆ 三 ㇌ 妻 妻	wife chài — qī
639 *	妾	' 亠 立 立 妾	concubine chip — qiè

640 **	妹	女 女 女 妹 妹	younger sister *múi* · *mèi*
641 *	姊	女 女 女 姊 姊	older sister *jí* · *zǐ*
642 ***	姐	女 女 如 姐 姐	Miss; older sister *jé* · *jiě*
643 *	姑	女 女 女 姑 姑 姑	father's sister, aunt, husband's sister, unmarried female *gù* · *gū*
644 **	始	女 女 女 始 始 始	beginning, start, origin *chí* · *shǐ*
645 ***	姓	女 女 女 姓 姓 姓	family name, surname *sing* · *xìng*
646 **	委	ノ ニ 千 チ 禾 委	to delegate, entrust, commit *wái* · *wěi*
647 *	姆	女 女 姆 姆 姆 姆	baby sitter *móuh* · *mǔ*
648 *	姨	女 女 姨 姨 姨 姨	aunt, mother's sister, wife's sister *yìh* · *yí*
649 *	姻	女 女 姻 姻 姻 姻 姻	marriage *yàn* · *yīn*
650 *	姿	丶 冫 冫 次 次 姿	posture, manner *jī* · *zī*
651 *	威	一 厂 厂 厔 威 威	dignity; solemn *wài* · *wēi*
652 *	姦	女 姦 姦	adultery; to rape *gàan* · *jiān*

653 *	娃	女 女 女 女 娃	baby, little girl	
			wà	*wá*
654 *	姪	女 女 女 妷 妷 妷 姪	nephew, niece	
			jaht	*zhí*
655 **	娘	女 女 妁 妁 妁 娘 娘 娘	mother, young lady	
			neùhng	*niáng*
656 *	娟	女 女 女 娟 娟 娟 娟	elegant, graceful	
			gyùn	*jūan*
657 *	娛	女 女 妁 妁 娓 娓 娛 娛	to amuse; joy, pleasure	
			yùh	*yú*
658 *	娩	女 女 女 女 娩 娩 娩 娩 娩	to give birth to	
			míhn	*miǎn*
659 **	婚	女 女 妒 妒 妮 婬 婚 婚 婚	marriage	
			fàn	*hūn*
660 **	婦	女 女 妇 妇 妇 妇 婦 婦	woman, wife	
			fúh	*fù*
661 **	婆	氵 氵 沪 沖 波 波 婆	old lady, husband's mother, mother-in-law, father's mother, grandmother	
			pòh	*pó*
662 *	婢	女 女 妁 妁 妁 妁 婢 婢 婢	slave girl, maid	
			péih	*bi̍*
663 *	婊	女 女 女 娃 娃 娃 婊 婊	prostitute	
			biù	*biǎo*
664 *	婪	一 十 オ 木 林 婪	greedy	
			laàhm	*lán*
665 *	婉	女 女 妁 妒 妒 妒 妒 婉 婉	tactful, graceful, diplomatic	
			yùn	*wǎn*

666 *	娶	一丁丌丌丌取　取娶	to marry a wife
			chéui　　　　qǔ
667 *	娼	女 女' 女ロ 女ロ 女ロ　娼	prostitute
			cheùng　　　chāng
668 *	媒	女 女┤ 女┼ 女卄 女卅　女卄 女某 女媒 媒 媒	match-maker
			mùih　　　　méi
669 *	婿	女 女⌐ 女⌐ 女㇏ 女⌐ 婎　婎 婿 婿	son-in-law, husband
			sai　　　　　xù
670 *	嫂	女 女' 女ᄀ 女ᄀ 女ᄀᄀ 女ᄀᄀ　女ᄀ 女ᄆ 嫂 嫂	older brother's wife, sister-in-law
			sóu　　　　　sǎo
671 *	嫁	女 女' 女' 女宀 女宀 女疒　女疒 女家 嫁 嫁	to marry a husband
			ga　　　　　jià
672 *	媳	女 女' 女ʼ 女自 女自 女息　媳 媳 媳 媳	son's wife, daughter-in-law
			sīk　　　　　xí
673 *	嫉	女 女' 女疒 女疒 女疒　女疒 女疾 嫉 嫉 嫉	to envy, be jealous
			jaht　　　　jí
674 *	嫌	女 女' 女ʽ 女ʽ 女兼　女兼 嫌 嫌 嫌	to dislike, suspect, doubt
			yìhm　　　　xián
675 **	媽	女 女ᄀ 女ᄀ 女匚 女馬　媽 媽	mother
			mà　　　　　mā
676 *	嫡	女 女' 女ʼ 女ʼ 女商 嫡　嫡 嫡 嫡 嫡 嫡	legitimate, legally related
			dīk　　　　　dí
677 *	嫩	女 女' 女ʼ 女束 女束 女束　女束 媡 嫩 嫩 嫩 嫩	tender, delicate
			nyuhn　　　nèn
678 *	嬌	女 女' 女ʼ 女ʼ 女夭 女夭　嬌 嬌 嬌 嬌 嬌	charming, cute
			gìu　　　　　jiāo

679 *	嫺	女 刞 奷 奷 奷 奷 奷 奷 嫺 嫺 嫺 嫺	gracious, refined	
			hàahn	xián
680 *	嬉	女 女 女 女 女 娃 娃 娃 娃 嬉 嬉	to play; amusement	
			hèi	xī
681 *	嬰	l П Ħ ㅂ 貝 賏 嬰	infant, baby	
			yīng	yīng
682 *	嬸	女 女 好 好 好 嫅 娌 嫅 嫅 嫅 嫅 嬸	aunt	
			sám	shěn
683 *	孀	女 女 好 奸 婶 娾 婶 婶 嬬 孀 孀 孀	widow	
			sèung	shuāng

子　　Section

684 ***	子	ㄱ 孒 子	son, boy	
			jí	zǐ
685 *	孑	ㄱ 孑	alone, single	
			kit	jié
686 *	孔	孑 孔	hole	
			húng	kǒng
687 *	孕	孑 乃 孕	to conceive; pregnant	
			yahn	yùn
688 ***	字	` 宀 宀 字	word, character	
			jih	zì
689 **	存	一 ナ 才 存	to exist, save, keep	
			chyùhn	cún
690 *	孝	一 十 土 尹 孝	to pay respect to parents	
			haau	xiào

691 *	孤	子 孑 孑 孤 孤 孤	orphan, lonely gù　　　　　　gū
692 **	季	ノ 二 千 禾 禾 季	season gwai　　　　　　jì
693 *	孟	子 孑 孟 孟 孟	senior, oldest maahng　　　　mèng
694 **	孩	子 孑 孑 孩 孩 孩 孩	child, baby haàih　　　　　hái
695 **	孫	子 孑 孑 孫 孫 孫 孫 孫	grandchild syùn　　　　　sūn
696 *	孰	﹑ 二 宀 六 言 享 享 孰 孰	who? which? what? suhk　　　　shú
697 *	孵	ノ ﹢ ﹢ 身 卵 卵 卵 卵 卵 孵	to hatch fù　　　　　　fū
698 ***	學	ノ ﹤ ﹤ ﹤ 段 臼 臼 臼 學 學	to learn; knowledge, study hohk　　　　xué
699 *	孺	子 孑 孑 孑 孺 孺 孺 孺 孺 孺 孺 孺	child yùh　　　　　rú
700 *	孿	﹑ 二 言 言 言 言 綜 綜 綜 綜 孿	twins lyùhn　　　　luán

| | 宀　　Section | |

| 701 * | 它 | ﹑ ﹑ 宀 宁 它 | it
tà　　　　　　tā |
| 702 * | 宅 | 宀 宀 宀 宅 | residence
jaahk　　　　zhái |

No.	Character	Stroke Order	Meaning / Pronunciation
703 **	守	⼧ ⼧ 宁 守	to guard, keep sáu shǒu
704 **	安	⼧ ⼧ 安 安	peaceful, safe, secure òn ān
705 *	宇	⼧ ⼧ 宇	house, universe yuh yǔ
706 *	宋	⼧ 宁 宋 宋 宋	the Sung Dynasty sung sòng
707 ***	完	⼧ 宀 宇 完	to finish, complete; finished, completed yùhn wán
708 *	宏	⼧ 宀 宏 宏 宏	vast, great wàhng hóng
709 ***	定	⼧ 宀 宀 宇 定 定	certain, decided, finalized; to decide dihng dìng
710 *	宙	⼧ 宀 宀 宙 宙 宙	universe jauh zhòu
711 **	官	⼧ 宀 宀 官 官	officer, official, bodily organ gùn guān
712 **	宗	⼧ 宀 宇 宇 宗	ancestor, clan jùng zōng
713 *	宜	⼧ 宀 宀 宜 宜	suitable, proper yìh yí
714 **	室	⼧ 宀 宏 宏 宏 宰 室	room, office sàt shì
715 **	宣	⼧ 宀 宀 宗 宣 宣 宣	to announce, declare syùn xuān

716 ***	客	宀 宀 宀 灾 灾 客 客	guest, customer, visitor	
			haak	kè
717 ***	容	宀 宀 宀 灾 宕 容 容	to contain, endure; appearance	
			yùhng	róng
718 ***	家	宀 宀 宀 宁 宇 家 家	home, family, household	
			gà	jiā
719 *	宮	宀 宀 宁 宮 宮	palace, temple	
			gùng	gōng
720 *	宴	宀 宀 宀 宦 宦 宴 宴 宴	to feast, entertain; feast, banquet	
			yin	yàn
721 **	害	宀 宀 中 宇 宝 害 害 害	to harm, hurt; misfortune	
			hoih	hài
722 **	寄	宀 宀 宁 宀 宝 宋 害 寄 寄	to send, stay at	
			gei	jì
723 *	宿	宀 宀 宁 宁 宁 宿 佑 宿 宿	dormitory; lodging	
			sùk	sù
724 **	密	宀 宀 宀 宓 宓 宓 密 密 密	dense, secret, intimate; secret	
			maht	mì
725 *	寂	宀 宀 宁 宀 宇 宋 宋 寂 寂	silent, lonely	
			jihk	jì
726 *	寇	宀 宀 宇 完 完 完 寇 寇	plunderer, robber	
			kau	kòu
727 *	寃	宀 宀 宁 宀 宛 宛 宛 寃 寃 寃	injustice	
			yùn	yuān
728 **	富	宀 宀 宁 宁 宁 宫 富 富 富 富	rich, wealthy	
			fu	fù

729 **	寒	宀宀宀宀宀宓寔寒寒 寒	cold, chilly
			hòhn　　　　　　hán
730 ***	實	宀宀宀宀宀宀宀宀 宀宀宀實實實	solid, true, real, sincere
			saht　　　　　　shí
731 *	寧	宀宀宀宀宀宀 宀宀宀宀寧	peaceful; rather
			nìhng　　　　　níng
732 *	寥	宀宀宀宀宀宀 寥	very few; empty
			liùh　　　　　　liáo
733 **	察	宀宀宀宀宀宀 宀宀察察察	to observe, inspect
			chaat　　　　　chá
734 *	寢	宀宀宀宀宀宀 宀宀宀宀寢寢	to sleep, go to bed, stop
			chám　　　　　qǐn
735 *	寡	宀宀宀宀宀宀 宀宀真寡寡	few, alone; widowhood
			gwá　　　　　　guǎ
736 *	寞	宀宀宀宀宀宀 宀宀宣寞寞	lonely
			mohk　　　　　mò
737 **	寬	宀宀宀宀宀宀 宀宀實寬寬	wide, broad
			fùn　　　　　　kuān
738 *	審	宀宀宀宀宀宀 宀宀寄寄審審	to examine, judge
			sám　　　　　　shěn
739 ***	寫	宀宀宀宀宀宀 宀宀寫寫	to write, compose
			sé　　　　　　　xiě
740 *	寵	宀宀宀宀宀宀 宀宀宀寵寵寵	to love, spoil, favor
			chúng　　　　chǒng
741 **	寶	宀宀宀宀宀宀宀 宀宀宀寶寶寶寶	precious; treasure, jewel
			bóu　　　　　　bǎo

		寸　　Section	

742 **	寸	一 寸 寸	Chinese inch
			chyun　　　　　*cùn*

743 *	寺	一 十 土 寺	temple, Buddhist monastery
			jí　　　　　*sì*

744 **	封	一 十 土 圭 封	to seal, close; measure word for correspondence
			fùng　　　　　*fēng*

745 *	射	ノ イ 竹 身 身 身 射	to shoot, squirt
			seh　　　　　*shè*

746 **	將	㇄ ㇄ ㇄ 爿 ㇓ ㇓ ㇓ 將	[1] will, [1] shall; [1] soon; [1] to take; [2] commander
			[1] *jèung*; [2] *jeung*　　[1] *jiāng*; [2] *jiàng*

747 **	專	一 厂 币 百 叀 車 叀 叀 專	to concentrate; special
			jyun　　　　　*zhuān*

748 *	尉	㇖ ㇌ 尸 尼 屈 尉 尉 尉	military officer
			wai　　　　　*wèi*

749 *	尊	㇑ ㇒ 产 产 严 酋 酋 酋 尊	to respect, honor
			jyun　　　　　*zūn*

750 *	尋	㇆ ㇗ ㇕ ㇕ ㇕ ㇕ 寻 寻 寻 寻	[1] to find, [1] search, [1] look for, [2] beg
			[1][2] *chàhm*　　[1] *xún*; [2] *xín*

751 ***	對	㇑ ㇑ ㇑ 业 业 业 业 業 業 業 對	to oppose, compare, deal with; towards; couple
			deui　　　　　*dùi*

752 *	導	㇑ ㇒ ㇒ ㇒ 产 首 首 道 道 道 道 導	to lead, direct
			douh　　　　　*dǎo*

		小　　Section	

753 ***	小	亅 小 小	small, little
			síu　　　　　　　　*xiǎo*
754 ***	少	小 少	[1] a few; [2] young
			[1] *síu*; [2] *siu*　　　　[1] *shǎo*; [2] *shào*
755 **	尖	小 尖	pointed, sharp
			jìm　　　　　　　　*jiān*
756 *	尚	小 小 尚 尚 尚 尚	to hold in esteem; yet, still
			seuhng　　　　　　*shàng*

尢　Section

757 *	尤	一 尢 尢 尤	especially; fault; to blame
			yàuh　　　　　　　*yóu*
758 ***	就	丶 亠 亠 六 古 亨 京 就	then; at once; only; success
			jauh　　　　　　　*jiù*
759 *	尷	尢 尤 尬 尬 尴 尴 尴 尴 尴 尷 尷 尷	awkward, embarrassing
			gaam　　　　　　　*gān*

尸　Section

760 **	尺	𠃍 コ 尸 尺	Chinese foot (measurement), ruler
			chek　　　　　　　*chǐ*
761 *	尼	尸 尸 尼	nun
			nèih　　　　　　　*ní*
762 **	尾	尸 尸 尸 尾 尾	tail, the last, end
			méih　　　　　　　*wěi*
763 **	局	尸 局 局 局 局	bureau, circumstances
			guhk　　　　　　　*jú*

764 *	尿	尸 尸 尸 尿 尿	urine
			niuh niào
765 *	居	尸 尸 尼 尼 居 居	to reside; residence
			geùi jū
766 *	届	⌐ 尸 尼 届 届 届	to reach; term
			gaai jiè
767 *	屈	尸 尼 尼 屈 屈	to bend, stoop
			wàt qū
768 **	屋	尸 尸 居 屈 居 居 屋	house, room
			ùk wū
769 *	屎	尸 尸 屈 屎 屎 屎	excrement
			sí shǐ
770 *	屍	尸 尸 尸 屄 屄 屄 屍	corpse
			sì shī
771 **	展	尸 尸 尸 屈 屈 展 展 展	to spread, expand, exhibit
			jín zhǎn
772 *	屑	尸 尸 尼 屄 屄 屑	fragment, powder
			sit xiè
773 *	屐	尸 尸 尸 屑 屑 屏 屏 屐	wooden slippers, clogs
			kehk jī
774 *	屏	尸 尸 尼 居 屋 屏	screen, shelter
			pihng píng
775 *	屜	尸 尸 尼 尸 屏 屜 屜 屜	drawer
			tai tì
776 *	屠	尸 尸 尸 居 居 屠 屠 屠 屠 屠	to slaughter, butcher
			tòuh tú

777 *	屢	尸 尸 屄 屄 屄 屄 屄 屄 屄 屚 屚 屚 屢	frequent, often leuih lǚ
778 *	履	尸 尺 屄 屄 屄 屄 屄 屄 屄 屄 屄 履	shoes; to act, carry out, walk leuih lǚ
779 **	層	尸 尺 尸 屄 屄 屄 屄 屄 層 層 層	story (in a building), layer chàhng céng
780 *	屬	尸 尺 尸 屄 屄 屄 屄 屄 屄 屬 屬 屬 屬 屬 屬	to belong to, subject to suhk shǔ

屮 Section

781 *	屯	一 亡 屮 屯	to store up, collect together tyùhn tún

山 Section

782 ***	山	丨 屮 山	mountain, hill saàn shān
783 *	岔	丿 八 分 分 岔	intersection; contradictory chà chà
784 *	岳	丿 亻 ⺊ 圷 丘 岳	tall mountain, wife's parent, parent-in-law ngohk yuè
785 *	岸	山 屵 屵 岸 岸	shore ngohn àn
786 *	岩	山 屵 屵 岩 岩 岩	rock ngàahm yán
787 *	島	丿 亻 ⼍ 烏 烏 烏 烏 島	island dóu dǎo

- 101 -

788 *	峭	山 山' 山" 山" 山" 峭	steep, severe
			chiu　　　　qiào
789 *	峰	山 山' 山" 山" 峰 峰	peak
			fùng　　　　fēng
790 *	峽	山 山" 山" 山" 山" 山" 峽	mountain pass, gorge
			hahp　　　　xiá
791 *	峻	山 山' 山" 山" 山" 山" 峻 峻 峻	steep, lofty
			jeun　　　　jùn
792 *	崩	山 ゲ ゲ 岸 崩	to collapse
			bàng　　　　bēng
793 *	崗	山 山" ゲ 岜 岜 岗 岗 崗	ridge of a hill, mound
			gòng　　　　gǎng
794 *	崖	山 ゲ 庐 庐 岸 崖 崖	cliff
			ngàaih　　　yá
795 *	崇	山 ゲ 崇 崇 崇 崇 崇 崇	lofty, high; to worship, respect
			sùhng　　　chóng
796 *	崎	山 山" 山" 山" 山" 崎 崎 崎 崎	rugged, craggy, rough
			kèi　　　　qí
797 *	嵌	山 ゲ 甘 甘 甘 甘 甘 甘 嵌 嵌	to inlay
			hahm　　　qiàn
798 *	嶇	山 山" 屺 屺 屺 屺 嶇 嶇	rugged, craggy, rough
			keùi　　　qū
799 *	嶺	山 ゲ 尖 岺 岺 岺 岺 岺 岺 嶺 嶺 嶺 嶺	mountain range
			lihng　　　lǐng
800 *	嶼	山 山" 山" 峅 峅 峅 峅 峅 峅 峅 嶼 嶼	[1] small island, [2] one of the Hong Kong islands
			[1] jeuih; [2] yùh　　[1] [2] yǔ

801 *	巓	山 屵 屵 峕 峕 峕 巅 巅 巅 巓 巓 巓 巓	peak, mountain top
			dīn 　　　　　　*diān*

<<< Section

802 *	川	))) 川	stream, flow; Zichuan
			chyùn 　　　　　*chuān*

803 *	州	) ナ 州 州 州 州	state, region
			jàu 　　　　　　*zhōu*

804 *	巢	く 巛 巛 岑 峃 峃 峃 巣 巢 巢	nest
			chaàuh 　　　　*cháo*

工　Section

805 ***	工	一 丁 工	to work, labor; workman, laborer
			gùng 　　　　　*gōng*

806 **	左	一 ナ 左	the left side
			jó 　　　　　　*zuǒ*

807 *	巧	工 工 巧	skillful, dexterous
			haáu 　　　　　*qiǎo*

808 *	巨	一 丁 尸 戸 巨	huge, enormous, gigantic
			geuih 　　　　　*jù*

809 *	巫	一 丁 丌 巫 巫 巫	wizard, witch
			mòuh 　　　　　*wū*

810 ***	差	` ` ` ` ` ` 羊 差	[1] difference, [1] mistake, [4] order; [2] bad; [3] to send
			[1][2] *chà*; [3] *chaài*; [4] *chī* [1] *chā*; [2] *chà*; [3] *chāi*; [4] *cī*

己　Section

811 **	己	フ コ 己	oneself géi　　　　jǐ
812 ***	已	フ コ 已	already; stopped yíh　　　　yǐ
813 *	巳	フ コ 巳	the 6th of the branches jih　　　　si
814 *	巴	フ コ コ 巴	to attach to bà　　　　bā
815 *	巷	丨 十 艹 芷 芋 共 芸 茶 巷	alley hohng　　　　xiàng

巾　Section

816 *	巾	丨 冂 巾	towel, napkin, kerchief gàn　　　　jīn
817 **	布	一 ナ 大 右 布	cloth, fabric bou　　　　bù
818 **	市	丶 亠 市	market, city, town síh　　　　shì
819 *	帆	巾 巾丶 帆 帆	sail, canvas faàhn　　　　fán
820 **	希	ノ メ 乂 圶 希	to hope, wish; scarce hèi　　　　xī
821 *	帕	巾 巾丶 帕 帕 帕 帕	kerchief paak　　　　pà
822 *	帚	フ ヨ ヨ 帚 帚 帚	broom jáau　　　　zhǒu

823 *	帛	丿 亻 白 白 白 帛	silk, fabric
			baahk bó
824 *	帖	巾 巾丨 巾十 巾圤 帖 帖	[1] invitation, [2] practice book for characters
			[1][2] tip [1] tiě, [2] tiè
825 **	帝	丶 二 亠 立 产 帝	emperor
			dai dì
826 *	帥	丿 亻 亡 𠂤 帥	general, leader, commander in chief
			seui shuài
827 **	師	丿 亻 亡 𠂤 師 師	teacher, instructor
			si shī
828 **	席	丶 二 广 广 产 庐 庐 席	mat, table, feast
			jihk xí
829 *	帷	巾 巾丨 巾丨 帏 帏 帷 帷	curtain, screen
			waih wéi
830 ***	帶	一 十 丗 丗 丗 丗 丗 丗 帶	belt, band; to carry, lead, bring
			daai dài
831 **	帳	巾 巾丨 巾丨 帐 帐 帳 帳 帳	curtain, screen
			jeung zhàng
832 ***	常	丨 丷 丷 兴 兴 学 学 常	regular, frequent
			seuhng cháng
833 *	幀	巾 巾丨 巾丨 帖 帖 帕 幀 幀	measure word for pictures
			jing zhèng
834 *	幅	巾 巾丨 巾丨 帄 帄 帾 帾 幅 幅	width, roll
			fuk fú
835 **	帽	巾 巾丨 巾丨 帜 帽 帽 帽 帽	cap, hat
			mouh mào

836 *	幕	`丶 亠 艹 芦 节 苩 苩` `莫 莫 莫 幕`	curtain	
			mohk	mù
837 *	幣	`丿 兴 兴 片 朮 尚 敝` `敝 敝 敝 幣`	money, currency	
			baih	bì
838 *	幟	`巾 巾 巾 忄 帄 帜 帜` `帜 帜 幟 幟 幟`	banner, flag	
			chi	zhì
839 **	幫	`一 十 土 主 圭 封 封` `封 封 封 封 封 幫`	to help; gang	
			bòng	bāng
840 *	幪	`巾 巾 巾 忄 忄 忄 帩` `帩 帩 幪 幪 幪`	to cover up	
			mùhng	méng

干　　　Section

841 **	干	`一 二 干`	to interfere	
			gòn	gān
842 **	平	`一 亓 平 平`	level, even, ordinary, peaceful	
			pìhng	píng
843 ***	年	`丿 仁 仁 午 乍` `年`	year, age	
			nìhn	nián
844 **	幸	`一 十 土 去 幸`	fortunate; luck	
			hahng	xìng
845 **	幹	`一 十 土 古 古 古` `卓 卓 斡 幹`	to do, manage	
			gon	gàn

幺　　　Section

| 846 * | 幻 | `乚 幺 幺 幻` | imaginary, unreal; fantasy; to fantasize | |
| | | | waahn | huàn |

847 *	幼	幻 幼	young; early age
			yau　　　　　　yòu
848 *	幽	｜ 幻 峰 幽 幽	dark, refined
			yàu　　　　　　yōu
849 ***	幾	幺 幺幺 丝 丝丝 幾 幾 幾	[1] several, [1] some; [2] almost
			[1] géi; [2] gèi　　[1] jǐ; [2] jī

广　Section

850 *	序	、 ー 广 广 庐 序 序	order, preface
			jeuih　　　　　xù
851 *	庇	广 广 店 庇 庇	to shelter, protect
			bei　　　　　　bì
852 *	床	广 广 庁 床 床	bed
			chohng　　　　chuáng
853 **	底	广 广 庐 店 底 底	bottom, base; under
			dái　　　　　　dǐ
854 ***	店	广 广 庄 庄 店 店	store, shop
			dim　　　　　　diàn
855 **	府	广 广 庁 斤 府 府	government, residence
			fú　　　　　　　fǔ
856 **	度	广 广 庐 庐 庐 度 度	[1] to measure, [1] estimate, [1] pass, [2] conjecture; [1] degree
			[1] douh; [2] dohk　[1] dù; [2] duó
857 *	庭	广 广 庁 床 庄 庭 庭 庭	courtyard
			tihng　　　　　tíng
858 *	座	广 广 广 庐 庐 座 座	seat, stand
			joh　　　　　　zuò

859 *	庫	广 广 庐 庐 庐 庐 庫 庫	depot, storehouse
			fu 　　　　*kù*
860 *	庶	广 广 庐 庐 庐 庶	many, various; people
			syu 　　　　*shù*
861 *	庸	广 广 庐 庐 庐 庐 肩 庸	common, ordinary
			yùhng 　　　　*yōng*
862 *	康	广 广 庐 庐 庚 庚 庚 康 康	healthy, peaceful
			hòng 　　　　*kāng*
863 *	廂	广 广 厈 庌 床 床 廂 廂 廂	a side room
			seùng 　　　　*xiāng*
864 *	廁	广 广 庁 庌 庌 庌 庌 庌 庌	toilet
			chi 　　　　*cè*
865 *	廊	广 广 庐 庌 庌 庌 庌 廊 廊	porch
			lòhng 　　　　*láng*
866 *	廈	广 广 庐 庐 庐 盾 盾 盾 廈 廈	large house, building
			hah 　　　　*shà*
867 *	廉	广 广 庐 庌 庐 庐 廉 廉 廉	honest, low-priced
			lìhm 　　　　*lián*
868 *	廟	广 广 庐 庐 庐 庐 庐 庫 庫 廟 廟	temple
			miú 　　　　*miào*
869 *	廢	广 庐 庐 庁 庂 庂 庂 庲 庲 麿 麿 廢	to abandon; waste, ruined
			fai 　　　　*fei`*
870 **	廠	广 广 庐 庐 庌 庌 庌 庌 廂 廂 廠 廠	factory, mill, plant
			chóng 　　　　*chǎng*
871 **	廣	广 广 庐 庐 庌 庌 庫 庯 庯 廣 廣 廣	broad; to enlarge; width
			gwóng 　　　　*guǎng*

872 *	廚	广 广 广 庐 庐 庐 庐 庐 庐 廚 廚 廚 廚	kitchen, cook
			chèuih chú
873 *	龐	广 广 广 庐 庐 床 庐 庐 庐 庐 庐 龐 龐	huge
			pòhng páng
874 *	廳	广 庐 庐 庐 庐 庐 庐 庐 庐 庐 庐 庐 庐 庐 庐 廳 廳 廳	hall, living room
			tìng tīng

又 Section

875 *	廷	ノ ー 千 壬 壬 廷 廷	palace, imperial court
			tìhng tíng
876 *	延	ノ ノ 千 壬 正 延	to lengthen, postpone, delay
			yìhn yán
877 **	建	ｺ ｺ ｺ ｺ ｺ 聿 建	to establish, build, suggest
			gin jiàn

廾 Section

878 **	弄	ー 丁 王 王 弄	to make, play, cause
			nuhng nòng
879 *	弊	' 丷 丷 为 尚 尚 尚 敝 敝 弊	defects, corruption
			baih bì

弋 Section

880 *	貳	一 二 三 貳 貳	two
			yih èr
881 **	式	一 二 三 式 式 式	form, formula, style
			sìk shì

882 *	弑	ノ メ ㄨ 二 辛 矛 杀 杀 弑	to murder a superior si shì

弓   Section

883 *	弓	ㄱ ㄱ 弓	bow (for arrow) gùng gōng
884 **	引	弓 引	to pull, lead, guide, introduce yáhn yǐn
885 *	弔	弓 弔	to offer condolences, hang diu diào
886 *	弛	弓 弓ㄱ 弓� 弛	to loosen, relax chìh chí
887 **	弟	ヽ 苎 弟 弟	younger brother daih dì
888 *	弧	弓 弓 弘 弧 弧 弧	wooden bow, arc wùh hú
889 *	弦	弓 弓 弘 弦 弦 弦	string of a bow, string of a musical instrument yìhn xián
890 **	弱	弓 弓 弱	weak, young yeuhk ruò
891 ***	張	弓 弓 弘 弜 弝 張 張 張	to stretch, open; sheet jeùng zhāng
892 **	強	弓 引 弘 弘 弜 弲 強 強	[1] strong, [1] rough; [2] to force [1] keùhng; [2] keúhng [1] qiáng; [2] qiǎng
893 **	彈	弓 弓 弘 弜 弲 弾 弾 彈 彈 彈 彈	[1] bullet; [2] to flick, [2] play music [1] daahn; [2] tàhn [1] dàn; [2] tán

894 *	彌	弓 弓 弜 弜 弜 弥 弥 弥 弥 弥 弥	full	
			nèih	mí
895 *	彎	、 亠 亖 言 言 信 信 絃 結 䜌 彎	to bend; curve	
			wàan	wān

彐 Section

896 *	彗	三 丰 拝 彗 彗 彗	broom	
			seuih, waih	huì
897 *	彙	乚 彑 立 血 血 岛 岛 彖 彖 彙 彙 彙	to gather	
			wuih	huì

彡 Section

898 **	形	二 开 形	shape, figure, appearance	
			yìhng	xíng
899 *	彥	、 亠 文 立 产 彦	educated and gentlemanly	
			yihn	yàn
900 *	彩	丿 爫 爫 平 采 采 彩	beautiful colors	
			chói	cǎi
901 *	彫	丿 冂 月 用 周 周 周 周 彫	to carve, engrave	
			diù	diāo
902 *	彪	丨 𠂉 𠃑 广 卢 虍 虎 虎 彪	little tiger, tiger stripes	
			biù	biāo
903 *	彬	一 十 才 木 林 彬	elegant and refined	
			bàn	bīn
904 *	彰	、 亠 立 立 产 音 音 音 音 章 彰	apparent; to show	
			jeung	zhāng

905 **	影	丶 冂 冂 日 旦 里 昙 昙 昜 景 景 影	shadow, image, movie; to make photocopies, take pictures yíng _____ yǐng

彳	Section

906 *	役	丶 彳 彳 彳 彳 役	event, service, work, servant yihk _____ yì
907 *	彷	彳 彳 彳 彷 彷	resembling, alike fóng _____ fǎng
908 ***	往	彳 彳 彳 往 往 往	to go; formerly, toward wóhng _____ wǎng
909 *	征	彳 彳 彳 征 征 征	to attack, tax jìng _____ zhēng
910 *	彼	彳 彳 彳 彼 彼 彼	that, those, he, she, it, they béi _____ bǐ
911 ***	後	彳 彳 衫 後 後 後 後	back, behind, later, after hauh _____ hòu
912 ***	很	彳 彳 彳 彳 很 很 很	very hán _____ hěn
913 **	待	彳 彳 彳 待 待 待 待	to wait, treat, handle; salary doih _____ dài
914 **	律	彳 彳 彳 律 律 律 律	laws, rules leuht _____ lü
915 *	徊	彳 彳 彳 徊 徊 徊	to go back and forth wùih _____ huái
916 *	徐	彳 彳 彳 徐 徐 徐 徐	slow, at ease chèuih _____ xú

917 *	徒	彳 彳 彳 샤 샤 샤 샤 徙 徒	bad person, follower, disciple
			tòuh　　　　　tú
918 *	徑	彳 彳 샤 샤 샤 徑	path
			ging　　　　　jìng
919 *	徘	彳 彳 샤 徘 徘	to walk aimlessly
			pùih　　　　　pái
920 ***	從	彳 彳 샤 샤 샤 샤 샤 從	from; to follow, obey, join
			chùhng　　　　cóng
921 *	徙	彳 彳 샤 샤 샤 샤 샤 徙	to move, shift
			saái　　　　　xǐ
922 ***	得	彳 彳 샤 샤 샤 샤 得 得	[1] to get, [1] gain; [1] can, [1] may; [1] finished; [2] must
			[1] [2] dàk　　　[1] dé; [2] děi
923 *	御	彳 彳 샤 샤 샤 샤 御 御	to drive, manage
			yuh　　　　　yù
924 *	徧	彳 彳 샤 샤 샤 샤 徧 徧	everywhere
			pin　　　　　biàn
925 **	復	彳 彳 샤 샤 샤 샤 샤 復 復	to recover, return
			fuhk　　　　　fù
926 *	徨	彳 彳 샤 샤 샤 샤 徨	hesitating, confused
			wòhng　　　　huáng
927 *	循	彳 彳 샤 샤 샤 샤 循 循	to follow, accord
			chèuhn　　　　xún
928 *	徬	彳 彳 샤 샤 샤 徬 徬 徬	uncertain, in a dilemma
			pòhng　　　　páng
929 *	微	彳 彳 샤 샤 샤 샤 샤 微 微	small, tiny
			mèih　　　　　wéi

930 *	徵	彳 彳' 彳# 彳# 彳# 彳# 徨 徨 徵 徵 徵	to levy, collect
		jìng	zhēng
931 **	德	彳 彳 彳# 彳# 德 德 德 德 德 德 德	morality, virtue; Germany; German
		dàk	dé
932 *	徹	彳 彳 彳# 彳# 彳# 循 循 循 循 徹 徹 徹	throughout, thorough
		chit	chè
933 *	徽	彳 彳 彳# 彳# 彳# 徨 徨 徨 徨 徽 徽 徽 徽	symbol, badge
		fài	huī

心　Section

934 ***	心	丶 心 心 心	heart, mind, mood, motive
		sàm	xīn
935 ***	必	心 必 必	surely, certainly, must
		bìt	bì
936 *	忍	刁 刀 刃 忍	to endure, bear; patience
		yán	rěn
937 *	忌	刁 刁 己 忌	to avoid; jealous
		geih	jì
938 **	忘	丶 亠 亡 忘	to forget, neglect
		mòhng	wàng
939 **	志	一 十 士 志	will, target, determination, intention
		ji	zhì
940 **	忙	丶 刂 忄 忄 忙 忙	busy, occupied, hurried
		mòhng	máng
941 *	忠	丶 冖 口 中 忠	loyal, faithful, sincere
		jùng	zhōng

942 ***	念	丿 亻 𠆢 今 念	to think about; thought *nihm*　　　*niàn*
943 **	忽	丿 勹 勿 忽	suddenly; to neglect *fàt*　　　*hū*
944 ***	快	忄 忄 忆 忰 快	cheerful, straightforward, rapid; almost *faai*　　　*kuài*
945 **	性	忄 忄 忰 忰 性	nature, gender, sex, disposition *sing*　　　*xìng*
946 **	急	丿 ⺈ 刍 刍 刍 急	hasty, urgent, anxious *gàp*　　　*jí*
947 *	怒	乚 𡿨 女 奴 奴 怒	angry; anger *nouh*　　　*nù*
948 ***	思	丶 冂 曰 甲 田 思	to think, miss; thought *sì*　　　*sī*
949 *	怠	乚 厶 台 台 台 怠	lazy, idle *tóih*　　　*dài*
950 **	怪	忄 忄 忆 怪 怪 怪	strange; to blame *gwaai*　　　*guài*
951 **	怎	丿 ⺅ 个 乍 怎	how, why *jám*　　　*zěn*
952 **	怕	忄 忄 忄 怕 怕 怕	to fear, guess *pa*　　　*pà*
953 *	怯	忄 忄 忓 怯 怯 怯	timid, cowardly *hip*　　　*qiè*
954 *	怨	丿 夕 夕 夕 夗 怨	hatred; to grumble, complain *yun*　　　*yuàn*

955 *	怖	忄 忄 忙 忙 怖 怖	terror
			bou bù
956 *	恒	忄 忄 忙 恒 恒 恒 恒	permanent, constant
			hàhng héng
957 **	恩	丨 冂 冃 因 因 因 恩	favor, benevolence
			yàn ēn
958 **	恨	忄 忄 忖 忖 忆 恨 恨	to hate; resentment
			hahn hèn
959 **	息	丿 亻 自 自 自 息	breath, interest, news; to stop, rest
			sik xī
960 *	恕	乁 夂 女 如 如 如 恕	to pardon, excuse, forgive
			syu shù
961 *	恙	丷 丷 羊 羊 恙	sickness, illness, worry
			yeuhng yàng
962 *	恢	忄 忄 忙 恢 恢 恢	great; to recover, restore
			fùi hūi
963 **	恐	一 丁 工 邛 巩 巩 恐	to fear, threaten
			húng kǒng
964 *	恭	丶 十 艹 艹 芇 芣 荅 恭	to respect
			gùng gōng
965 *	恰	忄 忄 忄 忄 恰 恰 恰	just, exactly
			hàp qià
966 *	耻	一 丁 丆 耳 耳 耻	shame; shameful
			chí chǐ
967 *	恤	忄 忄 忄 恤 恤 恤	to pity, sympathize
			syùt xù

No.	Character	Stroke order	Meaning / Pronunciation
968 *	悔	忄 忄' 忙 忻 悔 悔 悔 悔	to regret, repent *fui*　　　*huǐ*
969 *	悟	忄 忄一 忏 忏 怄 悟 悟 悟	to apprehend, understand, become aware *ngh*　　　*wù*
970 *	悠	ノ イ 亻 亻 攸 攸 攸 悠	long (period of time), sad *yàuh*　　　*yōu*
971 *	您	ノ イ 亻 你 你 你 你 您	respectful form of "you" *néih*　　　*nín*
972 *	患	、 冖 口 串 患	worry, tragedy, trouble, distress *waahn*　　　*huàn*
973 *	悦	忄 忄ˊ 忄 悦 悦 悦 悦	delighted, pleasant *yuht*　　　*yuè*
974 *	悉	ノ 厶 立 平 釆 釆 悉	to know, comprehend; all; completely *sīk*　　　*xī*
975 *	悄	忄 忄' 忄' 忄' 悄 悄	[1] quiet, [1] sorrowful; [2] to whisper [1] [2] *chiu*　　[1] *qiǎo*; [2] *qiǎo*
976 *	惟	忄 忄' 忄' 忄' 忙 忙 惟	to think about; only, but, however *wàih*　　　*wéi*
977 *	惋	忄 忄 忄 忄 忄 忄 忄 惋	to sympathize *yún*　　　*wǎn*
978 *	悽	忄 忄 忏 忏 悽 悽 悽 悽 悽	grieved; sorrowful *chài*　　　*qī*
979 ***	情	忄 忄 忄 忄 情 情 情	feelings, affection, favor, condition *chìhng*　　　*qíng*
980 **	惡	一 丅 丁 亞 亞 惡 惡 亞 惡	[1] bad, [1] wicked, [2] disgusting [1] *ok*; [2] *wu*　　[1] *è*; [2] *wù*

981 *	悼	ㄐ ㄐ' ㄐ^ ㄐ= 忄占 忄占 忄卓 悼	to lament
			douh / daò
982 *	悴	ㄐ ㄐ' ㄐ^ 忄ゥ 忄ゥ 忄卒 悴 悴	haggard
			seúih / cùi
983 *	悲	l ㅋ 非 非 非 悲	sad, pessimistic
			bēi / bēi
984 *	惕	ㄐ ㄐ' 忄' 忄ワ 忄ワ 忄ワ 惕 惕	cautious, watchful
			tik / tì
985 *	悶	l ㄏ ㄏ ㄋ ㄋl ㄋ| ㄋ| 門 門 悶	bored, melancholy, sultry, suffocating
			muhn / mèn
986 *	惦	ㄐ ㄐ' 忄' 忄广 忄广 忄广 忄店 忄店 惦 惦	to think of someone
			dim / diàn
987 *	惆	ㄐ ㄐ' 忄] 忄] 忄冂 忄冂 忄冂 惆 惆	disappointed, vexed, grieved
			chàuh / chóu
988 *	惠	一 ㄏ 币 市 市 軎 重 重 惠	favor, kindness
			waih / huì
989 **	惜	ㄐ ㄐ' 忄' 忄世 忄世 忄世 惜 惜 惜	to treasure, regret; pity
			sik / xī
990 *	惑	一 ㄈ ㄈ 戓 可 或 或 或 惑 惑	to doubt; suspicion
			waahk / huò
991 **	感	一 ㄏ ㄏ 反 咸 咸 咸 咸 咸 感 感	to feel, influence; feeling, emotion
			gám / gǎn
992 ***	愛	ʼ ʼʼ ʼʼʼ 爫 爫 愛 愛 愛 愛	to love, be fond of; love
			oi / aì
993 **	想	一 十 オ オ 木 木 相 相 相 想	to think, miss, want, consider
			seúng / xiǎng

994 *	惰	忄 忄 忄 忄 忰 忰 / 忰 惰 惰	lazy, sluggish, idle
			doh　　　　　　　*duò*
995 *	愚	丶 口 口 日 旦 禺 / 禺 禺 禺 愚	stupid, foolish; to fool
			yùh　　　　　　　*yú*
996 *	惶	忄 忄 忄 忄 忄 / 忷 忷 悼 惶	frightened, fearful
			wòhng　　　　　*huáng*
997 *	愉	忄 忄 忄 忄 忄 忏 / 愉 愉 愉	happy
			yùh　　　　　　　*yú*
998 *	愎	忄 忄 忄 忄 忄 愊 / 愊 愊 愎 愎	stubborn
			bīk　　　　　　　*bì*
999 ***	意	丶 亠 立 立 音 音 音 / 音 意	thought, opinion, idea; Italy; Italian
			yi　　　　　　　　*yì*
1000 *	惻	忄 忄 忄 忄 恻 恻 / 恻 惻 惻	to grieve for, pity
			chàk　　　　　　*cè*
1001 *	愈	丿 人 亼 今 合 俞 / 俞 俞 愈	more, further
			yuht　　　　　　*yù*
1002 *	惱	忄 忄 忄 忄 惱 / 惱 惱 惱	irritated, distressed; to be upset at
			nóuh　　　　　　*nǎo*
1003 *	愕	忄 忄 忄 愕 愕 / 愕	startled, frightened
			ngohk　　　　　*è*
1004 **	愁	丿 亠 千 禾 禾 禾 / 禾 秋 秋 愁	to worry; sad, gloomy
			sàuh　　　　　　*chóu*
1005 *	惹	丶 丷 艹 艹 若 / 芋 若 若 惹	to incite, cause, tease
			yéh　　　　　　　*rě*
1006 *	愧	忄 忄 忄 忄 愧 愧 / 愧 愧 愧 愧 愧	ashamed
			kwáih　　　　　*kuì*

1007 *	慭	ノ 亻 冃 冃 臬 臬 肻 肸 殷 慭	sorrowful, enthusiastic
			yàn	*yīn*
1008 **	態	ㅗ ㅿ 角 角 肖 肖 能 能 態	form, attitude, behavior
			taai	*tài*
1009 *	慌	ㅐ ㅐ 忄 忄 忙 忙 忙 恍 慌 慌	to fear; alarmed, nervous
			fòng	*huāng*
1010 *	愴	ㅐ 忄 忄 怜 怜 怜 怜 愴 愴 愴	sad
			chong	*chuàng*
1011 *	慈	ㅛ 兰 芦 玄 兹 兹 慈	kind, motherly
			chìh	*cí*
1012 *	慎	ㅐ 忄 忄 忤 恂 恟 恾 恾 愼 慎	careful, cautious
			sahn	*shèn*
1013 **	慶	ㆍ ㅗ 广 户 户 庐 庐 庐 廖 廖 慶 慶	to celebrate; celebration
			hing	*qìng*
1014 *	慨	(慨) ㅐ 忄 忓 忮 忮 忯 恨 恨 慨 慨 慨	resentment, generous, noble
			koi	*kǎi*
1015 *	慰	フ ㄱ 尸 尼 尽 层 层 尉 尉 尉 慰	pleased, comfortable; to console
			wai	*wèi*
1016 *	慾	ノ 八 公 欠 谷 谷 谷 谷 欲 慾	appetite, desire, lust
			yuhk	*yù*
1017 *	慷	ㅐ 忄 忄 忭 忭 忭 慷 慷 慷 慷 慷	generous, bountiful
			hóng	*kāng*
1018 ***	慢	ㅐ 忄 忙 忙 忆 愠 愠 愠 愠 慢 慢	slow, negligent
			maahn	*màn*
1019 *	憂	ㆍ ㄱ 了 丆 冇 百 百 直 惪 惪 夢 夢 憂	to worry; distress, sorrow
			yàu	*yōu*

1020 *	慮	一 ト ゲ 卢 卢 虎 虏 虏 虏 虜 慮	to think through, worry; concerned
			leuih *lù*
1021 *	慟	ㅏ ㅑ ㅑ 忄 忄 恒 恒 恒 恒 慟 慟	grief; sorrowful
			duhng *tòng*
1022 *	慣	ㅏ 忄 忄 忡 忡 忡 忡 惜 惜 慣	habitual, accustomed; habit
			gwaan *guàn*
1023 *	慘	ㅏ 忄 忄 忄 忲 忴 恔 慘	tragic, cruel
			cháam *cǎn*
1024 *	慫	ㄅ 彳 彳 彳 彳 從 彴 彴 從 慫	to instigate, urge
			súng *sǒng*
1025 *	慚	ㅏ 忄 忄 忄 恒 恒 恒 惶 惶 慚 慚 慚	ashamed
			chàahm *cán*
1026 *	慧	三 丰 封 封 封 彗 彗 慧	wise, intelligent; wisdom, intelligence
			waih *hùi*
1027 *	憔	ㅏ 忄 忄 忄 忭 忭 惟 憔	haggard
			chìuh *qiáo*
1028 *	憎	ㅏ 忄 忄 恺 恺 恺 憎 憎 憎 憎 憎	to dislike, hate
			jàng *zēng*
1029 *	憐	ㅏ 忄 忄 忡 烊 烊 烊 烊 烊 憐 憐	to pity, sympathize
			lihn *lián*
1030 *	憫	ㅏ 忄 忄 忊 忊 忊 忟 惆 悶 憫 憫 憫	sad; to pity, sympathize
			máhn *mǐn*
1031 *	憮	ㅏ 忄 忄 忙 惇 憮 憮	disappointed, depressed; to cherish
			móuh *wǔ*
1032 *	憑	冫 冫 冮 冯 馮 馮 憑	to lean on, depend on; proof
			pàhng *píng*

1033 *	憤	忄 忄 忄 忄 忱 忱 忱 忱 憤 憤	indignant; indignation, anger
			fáhn 　　　　　　*fèn*
1034 *	憲	丶 ﾉ 宀 宀 宀 宝 宝 宝 寓 寓 寓 憲	law, constitution
			hin 　　　　　　*xiàn*
1035 ***	應	丶 一 广 广 广 府 府 府 雁 雁 應	¹ should; ² to reply
			¹ *yīng*; ² *yìng* 　　¹ *yīng*; ² *yìng*
1036 *	憶	忄 忄 忄 忄 忄 忱 忱 忱 憶 憶	to recall, remember
			yik 　　　　　　*yì*
1037 ***	懂	忄 忄 忄 忄 忄 忱 忱 忱 懂 懂 懂 懂 懂.	to understand, comprehend
			dúng 　　　　　*dǒng*
1038 *	懊	忄 忄 忄 忄 忱 忱 忱 忱 懊 懊 懊	to regret; irritated
			ou 　　　　　　*aò*
1039 *	懇	ノ ⺈ 夕 夕 豸 豸 豸 豸 豺 豺 豺 懇 懇 懇	sincere; to beg
			hán 　　　　　　*kěn*
1040 *	憾	忄 忄 忄 忄 忱 忱 忱 忱 憾 憾 憾 憾	unpleasant, regretful
			hahm 　　　　　*hàn*
1041 *	懈	忄 忄 忄 忄 忱 忱 忱 忱 懈 懈 懈 懈 懈	lazy, idle; liquefy
			haaih 　　　　*xiè*
1042 *	懦	忄 忄 忄 忄 忱 忱 忱 忱 懦 懦 懦 懦 懦	weak, cowardly
			noh 　　　　　　*nuò*
1043 *	懲	ノ 彳 彳 彳 彳 彳 衧 衧 徨 徨 徵 徵 徵	to punish
			chìhng 　　　　*chéng*
1044 *	懸	l 冂 月 目 旦 早 県 県 縣 縣 縣 縣 懸 懸	to hang, suspend; dangerous, different
			yùhn 　　　　　*xuán*
1045 **	懶	忄 忄 忄 忄 忱 忱 忱 忱 懶 懶 懶 懶 懶 懶	lazy, idle
			laahn 　　　　*lǎn*

1046 *	懷	to embrace, carry, think of; mind
		wàaih 　　　 *huái*

1047 *	懺	to regret, repent
		chaam 　　　 *chàn*

1048 *	懼	to fear; afraid
		geuih 　　　 *jù*

1049 *	戀	to long for, love; love
		lyún 　　　 *liàn*

戈　　　Section

1050 *	戊	5th of the 10 stems
		mouh 　　　 *wù*

1051 *	戌	the 11th of the 12 branches
		seùt 　　　 *xū*

1052 *	戎	weapon, troop, military matter
		yùhng 　　　 *róng*

1053 *	戍	to guard the frontier
		syu 　　　 *shù*

1054 **	成	to finish, succeed, become; successful
		sìhng 　　　 *chéng*

1055 ***	我	I, me
		ngóh 　　　 *wǒ*

1056 *	戒	to warn, caution, abstain
		gaai 　　　 *jiè*

1057 ***	或	or; perhaps, probably
		waahk 　　　 *huò*

1058 *	戚	一 厂 厂 厂 厉 厉 厉 咸 戚 戚	relative, sorrow; sad chìk qī
1059 *	截	一 十 土 圥 圥 圥 圥 亦 聟 截 截 截	to cut off, intercept jiht jié
1060 **	戰	丨 冂 口 吅 咒 罒 罒 罒 單 單 單 戰	to fight, fear, tremble; battle, war jin zhàn
1061 **	戲	丨 卜 占 卢 卢 虎 虎 虍 虛 虗 虛 虘 戲	to play, joke; game, play hei xì
1062 *	戴	十 土 圥 吉 直 喜 喜 喜 喜 壹 壹 載 戴	to wear, respect daai dài
1063 *	戳	⁊ ⁊ ⁊⁊ 羽 羽 翟 翟 翟 翟 戳	to stab; stamp, seal cheuk chuō

户   Section

1064 **	户	丶 ㇇ 亠 户	door, household wuh hù
1065 **	房	户 户 庐 庐 房 房	room, house, apartment fòhng fáng
1066 ***	所	⼁ ㇒ 斤 斤 斤 所 所 所	place; that which só suǒ
1067 *	扁	户 户 启 启 扁	flat bín biǎn
1068 *	扇	户 戽 肩 扇	[1] fan, [1] leaf of a door; [2] to fan [1] [2] sin [1] shàn; [2] chān
1069 *	扉	户 戽 肩 扉 扉	one-leaf door, back cover of a book fèi fēi

手 Section

1070 ***	手	ノ 二 三 手	hand, arm	*sáu*	*shǒu*
1071 ***	才	一 十 才	ability, talent; just, only if	*chòih*	*cái*
1072 *	扎	一 寸 扌 扎	to prick, pierce, tie up	*jaat*	*zhā*
1073 **	打	扌 扌一 打	to strike, hit; dozen	*dá*	*dǎ*
1074 *	扒	扌 扌丿 扒	to scratch, pick a pocket; pickpocket	*pàh*	*pá*
1075 *	扔	扌 扌乃 扔	to throw	*yìng*	*rēng*
1076 *	托	扌 扌丿 扌乇 托	to support with the hand, entrust	*tok*	*tuō*
1077 *	扛	扌 扌一 扌丅 扛	[1] to carry with both hands, [2] carry on shoulders	[1 2] *gòng*	[1] *gāng;* [2] *káng*
1078 **	扣	扌 扌丨 扌冂 扣	to hold, deduct, knock	*kau*	*kòu*
1079 *	抓	扌 扌丿 扌厂 扌爪 抓	to scratch, seize	*jáau*	*zhuā*
1080 **	投	扌 扌几 扌几 扌殳 投	to throw	*tàuh*	*tóu*
1081 ***	把	扌 扌巴 扌巴 扌巴 把	to hold, take; measure word for things with handles	*bá*	*bǎ*

1082 **	折	才 才 打 折 折	to break, discount; discount *jit* *zhé*
1083 *	技	才 才 扩 拮 技	skill, technique *geih* *jì*
1084 **	批	才 才 扎 批 批	to criticize, sell wholesale *pài* *pī*
1085 **	找	才 扌 扌 找 找	to seek, look for, find *jáau* *zhǎo*
1086 **	承	了 了 矛 承 承 承	to receive, acknowledge *sìhng* *chéng*
1087 *	扭	才 打 扣 扭 扭	to twist *náu* *niǔ*
1088 *	扮	才 扌 扒 扮 扮	to dress up, disguise *baahn* *bàn*
1089 *	抄	才 扌 扌 抄 抄	to confiscate, copy *chàau* *chāo*
1090 **	抗	才 扌 扩 扩 抗	to resist, object, oppose *kong* *kàng*
1091 *	扶	才 扌 扙 扶 扶	to support, assist *fùh* *fú*
1092 *	抒	才 扌 扝 抒 抒	to express, pour out, state freely *syù* *shū*
1093 *	扯	才 扌 扖 扯 扯	to tear, pull, drag *ché* *chě*
1094 *	抑	才 扌 扝 押 抑	to restrain, repress; or *yìk* *yì*

1095 *	抖	扌 扗 扗 抖	to shake, tremble *dáu*　　　　*dǒu*
1096 *	拜	´ 三 手 拜 拜	to worship *baai*　　　　*bài*
1097 *	拒	扌 扌 扪 扪 拒 拒	to resist, refuse, reject *kéuih*　　　　*jù*
1098 **	抛	(抛) 扌 扌 扚 执 抛	to throw, cast *paàu*　　　　*pāo*
1099 *	拖	扌 扌 扩 拖 拖 拖	to drag, tow, delay *tò*　　　　*tuō*
1100 *	拘	扌 扌 扚 扚 扚 拘	to arrest, restrict; restraint *keūi*　　　　*jū*
1101 *	押	扌 扌 扣 押 押 押	to mortgage, arrest *ngaat*　　　　*yā*
1102 *	拔	扌 扌 扩 扐 拔 拔	to pull, pluck *baht*　　　　*bá*
1103 *	抬	扌 扌 扪 抬 抬 抬	to lift, raise, carry between 2 people *tòih*　　　　*tái*
1104 **	抵	扌 扌 扡 扺 抵 抵	to resist, arrive, mortgage *dái*　　　　*dǐ*
1105 *	招	扌 扌 扟 扣 招 招	to beckon, cause, confess, invite *jiū*　　　　*zhāo*
1106 **	抽	扌 扌 扣 抽 抽 抽	to pull, draw *chàu*　　　　*chōu*
1107 *	拌	扌 扌 扞 拌	to stir, mix *buhn*　　　　*bàn*

1108 *	披	扌 扌 扩 扴 抜 披	to spread out, put on
			pèi　　　　　　pī
1109 *	拐	扌 扌 扩 扩 拐 拐	to kidnap, swindle
			gwáai　　　　　guǎi
1110 **	抱	扌 扌 扩 抝 抩 抱	to embrace, carry in the arms
			póuh　　　　　bào
1111 *	拍	扌 扌 扩 折 拍 拍	to pat, clap, hit; beat, rhythm
			paak　　　　　pāi
1112 *	拙	扌 扌 扩 扗 拙	clumsy, awkward
			chyut　　　　　zhuō
1113 **	拉	扌 扌 扩 拉 拉	to pull
			laai　　　　　lā
1114 *	拇	扌 扎 扔 拐 拇 拇	thumb
			móuh　　　　　mǔ
1115 *	拂	扌 扌 扫 拐 拂	to shake off, wipe off
			fàt　　　　　fú
1116 *	拆	扌 扌 扣 折 折 拆	to undo, pull down, break, destroy
			chaak　　　　chāi
1117 *	抹	扌 扫 抟 抹	[1] to rub, [1] wipe, [1] spread, [1] clear away, [2] slap on and spread (mortar)
			[1][2] mut　　　　[1] mǒ; [2] mā
1118 *	拼	扌 扌 扩 拧 拧 拼	to combine, spell, pronounce, do one's best
			ping　　　　　pīn
1119 **	挑	扌 扚 扸 挑 挑	to carry on shoulder, select; frivolous
			tiu　　　　　tiāo
1120 **	按	扌 扌 扌 扩 挼 按 按	according to; to press, stop
			on　　　　　àn

1121 *	挖	扌 扌 扩 扩 扮 扲 挖	to scoop, dig, excavate	waat	wā
1122 *	拷	扌 扌 扩 拧 拷 拷 拷	to beat, flog, torture	haáu	kǎo
1123 **	拾	扌 扌 扒 扲 拾 拾 拾	to pick up, collect; ten	sahp	shí
1124 *	括	扌 扌 扩 扞 括 括 括	to include	kut	kuò
1125 **	持	扌 扌 扩 扩 持 持 持	to hold, support	chìh	chí
1126 *	拭	扌 扌 扩 扩 扗 拭 拭	to rub, wipe	sik	shì
1127 **	指	扌 扌 扡 扡 指 指 指	finger; to point, point out, indicate	jí	zhǐ
1128 *	拴	扌 扌 扒 扲 拴 拴	to fasten, tie	saàn	shuān
1129 ***	拿	丿 人 人 合 合 合 拿	to take, hold, bring	nàh	ná
1130 *	拳	丷 半 半 半 拳 拳	fist, boxing	kyùhn	quán
1131 *	挈	一 十 主 初 初 挈	to lift, carry	kit	qiè
1132 *	挪	扌 扌 扐 挪 挪 挪 挪	to shift, move	nòh	nuó
1133 *	挫	扌 扌 扩 扩 挫 挫	obstruction	cho	cuò

1134 *	振	扌 扩 扩 振 振 振	to stimulate, shake *jan* *zhèn*
1135 **	捉	扌 扌 扩 护 护 扣 扭 捉	to catch, arrest *jùk* *zhuō*
1136 *	捕	扌 扌 扩 扩 扣 捕 捕	to arrest, catch *bouh* *bǔ*
1137 *	捆	扌 扛 扣 捆 捆 捆 捆	to tie together; a bundle *kwán* *kǔn*
1138 *	挾	扌 扌 扩 护 挟 挟 挾	to hold under the arm, intimidate *hip* *xié*
1139 *	捍	扌 扌 扩 扞 捍 捍 捍	to guard, defend *hohn* *hàn*
1140 *	捎	扌 扌 扩 扩 扚 捎	to carry, send *saàu* *shāo*
1141 *	挨	扌 扩 扩 扩 挓 挨 挨	near; to lean *aai* *āi*
1142 *	捐	扌 扌 扩 护 护 捐 捐	to contribute *gyùn* *juān*
1143 *	挺	扌 扌 扩 抂 抂 挺 挺 挺	to stiffen, straighten; upright *tíhng* *tǐng*
1144 *	捌	扌 扌 扩 护 护 拐 捌 捌	eight *baat* *bā*
1145 *	挽	扌 扌 扩 护 护 挩 挽 挽 挽	to pull, save, rescue *wáahn* *wǎn*
1146 **	採	扌 扌 扩 拦 拦 採	to pick, select *chói* *cǎi*

1147 **	推	扌 扌 扚 扚 扚 折 推	to push, refuse, delay *teùi*　　　　*tūi*
1148 **	掛	扌 扌 扩 挂 挂 掛 掛	to hang up, register *gwa*　　　　*guà*
1149 *	捨	扌 扌 扒 扲 拎 拎 捨 捨	to give up, bestow *se*　　　　*shě*
1150 **	掃	扌 扌 扫 扫 扫 扫 掃 掃	[1] to sweep; [2] broom [1] [2] *sou*　　[1] *sǎo;* [2] *saò*
1151 *	措	扌 扌 扩 扩 拱 拱 措 措 措	to place, arrange, manage *chou*　　　　*cuò*
1152 *	掌	丨 丷 丷 些 尚 尚 尚 掌	palm, bottom of shoes, manage *jeúng*　　　　*zhǎng*
1153 *	掀	扌 扌 扚 扤 折 折 扴 掀 掀	to raise, stir up *hìn*　　　　*xiān*
1154 *	掂	扌 扌 扩 扩 扩 扩 扗 掂 掂	to weigh in the hand *dim*　　　　*diān*
1155 *	掘	扌 扌 扛 护 挕 挕 扮 掘	to dig, excavate *gwaht*　　　　*jué*
1156 *	授	扌 扌 扩 扩 扩 扮 授 授	to give, confer, impart *sauh*　　　　*shòu*
1157 *	捧	扌 扛 抃 扶 捧 捧	to hold by both hands, eulogize *búng*　　　　*pěng*
1158 *	掖	扌 扌 扩 扩 扩 挤 挤 掖 掖	to support, lead by the arm *yihk*　　　　*yè*
1159 *	掮	扌 扌 扩 扩 护 护 掮 掮	to carry on the shoulder *gìn*　　　　*qián*

No.	Character	Strokes	Meaning	Cantonese	Mandarin
1160 *	捲	扌 扌 扩 捗 挾 捲 捲	to roll up; roll	gyún	juǎn
1161 *	掠	扌 扌 扩 扩 护 护 掠 掠	to rob, plunder	leuhk	lüè
1162 *	捶	扌 扌 扩 扩 挿 捶 捶 捶	to beat, strike	cheùih	chúi
1163 **	掉	扌 扌 扌 护 护 护 掉 掉 掉	to fall, drop, lose, turn	diuh	diào
1164 **	排	扌 扌 挂 挑 排	line, rank, row; to push	paàih	pái
1165 *	掙	扌 扌 扌 护 护 挣 掙	[1] to get free from, [1] struggle, [2] work hard to make money	[1] jàng; [2] jaahng	[1] zhéng; [2] zhèng
1166 *	掏	扌 扌 扚 扚 掏 掏 掏	to draw out	toùh	tāo
1167 *	探	扌 扌 扩 护 护 挥 探	[1] to search, [1] visit, [1] test, [2] try	[1] [2] taam	[1] tàn; [2] tān
1168 *	控	扌 扌 扌 扩 护 护 控 控 控	to control, impeach	hung	kòng
1169 *	捫	扌 扌 扑 扪 押 押 押 捫 捫	to feel	mùhn	mén
1170 **	接	扌 扌 扩 护 控 接 接 接	to receive, connect, accept	jip	jiē
1171 *	捷	扌 扩 扫 护 护 护 捷 捷 捷	prompt; to win	jiht	jié
1172 *	掩	扌 扩 扩 扶 扶 掩 掩 掩 掩	to cover, close, shut	yím	yǎn

1173 *	掣	丿 亇 缶 制 掣	to obstruct, pull	jai　　　chè
1174 **	換	扌 扩 扩 护 拘 捣 换 換	to switch, change, exchange	wuhn　　huàn
1175 *	揚	扌 扌 扌 扩 担 护 揚 揚	to raise, wave, praise, spread	yeùhng　yáng
1176 **	提	扌 扌 扩 担 担 担 捍 捍 提	to lift, withdraw, suggest, mention	taìh　　　tí
1177 *	描	扌 扌 扩 扩 扩 抬 抬 描 描	to sketch, draw, describe	miuh　　miáo
1178 *	揸	扌 扌 扪 抹 抹 抹 抹 措 揸 揸	to squeeze, hold	jà　　　zhǎ
1179 *	揶	扌 扌 扛 扛 扫 拝 捙 揶 揶	to ridicule	yèh　　　yé
1180 *	揮	扌 扌 扩 扩 护 挦 挦 挦 揮 揮	to shake, wave	faì　　　huī
1181 **	插	扌 扌 扩 杵 杵 栟 栬 揣 揣 插	to insert, interrupt	chaap　　chā
1182 *	揀	扌 扌 扩 扫 扬 扡 捗 捗 揀	to choose, select	gaán　　jiǎn
1183 *	握	扌 扌 护 护 护 捉 捉 捏 捏 握	to grasp, hold	ngàak　　wò
1184 *	揹	扌 扌 扌 扪 扰 批 扝 揹 揹	to carry on the back	bui　　　bēi
1185 *	揑	扌 扌 扩 护 护 护 担 担 捊 揑	to hold with two fingers	nip　　　niē

1186 *	援	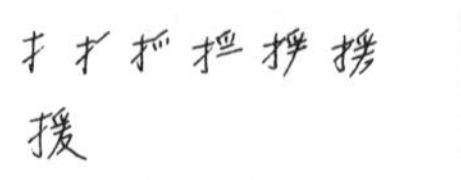	to rescue, help	wùhn	yuán
1187 *	揉	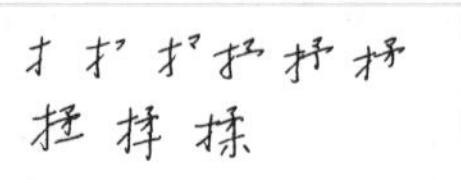	to rub, twist	yàuh	róu
1188 *	揍		to beat up	jau	zòu
1189 *	揩	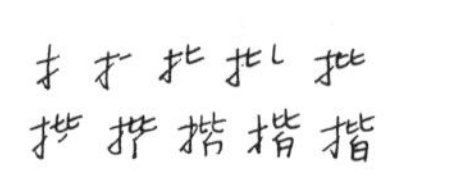	to wipe	hàai	kāi
1190 *	揖	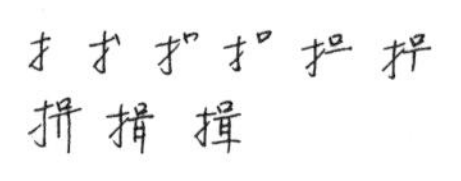	to bow, salute	yàp	yī
1191 *	揭	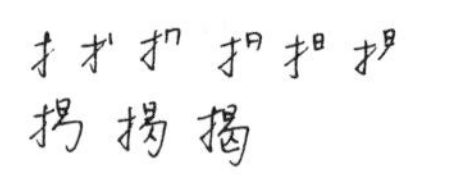	to raise, lift up, uncover	kit	jiē
1192 *	揪	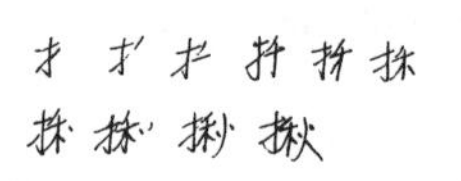	to grasp	chàu	jiū
1193 *	搜	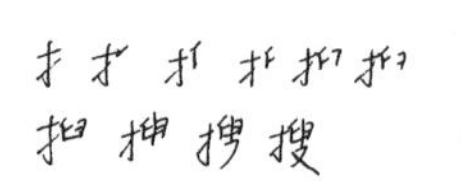	to search	sáu	sōu
1194 *	搥	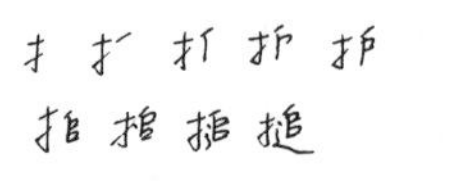	to beat, strike	chèuih	chúi
1195 **	搖		to shake, swing	yìuh	yáo
1196 *	搗	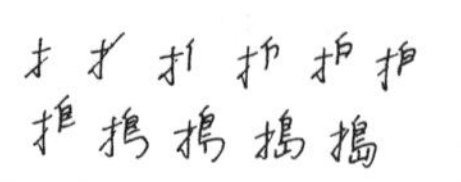	to pound, attack, make trouble	dóu	daǒ
1197 *	搓	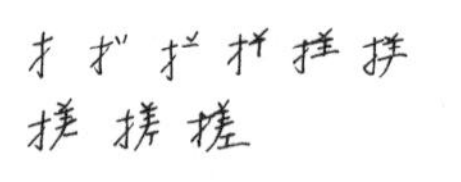	to rub, rub the hands, roll between hands	chò	cuō
1198 *	搞	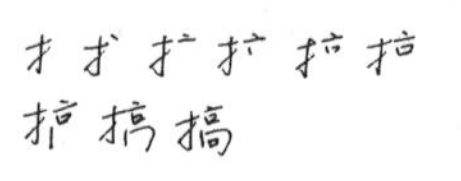	to make, do, disturb	gáau	gaǒ

1199 *	搧	扌 扌 扩 护 护 搊 搧	to fan		
			sin	shān	
1200 *	搾	扌 扌 扩 扩 扩 扩 扩 扩 搾 搾	to squeeze		
			ja	zhà	
1201 *	搬	扌 扌 扚 扚 扚 扚 拥 拥 搬 搬	to move		
			bùn	bān	
1202 *	搭	扌 扌 扌 扩 扩 扙 扲 搭 搭 搭	to build, join, cover, ride		
			daap	dā	
1203 **	損	扌 扌 扩 扩 扩 掃 損 損 損 損	to hurt, injure, damage		
			syún	sǔn	
1204 **	搶	扌 扩 扙 扲 拎 拎 拎 挣 揝 搶 搶	to rob, snatch, plunder		
			cheúng	qiǎng	
1205 *	搏	扌 扌 扌 扑 捕 捕 捕 搏 搏	to wrestle, fight		
			bok	bó	
1206 *	搽	扌 扌 扩 扩 扩 扙 搽 搽 搽 搽	to rub on		
			chàh	chá	
1207 *	搔	扌 扚 扱 扱 扱 掻 搔 搔 搔 搔	to scratch		
			sòu	sāo	
1208 *	摸	扌 扌 扌 扩 扩 拱 描 描 摸 摸 摸	to touch, feel		
			mó	mō	
1209 *	摧	扌 扌 扩 扩 扩 扩 扩 扩 拼 摧	to destroy, break		
			cheùi	cūi	
1210 *	摔	扌 扌 扩 扩 拉 扻 挩 捵 捵 摔	to throw down, fall down		
			syùt	shuāi	
1211 *	摟	扌 扌 扣 护 揩 揩 搢 揩 挬 摟 摟 摟	[1] to embrace, [2] drag		
			[1] láuh; [2] làu	[1] lǒu; [2] lōu	

1212 *	摒	(摒) 扌 扌 扩 护 护 据 摒	to expel, remove
			pihng · · · · · · · · bìng
1213 *	摻	扌 扌 扩 扲 扲 摻 换 摻	[1] to hold, [1] pull, [2] mix in
			[1] sáam; [2] chàam · · · · [1] shǎn; [2] chān
1214 *	摩	丶 亠 广 广 庐 庅 麻 摩	to rub, massage
			mò · · · · · · · · mó
1215 *	摑	扌 扪 扪 捆 捆 捆 捆 捆 搄 搄 摑	to slap
			gwok · · · · · · · · guāi
1216 *	摘	扌 扌 扩 护 护 护 捇 捇 摘 摘 摘	to pick
			jaahk · · · · · · · · zhāi
1217 *	摺	扌 扌 扪 扪 搁 搁 搁 捏 摺 摺	to fold
			jip · · · · · · · · zhé
1218 *	摹	丶 丷 艹 芢 芑 苩 苴 莫 莫 摹	to imitate, follow a pattern
			mouh · · · · · · · · mó
1219 *	撥	扌 扌 扩 护 扲 扲 搀 搀 摍 撥 撥 撥 撥	to move, allot
			buht · · · · · · · · bō
1220 *	撕	扌 扪 扩 扗 扗 捑 捑 捑 搟 搟 搟 撕 撕	to tear, break into pieces
			sì · · · · · · · · sī
1221 *	撚	扌 扌 扪 扚 扚 搻 搻 搻 搻 撚	[1] to twist, [2] tease
			[1] nín; [2] nán · · · · [1] [2] niǎn
1222 *	撤	扌 扌 扩 扗 护 护 捇 捇 搧 搧 撤 撤	to delete, dismiss, withdraw
			chit · · · · · · · · chè
1223 *	撮	扌 扌 扩 护 护 捍 捍 搟 搟 搟 搟 撮 撮	[1] to bring together; [2] pinch
			[1] [2] chyut · · · · [1] cuō; [2] zuǒ
1224 *	撲	扌 扌 扑 扑 扝 扝 扻 搏 撲	to jump onto, strike
			pok · · · · · · · · pū

1225 *	撓	扌 扌 扩 扩 扩 挟 挢 捞 撓	to scratch lightly, disturb *naàuh* *naó*
1226 *	撞	扌 扌 扩 扩 扩 护 挡 挡 撞 撞	to collide, offend *johng* *zhuàng*
1227 *	撈	扌 扌 扩 扩 扩 扐 扐 挧 捞 撈	[1] to dredge, [2] make money [1] *laàuh*; [2] *lòu* [1] [2] *lāo*
1228 *	撩	扌 扌 扩 扶 扶 扶 捊 捔 揋 挴 撩	[1] to stir up, [2] pull up, [2] water, [2] glance [1] *lìuh*; [2] *liù* [1] *liáo*; [2] *liāo*
1229 *	撬	扌 扌 扩 挬 撬 撬	to force open *giuh* *qiào*
1230 *	播	扌 扌 扩 扩 扩 挵 挸 揺 播 播	to spread, disseminate, broadcast *bo* *bō*
1231 *	撑	扌 扩 扩 扩 扩 扩 挿 挡 撑 撑 撑 撑	to prop up, support *chaang* *chēng*
1232 *	撇	扌 扑 扑 扑 扝 抴 扷 抴 撇 撇 撇 撇	[1] to abandon, [1] leave behind; [2] type of stroke in calligraphy (/) [1] [2] *pit* [1] *piě*; [2] *piě*
1233 *	撒	扌 扑 扩 扩 扗 扗 扗 挡 挡 撒 撒 撒	[1] to cast, [1] distribute, [2] spread, [2] scatter [1] [2] *saat* [1] *sǎ*; [2] *sǎ*
1234 *	撫	扌 扩 扩 扩 撫 撫 撫	to nurture, feel, touch, pat, console, foster *fú* *fǔ*
1235 *	撐	扌 扌 扩 扩 扩 扩 挡 挡 撐	to prop up, support *chaang* *chēng*
1236 *	撙	扌 扌 扩 扩 扐 扐 挷 挿 揗 揗 撙 撙	to economize, regulate *jyún* *zǔn*
1237 *	撻	扌 扌 扩 扩 扩 挞 挚 挚 挚 撻	to whip *taat* *tà*

No.	Char	Strokes	Meaning / Pronunciation
1238 *	撼	扌 扩 扩 扜 捄 捄 捄 捤 捤 撼 撼 撼	to be moved (emotionally) *hahm*　　　　*hàn*
1239 *	操	扌 扌 扩 扩 捄 捛 捤 捤 操	¹ to control, ¹ exercise, ¹ drill, ¹ manage; ² self-discipline ¹ *chòu;* ² *chou*　　¹ ² *cāo*
1240 *	擋	扌 扌 扗 扗 捰 捛 捛 捛 捛 捛 擋 擋	to block, resist, obstruct *dóng*　　　　*dǎng*
1241 *	擅	扌 扌 扩 扩 捛 捕 捕 捕 捛 捛 擅 擅 擅	to act without authority, be good in *sihn*　　　　*shàn*
1242 *	擎	丶 ⺊ 艹 艻 芍 芍 芶 苟 徇 敬 敬 敬 擎	to raise, lift up *kìhng*　　　　*qíng*
1243 **	擔	扌 扌 扌 扩 扩 护 捄 捄 捛 擔 擔 擔 擔	to carry on the shoulder, undertake *dàam*　　　　*dān*
1244 *	擁	扌 扌 扩 扩 扩 捛 捛 捛 捛 捛 捛 擁	to embrace, hug, crowd, block *yúng*　　　　*yōng*
1245 *	擂	扌 扌 扩 扩 捛 捇 捇 捇 捛 捛 擂 擂	¹ to grind, ¹ beat, ¹ drum; ² boxing ring ¹ ² *lèuih*　　　¹ *léi;* ² *lèi*
1246 *	擇	扌 扌 扌 捛 捛 捛 捛 捛 捛 擇 擇 擇	to choose, prefer *jaahk*　　　　*zé*
1247 **	據	扌 扌 扌 扩 扩 扩 扩 捛 捛 捛 擄 擄 據	to base on, occupy; according to; receipt *geui*　　　　*jù*
1248 *	擄	扌 扌 扩 护 扩 扩 捛 捛 捛 捛 捛 捛 擄	to seize, capture *lóuh*　　　　*lǔ*
1249 *	擊	一 ⺆ 百 百 目 車 車 車 軎 軎 鼔 鼔 擊	to strike, attack *gìk*　　　　*jí*
1250 *	擠	扌 扌 扩 护 捛 捛 捛 捛 捛 捛 擠 擠	to squeeze, crowd *jài*　　　　*jǐ*

1251 *	擱	扌 扣 押 押 押 押 捫 捫 捫 捫 擱 擱 擱	to put aside
			gok　　　　　　　gē
1252 *	擦	扌 扩 扩 护 挼 挼 挼 挼 摍 摖 擦 擦	to rub, brush
			chaat　　　　　　cā
1253 *	擰	扌 扩 扩 扩 扣 抨 挐 捲 捲 搱 擰 擰	[1] to twist, [1] spin; [2] stubborn
			[1][2] nihng　　　[1] nǐng; [2] nìng
1254 *	擬	扌 扩 扩 拼 拼 拼 挦 挦 摬 擬 擬 擬 擬 擬	to draft, plan, intend
			yíh　　　　　　ni
1255 *	擴	扌 扩 扩 扩 扩 护 护 护 挿 捸 擔 擔 擴	to stretch, enlarge, expand
			kong　　　　　kuò
1256 *	擾	扌 扩 扩 扝 抈 掮 摖 摵 摵 摵 摵 摵 擾	to disturb, annoy, trouble
			yiu　　　　　rǎo
1257 *	擲	扌 扩 扩 拼 挷 搐 揥 摸 摸 摷 擲 擲	to throw, fling
			jaahk　　　　zhì
1258 *	擺	扌 扩 扩 扣 扣 扣 押 掃 揭 揖 擺 擺	to place, display, swing, show
			báai　　　　bǎi
1259 *	攏	扌 扩 扩 拃 挢 挢 挢 捎 捎 撐 撐 攏	to collect, gather
			lúhng　　　　lǒng
1260 *	攔	扌 扣 押 押 押 押 捫 捫 捫 捫 捫 攔	to obstruct, block
			laahn　　　　lán
1261 *	攝	扌 扩 扩 抈 抈 抈 摠 攝	to absorb, manage, photograph
			sip　　　　shè
1262 *	攜	扌 扩 扩 扪 扩 护 护 拼 携 携 携 携 携	to carry, bring
			kwàih　　　xié
1263 *	攤	扌 扩 扩 护 扩 捎 捎 捎 捎 捎 摷 摷 摷 攤 攤	to spread, share, display; stall, vendor
			taàn　　　tān

1264 *	攅	扌 扩 扩 扩 扩 扩 挦 挦 撜 撜 攒 攒 攢 攢	¹ to store, ¹ save, ² collect, ² gather ¹ *jaán;* ² *chyùhn*　　¹ *zǎn;* ² *cuán*
1265 *	孿	丶 二 三 言 言 言 絟 絟 絟 結 纞 孿	bent, crooked *lyùhn*　　*luán*
1266 *	攪	扌 扌 扣 扚 扚 挖 挖 挖 挖 挌 挌 攪 攪 攪 攪	¹ to stir, ¹ mix, ² disturb, ² trouble ¹ ² *gáau*　　¹ *jiǎo;* ² *gǎo*
1267 *	攬	扌 扌 扫 扫 挡 挡 挡 抌 抌 挡 挡 挡 撺 撺 攬	to grasp, monopolize *laám*　　*lǎn*
		支　Section	
1268 **	支	一 十 ㄎ 支	branch, expense; to support, hold up *jì*　　*zhī*
		攴　Section	
1269 **	收	㇄ 丩 屮 屮 收 收	to keep, harvest, collect, receive, close; income *saù*　　*shōu*
1270 **	改	ㄱ ㄱ 己 改	to change, correct *gói*　　*gǎi*
1271 **	攻	一 T 工 攻	to attack, work at *gùng*　　*gōng*
1272 **	放	丶 亠 方 方 放	to set free, release, place, put *fong*　　*fàng*
1273 **	政	一 T 下 正 正 政	governmental; politics, administration *jing*　　*zhèng*
1274 **	故	一 十 十 古 古 故	reason; therefore; purposely; dead *gu*　　*gù*

1275 **	效	、一六亣交效	to imitate; effect
			haauh　　　　　*xiào*
1276 **	救	一十才求求救	to save, rescue
			gau　　　　　*jiù*
1277 ***	教	メ厶耂耂孝孝 敎	[1] to direct, [2] teach; [1] religion
			[1][2] *gaau*　　　[1] *jiào*; [2] *jiāo*
1278 **	敗	｜冂日目貝敗	to defeat, ruin; defeated
			baaih　　　　*bài*
1279 *	敏	ノ匕毎毎毎 毎敏	swift, clever
			máhn　　　　*mǐn*
1280 *	敍	ノ人今余余 剁鈙敍	to converse
			jeuih　　　　*xù*
1281 **	散	｜艹艹丗芇芇 菁散	[1] to scatter, [1] spread, [2] break up; [2] powder, [2] prose
			[1] *saan*; [2] *saán*　　[1] *sàn*; [2] *sǎn*
1282 **	敢	一丁工平严耳 耳敢	to dare
			gám　　　　*gǎn*
1283 *	敦	、一六亡言亨 亨享敦	honest
			dèun　　　　*dūn*
1284 *	敝	｜⺌⺌爿爿南 敝	bad, poor
			baih　　　　*bì*
1285 *	敞	｜⺌⺌炏尚尚 尚敞	spacious; to open, disclose
			tóng　　　　*chǎng*
1286 **	敬	、艹艹艻芍 苟苟敬	to respect; honorable
			ging　　　　*jìng*
1287 *	敲	、一六古言言高 高高髙敲敲	to knock, blackmail
			haàu　　　　*qiāo*

1288 **	敵	丶 亠 ⺊ 产 冏 咼 咼	enemy; to fight against
		咼 啇 啇 敵	dihk dí
1289 *	敷	一 十 寸 市 甫 甫 甫	to administer medicine; perfunctory
		車 車 尃 敷	fù fū
1290 **	數	丶 口 ⊟ 母 串 串 畠	[1] number; [1] several; [2] to count
		婁 婁 婁 妻 數	[1] sou; [2] sóu [1] shù; [2] shǔ
1291 *	整	一 厂 戸 束 束 敕	complete, whole, uniform, neat; to fix
		敕 敕 整 整 整	jíng zhěng
1292 *	斃	丿 丬 仆 汁 折 敝 敝	to die
		弊 弊 弊 弊 斃	baih bì

文   Section

1293 ***	文	丶 亠 𠂇 文	written language, literature, essay; gentle
			màhn wén
1294 *	斑	一 丁 王 王 玟	spot, stripe
		斑	baàn bān
1295 *	斐	丨 彐 非 非 斐	graceful, elegant
			féi féi
1296 *	斌	文 疒 斦 斨 疘	graceful, genteel
		疘 斌 斌 斌	bàn bīn

斗   Section

1297 *	斗	丶 丷 二 斗	10 pint measurement (for grain); big, small
			dáu dǒu
1298 **	料	丷 丷 半 米 料	material; to estimate, manage
			liuh liào

1299 *	斜	丿 𠆢 𠂉 今 余 斜	slanting
			chèh *xié*
1300 *	斟	丨 十 廿 甘 其 其 甚 斟	to pour a small amount, deliberate
			jàm *zhèn*

斤 Section

1301 **	斤	丿 丿 斤 斤	catty (16 oz)
			gàn *jīn*
1302 *	斥	斤 斥	to scold
			chìk *chì*
1303 *	斧	𠆢 𠆢 父 斧	axe, hatchet
			fú *fǔ*
1304 *	斫	一 丆 ア 石 石 斫	to chop, cut
			cheuk *zhuó*
1305 *	斬	一 厂 厃 厃 車 車 斬	to kill, cut into two, chop
			jaám *zhǎn*
1306 *	斯	丨 十 廿 甘 其 其 斯	this, these; such
			sì *sī*
1307 **	新	丶 亠 亠 立 辛 亲 新	new, modern, latest
			sàn *xīn*
1308 **	斷	丿 乞 幺 絲 絲 絲 絲 斷 斷	[1] [2] to sever, [3] judge; [2] discontinue; [3] certain
			[1] *dyuhn;* [2] *tyúhn;* [3] *dyun* [1] [2] [3] *duàn*

方 Section

1309 ***	方	丶 亠 𠃍 方	square; direction, method, prescription; just
			fòng *fāng*

1310 **	於	、 亠 亍 方 扩 於 於	at, in, on, with, by, to
			yù　　　　yú

1311 *	施	方 扩 扩 扩 扩 施	to arrange, distribute, give
			sì　　　　shī

1312 **	旁	、 亠 亠 方 产 旁	side
			pòhng　　　páng

1313 **	旅	方 扩 扩 扩 扩 旅 旅	to travel; trip
			léuih　　　lǚ

1314 **	族	方 扩 扩 扩 扩 族 族	family, clan, tribe, race
			juhk　　　zú

1315 *	旌	方 扩 扩 扩 扩 旌 旌 旌	flag; to show
			jìng　　　jīng

1316 *	旋	方 扩 扩 扩 扩 扩 旋 旋	[1] to roll around, [1] return; [2] tornado
			[1][2] syùhn　　[1] xúan; [2] xùan

1317 **	旗	方 扩 扩 扩 扩 扩 旗 旗 旗	flag
			kèih　　　qí

		旡　Section	

1318 **	旣	(既) フ ㄱ ㅋ ㄸ ㅌ 旣 旣 旣	finished; whereas, since
			gei　　　jì

		日　Section	

1319 ***	日	丨 冂 日 日	sun, day, Japan, Japanese
			yaht　　　rì

1320 *	旦	日 旦	dawn
			daan　　　dàn

1321 *	旭	ノ 九 旭	dawn, rising sun yùk　　　　　　xù
1322 ***	早	曰 旦 早	morning; early joú　　　　　　zǎo
1323 *	旨	一 匕 旨	meaning, purpose jí　　　　　　zhǐ
1324 *	旬	ノ 勹 旬	period of 10 days, decade cheùhn　　　　　　xún
1325 *	旱	曰 旦 早	dry weather, drought hóhn　　　　　　hàn
1326 ***	明	日 旫 明 明	bright, clear; to understand mìhng　　　　　　míng
1327 *	昂	曰 尸 尸 昂 昂	to rise; elevated ngòhng　　　　　　áng
1328 ***	易	日 尸 易 易	[1] to exchange, [1] change; [1] trade; [2] easy [1] yihk; [2] yih　　[1][2] yì
1329 *	昆	日 旦 尸 昆 昆	brothers, descendants, insects kwàn　　　　　　kūn
1330 *	昔	丶 十 卝 芷 昔	former, ancient, in the past sik　　　　　　xī
1331 *	昏	ノ 丆 圧 氏 昏	dusk; dim, dark, dizzy; to faint fàn　　　　　　hūn
1332 *	旺	日 日 旪 旺	prosperous, brilliant wohng　　　　　　wàng
1333 *	昌	日 昌	prosperous cheùng　　　　　　chāng

1334 *	昇	日 月 旦 昻 昇	to rise sìng　　　　　shēng
1335 **	昨	日 日′ 昨 昨 昨	yesterday, previously jok　　　　　zuó
1336 *	映	日 日 日″ 映 映	to shine, show a movie, reflect yíng　　　　　yìng
1337 *	昧	日 日二 昧 昧 昧	dull, dim, obscure muih　　　　　mèi
1338 **	星	日 月 旦 早 星	star, planet, performing artist sìng　　　　　xīng
1339 **	春	三 声 夫 春	spring season, young chèun　　　　　chūn
1340 ***	是	日 旦 早 昰 昰 是	to be; yes; correct sih　　　　　shì
1341 *	晏	日 早 旦 旦 旦 晏 晏 晏	late, tardy aan　　　　　yàn
1342 ***	時	日 日″ 旪 旪 旪 時 時	season, period, time, o'clock; stylish; always sìh　　　　　shí
1343 *	晉	一 云 云 亚 亚 晉 晉 晉	to enter, advance jeun　　　　　jìn
1344 *	晤	日 日″ 旺 昈 旺 晤 晤 晤	to meet; clear ngh　　　　　wù
1345 *	晦	日 日′ 昨 昑 晦 晦 晦 晦	last day of a month, dark night, unlucky fui　　　　　huì
1346 *	晝	ユ ユ ヨ 丰 丰 書 書 晝	daytime jau　　　　　zhòu

1347 *	晨	日 旦 尸 晨 晨 晨 晨	dawn, morning
			sàhn　　　　　chén
1348 ***	晚	日 日' 旷 旷 晚 晚 晚 晚 晚 晚	evening, late
			maáhn　　　　wǎn
1349 **	普	ソ ソ 並 並 並 普	general, common, universal
			póu　　　　　pǔ
1350 *	景	日 旦 早 早 昙 景 景 景 景	scenery, view, condition
			gíng　　　　　jǐng
1351 *	智	ノ ヒ タ 矢 知 知 知 智	wisdom
			ji　　　　　　zhì
1352 **	晴	日 旷 旷 旷 晴 晴 晴	clear sky
			chìhng　　　　qíng
1353 *	晰	日 旷 旷 盱 盱 盱 晰	clear
			sìk　　　　　　xī
1354 *	晾	日 日' 旷 旷 旷 晾 晾 晾	to dry in the air
			leuhng　　　　liàng
1355 *	晶	日 晶 晶	bright; crystal
			jìng　　　　　jīng
1356 *	暑	日 旦 早 昊 暑 暑 暑	hot weather, summer
			syú　　　　　shǔ
1357 *	暈	日 旧 昌 昌 量 暈 暈	to faint, feel dizzy
			wàhn　　　　yūn
1358 **	暗	日 日' 旷 旷 晓 暗	dark, secret
			am　　　　　àn
1359 **	暖	日 日' 旷 旺 暖 暖 暖	warm
			nyúhn　　　　nuǎn

1360 *	暢	日 申 甲 畀 𫳓 暢　暢	penetrating, delightful
			cheung　　　　　　　chàng
1361 *	暱	日 日 旫 旫 昵 昵　昵 眤 睨 暱 暱	intimate
			nìk　　　　　　　　　nì
1362 *	暮	⺊ ⺊ 艹 苩 苩 苩　莫 暮	dusk, evening, end of a period
			mouh　　　　　　　mù
1363 *	暴	日 日 早 昇 昱 昊　昊 暴 暴	[1] violent, [1] cruel, [1] sudden; [2] to expose
			[1] bouh; [2] buhk　　　[1] bào; [2] pù
1364 **	暫	一 日 亘 車 軒 斬 斬　斬 暫	short time, temporary
			jaahm　　　　　　　zàn
1365 *	曆	一 厂 厂 厈 厤 厤　厤 麻 曆	calendar
			lihk　　　　　　　　lì
1366 *	曉	日 日 日 日 旪 旪　旪 睦 睦 曉	dawn; to know, understand
			híu　　　　　　　　xiǎo
1367 *	曙	日 日 日 日 睭 睭　睭 睭 睼 睼 曙 曙	dawn, twilight
			chyúh　　　　　　　shǔ
1368 *	曠	日 旷 旷 旷 旷 旷　眶 曠 曠 曠 曠	extensive, desolate; to be absent
			kong　　　　　　　kuàng
1369 *	曝	日 日 旦 睍 睍 睍　暎 暴 曝 曝	to expose in the sun
			buhk　　　　　　　pù
1370 *	曦	日 旷 旷 旺 睢 睢　睢 曦 曦 曦 曦 曦	light of dawn
			hèi　　　　　　　　xī
1371 *	曬	日 日 胛 昂 睗 睗　睗 睛 睛 曘 曘 曬	to dry in the sun, develop photographs
			saai　　　　　　　　shài

日　　Section

1372 *	曰		to say, speak *yeuhk* *yuē*
1373 *	曳		to pull, draw, drag *yaih* *yè*
1374 *	曲		[1] crooked, [1] curved, [1] bent; [2] song, [2] tune [1] [2] *kùk* [1] *qū;* [2] *qǔ*
1375 ***	更	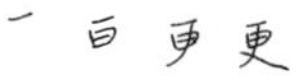	[1] to change; [2] more; [2] moreover [1] *gàng;* [2] *gang* [1] *gēng;* [2] *gèng*
1376 ***	書	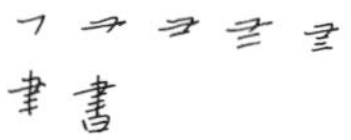	book, letter, writing, type style, document, to write *syù* *shū*
1377 *	曼		fine, long *maahn* *màn*
1378 *	曹	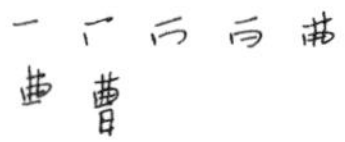	an official *chòuh* *caó*
1379 ***	最		the most; very, exceedingly, extremely *jeui* *zùi*
1380 **	替		to substitute, replace *tai* *tì*
1381 *	曾	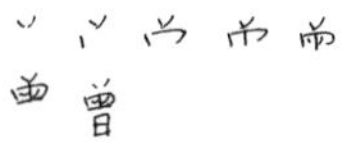	[1] great-grand-...(relative); [2] to have been; [2] already [1] *jàng;* [2] *chàhng* [1] *zēng;* [2] *céng*
1382 ***	會		[1] to meet, [2] be able; [1] moment, [1] chance, [2] association, [1] meeting, [3] accounting [1] [3] *wuih;* [2] *wúih* [1] [2] *hùi;* [3] *kuài*
月 Section			
1383 ***	月		moon, month *yuht* *yuè*

1384 ***	有	一 ナ 冇 有	to have yáuh　　　　　yǒu
1385 ***	朋	月 朋	friend, companion pàhng　　　　　péng
1386 **	服	月 朋' 肌 肌 服	clothes; to dress, take, be obedient fuhk　　　　　fú
1387 *	朗	、 ヲ 扂 良 朗	loud and clear lóhng　　　　　liǎng
1388 **	望	、 ン ヒ ゼ' 切 切 切 望 望 望	to see, look at, hope, expect; reputation mohng　　　　　wàng
1389 ***	期	丨 十 廿 甘 其 其 其 期	set time, time limit, period; to hope kèih　　　　　qī
1390 *	朝	一 十 ナ 古 占 卓 卓 朝	¹ morning, ² imperial court ¹ jiù; ² chiùh　　　¹ zhāo; ² cháo
1391 *	朦	月 月' 肌 朊 朊 朊 朊 腾 膝 膝 膝 朦	dim, hazy mùhng　　　　　méng

木　Section

1392 ***	木	一 十 才 木	wood muhk　　　　　mù
1393 **	未	一 未	not yet meih　　　　　wei
1394 ***	本	木 本	root, origin, volume; local bún　　　　　běn
1395 *	末	一 末	last; powder muht　　　　　mò

1396 *	朽	木 朽 朽	rotten, decayed *naú* *xiŭ*
1397 *	朱	丿 牛 朱	red *jyù* *zhū*
1398 *	朵	乃 乃 朵	measure word for flowers *dó* *duŏ*
1399 *	杜	木 杜 杜 杜	to stop, keep out *douh* *dù*
1400 *	李	木 本 李 李	plum *leíh* *lĭ*
1401 **	村	木 木 村 村	village *chyùn* *cūn*
1402 **	材	木 木 村 材	timber, materials, talent *chòih* *cái*
1403 *	杉	木 杉	cedar *chaam* *shān*
1404 *	杆	木 杵 杆	pole, post *gòn* *gān*
1405 *	杓	木 杓 杓 杓	ladle *biù* *biāo*
1406 *	杏	木 木 杏 杏	apricot *hahng* *xìng*
1407 *	束	一 亠 兩 亘 申 束	to tie up, restrain; a bunch *chùk* *shù*
1408 *	杖	木 木 村 杖	crutch, cane *jeúng* *zhàng*

No.	Char	Strokes	Meaning / Pronunciation
1409 *	枕	木 朩 朳 杚 枕	pillow *jám*　　　*zhěn*
1410 *	枉	木 朩 朾 枉	crooked; grievance; in vain *wóng*　　　*wǎng*
1411 *	杳	木 朩 杳 杳 杳	quiet; to disappear *míuh*　　　*yǎo*
1412 *	杷	木 朩 朳 杔 杔 杷	rake, loquat *pàh*　　　*pá*
1413 ***	東	一 厂 厅 百 百 東 東	east, orient *dùng*　　　*dōng*
1414 *	枇	木 朩 朼 杒 枇	loquat *pèih*　　　*pí*
1415 **	板	木 朩 朾 杤 板	board; dull *báan*　　　*bǎn*
1416 *	杪	木 朩 朳 杪 杪	branch, the end *míuh*　　　*miǎo*
1417 *	枝	木 朩 杧 枝 枝	branch, measure word for pens/cigarettes *jì*　　　*zhī*
1418 **	林	朩 林	woods, forest *làhm*　　　*lín*
1419 *	枚	木 朾 杪 枚 枚	piece, trunk of a tree *mùih*　　　*méi*
1420 *	松	木 朳 松 松	pine tree *chùhng*　　　*sōng*
1421 *	析	木 朩 朾 析 析	to analyze *sìk*　　　*xī*

1422 ***	果	丶 口 曰 日 果	fruit, results	
			gwó	*guŏ*
1423 *	杯	木 杧 杧 杯 杯	cup, glass	
			bùi	*bēi*
1424 *	柿	木 术 杧 杧 栉 柿	persimmon	
			chí	*shì*
1425 *	柩	木 术 札 杧 柩 柩	coffin with a corpse inside	
			gau	*jiù*
1426 *	柔	マ ヌ 予 予 矛 柔	mild, soft, tender; to act kindly	
			yàuh	*róu*
1427 *	查	木 术 杏 杏 杳 查	to examine, look up, investigate	
			chàh	*chá*
1428 *	柏	木 杧 杧 杧 栒 柏	cypress	
			paak	*bǎi*
1429 *	柑	木 杧 杧 杧 柑 柑	Mandarin orange	
			gàm	*gān*
1430 *	枯	木 木 杧 村 枯 枯	withered	
			fù	*kū*
1431 *	柚	木 木 杧 枏 柚 柚	pomelo	
			yáu	*yòu*
1432 *	某	一 十 廿 甘 甘 某	some, certain	
			máuh	*mŏu*
1433 *	柬	一 亠 亓 亓 柬 柬	invitation, letter	
			gáan	*jiǎn*
1434 *	柺	木 木 杧 杧 柺 柺	crutch, cane	
			gwáai	*guǎi*

1435 *	柳	木 术 杧 杧 杤 柳	willow *laúh*	*liǔ*
1436 *	柱	木 木 杧 杧 柱	pillar, column, post *chyúh*	*zhù*
1437 **	架	フ カ カ 加 加 架	shelf, frame; measure word for cars/planes *ga*	*jià*
1438 **	染	シ シ 氻 染	to dye, infect *yíhm*	*rǎn*
1439 *	柄	木 术 杧 杧 柄 柄	handle, power *bing*	*bǐng*
1440 *	栅	木 杧 杧 栅 栅	fence *chaak*	*zhà*
1441 **	柴	丨 卜 止 止 此 柴	firewood *chaàih*	*chái*
1442 ***	校	木 术 杧 杧 枌 校	¹ school; ² to compare, ² proofread ¹ *haauh;* ² *gaau*	¹ *xiào;* ² *jiào*
1443 **	格	木 术 杧 杦 枚 格 格	pattern, grid, personality *gaak*	*gé*
1444 *	桅	木 术 杧 杧 枂 桅 桅	mast of a ship *wàih*	*wéi*
1445 *	桃	木 杧 杧 桃 桃	peach *toùh*	*táo*
1446 *	核	木 术 杧 杧 杦 核 核	pit, core, nuclear; to examine *haht*	*hé*
1447 *	框	木 术 杧 杧 框 框	frame, sill *kwaàng*	*kuàng*

1448 *	栽	一 十 土 弎 栽 栽 栽	to plant, cultivate	
			jòi	zāi
1449 *	桑	フ ヌ ス 豕 桑	mulberry tree	
			sòng	sāng
1450 *	桐	木 朴 朾 桐 桐 桐 桐	paulownia	
			tùhng	tóng
1451 *	株	木 木 杧 杵 株	trunk of a tree	
			jyù	zhū
1452 *	案	丶 宀 宀 安 安 案	desk, file, record, court case	
			on	àn
1453 *	栗	一 亻 币 西 西 栗	chestnut	
			leuht	lì
1454 *	桔	木 木 村 杜 杜 桔 桔	Mandarin orange	
			gàt	jié
1455 *	桂	木 木 村 杜 桂	cassia, cinnamon	
			gwai	gùi
1456 **	根	木 木 朾 村 村 根 根	root, origin, foundation	
			gàn	gén
1457 **	桌	ⲓ 上 ⲓ 占 占 点 桌	table, desk	
			cheuk	zhuō
1458 *	栩	木 朾 栩 栩	pleased, lively	
			yihk	xǔ
1459 *	梁	氵 汈 沖 沙 梁	beam, ridge	
			leùhng	liáng
1460 *	梳	木 木 杧 杧 杭 栌 桥 梳	to comb; comb	
			sò	shū

1461 ***	條	ノ 亻 仏 伫 伫 佟 攸 條	strip, law; measure word for long, slender objects	
			tiùh	tiáo
1462 *	梆	木 杉 栏 栏 梆 梆	wooden cylinder	
			bòng	bāng
1463 *	梅	木 杓 杧 杧 栂 梅 梅 梅	prune	
			mùih	méi
1464 *	梭	木 朴 朳 朳 枀 杪 梭	shuttle	
			sò	suō
1465 *	桶	木 杧 杧 杧 柯 桶 桶	bucket, barrel, pail	
			túng	tǒng
1466 *	梗	木 杧 杧 桓 桓 桓 梗 梗	stalk, stem of a flower	
			gáng	gěng
1467 *	械	木 杧 杧 柿 械 械 械	weapon, tool	
			haaih	xiè
1468 *	桿	木 杧 杧 柯 桿 桿 桿	stick, rod, pole	
			gòn	gǎn
1469 *	梓	木 术 杧 杧 栏 梓	linden	
			jí	zǐ
1470 *	梯	木 杧 杧 栏 栏 梯 梯	stairs, ladder	
			tài	tī
1471 *	梢	木 杧 杧 杧 枂 梢	tip, end, end of a tree	
			saàu	shāo
1472 *	梨	ノ 二 千 禾 和 利 梨	pear	
			lèih	lí
1473 *	棕	木 术 杧 杧 柠 棕 棕	palm tree; tan color	
			jùng	zōng

1474 *	椅	木 杧 杧 杉 枍 梼 椅 椅 椅	chair	yi̍
			yi̍	yǐ
1475 *	棧	木 木 杧 杧 栈 棧	storehouse, warehouse, hotel, inn	
			jaán	zhàn
1476 *	棟	木 木 杧 柏 柏 栢 梀 楝	beam, pillar	
			duhng	dòng
1477 *	棋	木 利 杧 柑 柑 棋 棋	chess	
			kèih	qí
1478 *	棵	木 朳 柯 柙 棺 棵	measure word for trees	
			pò	kē
1479 *	植	木 木 杧 杧 柘 枯 植 植	to plant; plants	
			jihk	zhí
1480 *	椒	木 杧 杧 椒 椒 椒 椒	pepper	
			jiù	jiāo
1481 *	棒	木 杧 杧 挟 棒 棒	bat, club, stick	
			páahng	bàng
1482 *	森	木 木 森	bushy, stern, somber	
			sàm	sēn
1483 *	棗	一 匚 朿 朿 棗	date, jujube	
			jóu	zǎo
1484 *	棱	木 木 杧 杧 栌 枝 栈 楞 棱	angle	
			lìhng	léng
1485 *	棘	一 厂 匚 朿 朿 棘	bramble; troublesome	
			gìk	jí
1486 *	棚	木 利 枂 枂 棚	booth, shed, tent	
			pàahng	péng

1487 *	棠	丨 ㄴ ㄴ ㅛ 屵 屵 屵 棠	begonia
			tòhng táng
1488 *	棍	木 札 杧 柜 柜 柜 棍 棍 棍	stick, bat, club
			gwan gùn
1489 *	棲	木 木 杧 栖 栖 栖 棲 棲 棲	to stay at, roost
			chāi qī
1490 *	棺	木 木 杧 柠 柠 柠 棺 棺	coffin
			gùn guān
1491 **	棉	木 术 杧 杧 柏 柏 柏 棉 棉	cotton
			mìhn mián
1492 *	棄	丶 亠 亠 云 云 亝 亝 亝 棄 棄	to give up, discard
			hei qì
1493 ***	業	丨 刂 刂 业 业 业 业 業 業	profession, occupation, business, property
			yihp yè
1494 *	楷	木 术 柞 柞 柞 柞 柞 楷 楷 楷	model, pattern, Chinese script writing
			gàai kǎi
1495 *	楊	木 术 杧 栟 栟 栟 栟 楊 楊	willow, poplar, aspen
			yeùhng yáng
1496 *	椰	木 术 杧 杧 枡 枡 椰 椰 椰	coconut
			yèh yē
1497 *	楣	木 术 杧 杧 枂 枂 柟 柟 楣	lintel of a door
			mèih méi
1498 *	楓	木 术 机 机 机 枫 枫 枫 楓 楓	maple tree
			fùng fēng
1499 *	楚	木 林 林 梵 梵 梵 楚	suffering, clear
			chó chǔ

1500 **	極	木 朾 朾 朾 柯 柯 柯 極 極 極	extremely, the most, the end
			gihk jí
1501 *	槌	木 朾 朾 朾 柏 椎 椎 椎 槌	hammer, mallet
			cheùih chúi
1502 **	槍	木 朾 朳 朳 柃 柃 柃 柃 槍 槍	gun, spear, rifle
			cheùng qiāng
1503 *	榨	木 朾 朾 柠 柠 柠 柞 榨 榨	to squeeze
			ja zhà
1504 *	槓	木 朾 朾 杠 杠 杠 栢 槓 槓	pole
			gong gàng
1505 *	榜	木 朾 朾 柠 柠 柠 栌 椮 榜 榜	notice, model, example
			bóng bǎng
1506 **	榮	丷 丷 灳 炒 炏 炏 榮	glory, honor
			wihng róng
1507 *	構	木 朾 朾 柑 棋 棤 構 構 構 構	to build, compose, make; organization
			kau goù
1508 *	槐	木 朾 朾 柏 栒 枏 柪 槐 槐 槐	pagoda tree
			wàaih huái
1509 *	榴	木 朾 朾 朾 栌 栌 柳 桺 榴 榴	pomegranate
			laùh liú
1510 *	榻	木 朾 朾 柯 柯 桿 榻 榻	couch, bed
			taap tà
1511 *	樑	木 朾 柯 柯 柯 樑	beam, ridge
			leùhng liáng
1512 **	模	木 朾 朾 柑 柑 栉 栉 椹 椹 模 模	[1] pattern, [1] model, [2] mold
			[1] [2] moùh [1] mó; [2] mú

1513 *	標	木 朾 朾 朾 標 標 標 標 標	to specify; mark, sign
			biù biāo
1514 **	樓	木 朾 朾 朾 柜 柜 楼 楼 楼 楼 楼 樓	building, tower, floors of a building
			laùh lóu
1515 *	槽	木 朾 朾 朾 栖 槽 槽 槽 槽 槽	trough, groove
			chòuh cáo
1516 *	樁	木 杧 杧 枠 枠 椿 椿 椿 椿 椿	stake, post, measure word for matters
			jòng zhuāng
1517 *	概	(概) 木 朾 朾 柜 柜 柜 柜 柜 概 概	outline, concept; in general; to sum up
			koi gài
1518 **	樣	木 朾 朾 朾 样 样 样 栐 栐 樣 樣	figure, shape, model, style, fashion
			yeuhng yàng
1519 **	樂	′ 亻 白 白 白 自 鈍 鈍 樂 樂 樂	[1] music, [2] happiness, [2] joy; [2] happy
			[1] ngohk; [2] lohk [1] yùe; [2] lè
1520 *	樞	木 朾 朾 杞 杞 杞 枢 枢 樞	hinge, important point; central
			syù shū
1521 *	槳	㇀ 丬 丬 丬 뇌 뇌 꽈 꽈 將 將 槳	oar, paddle
			jéung jiǎng
1522 ***	機	木 朾 朾 杉 杉 杉 楼 楼 機 機 機	machine, opportunity
			gèi jī
1523 **	橋	木 朾 朾 杉 栐 栐 栝 栝 橋 橋 橋	bridge
			kiùh qiáo
1524 *	樽	木 朾 朾 朾 栌 栖 梅 梅 槽 樽 樽	wine glass
			jyùn zūn
1525 *	橙	木 朾 朾 朾 柊 柊 椌 椌 椌 橙 橙	orange
			chàang chéng

1526 *	橡	木 杧 杧 柠 柠 梌 椛 榉 椽 橡 橡 橡	oak tree, rubber	
			jeuhng	xiàng
1527 **	樹	木 木 杧 村 桔 桔 桔 桔 桔 桔 樹 樹	tree; to plant	
			syuh	shù
1528 *	樵	木 木 杧 杧 栌 枡 椎 樵	firewood; to chop firewood	
			chiùh	qiáo
1529 **	橫	木 木 杧 杧 杫 杫 梼 楛 椯 橫 橫 橫	[1] horizontal, [1] unexpected, [2] unreasonable	
			[1] wàahng; [2] wahng	[1] héng; [2] hèng
1530 *	樸	木 杧 杧 杚 杚 樸 樸 樸	plain, simple	
			pok	pǔ
1531 *	橘	杧 杧 杧 杪 杪 栿 橘 橘 橘 橘 橘 橘	orange	
			gwàt	jú
1532 *	檀	木 木 杧 杧 柠 栒 桓 檀 檀 檀 檀 檀 檀	sandalwood	
			taàhn	tán
1533 **	檢	木 木 朳 柃 柃 柃 柃 柃 検 檢	to examine	
			gím	jiǎn
1534 *	檔	杧 杧 杧 梢 梢 椙 椙 椙 椙 檔 檔 檔	cross-piece, record, file	
			dong	dàng
1535 *	檸	杧 杧 杧 杵 杵 梒 梒 梒 梒 梒 梒 檸	lemon tree, lemon	
			nihng	níng
1536 *	檬	木 木 杧 杧 杺 桩 梫 椚 椚 檬 檬	lemon	
			mùng	méng
1537 *	櫃	木 杧 杧 杞 杞 杞 枢 枢 枢 枢 櫃	closet, chest	
			gwaih	guì
1538 *	櫈	木 杧 杧 杧 柎 柎 梺 梺 梺 梺 櫈	stool	
			dang	dèng

1539 *	檯	木 木 ギ ギ ギ 梼 梼 梼 梼 梼 檯 梼 梼 檯 檯 檯	desk, table, stage
			tòih tái

1540 *	欄	木 木 杆 杆 柙 柙 楫 榈 榈 榈 榈 欄 欄 欄 欄	railing
			laàhn lán

1541 **	權	木 木 术 术 杧 杧 杧 梏 桃 楳 桙 楳 楳 權	power, authority, right
			kyùhn quán

欠   Section

1542 **	欠	ノ ⺈ ⺅ 欠	to lack, be short of, owe; deficient
			him qiàn

1543 ***	次	丶 冫 次	order, time; second, inferior, next
			chi cì

1544 *	欣	ノ 丿 斤 斤 欣	delighted, cheerful, joyful; to admire
			yàn xīn

1545 *	欲	八 公 公 谷 谷 欲	to want, wish; desire
			yuhk yù

1546 *	款	一 十 士 吉 夷 素 款	money, style; to entertain
			fún kuǎn

1547 *	欺	丨 十 艹 甘 其 其 欺	to deceive, cheat
			hèi qī

1548 *	欽	ノ 人 合 今 金 金 欽	to respect; imperial
			yàm qīn

1549 *	歇	丶 口 曰 日 尸 曷 曷 曷 曷 歇	to rest, stop
			hit xiē

1550 *	歉	丷 丷 丷 兰 芊 兼 兼 歉	[1] bad harvest; [2] sorry, [2] regretful
			[1] him; [2] hip [1] [2] qiàn

1551 **	歌	一 厂 厅 哥 哥 哥 哥 哥 歌	to sing; song
			gò　　　　　　　gē
1552 *	歐	一 匚 匚 匚 匚 匷 區 歐	Europe
			ngàu　　　　　　ōu
1553 *	歎	丶 一 廿 廿 甘 苗 苗 萛 莫 莫 歎	to sigh, moan
			taan　　　　　　tàn
1554 ***	歡	丶 艹 艹 艹 茾 萉 苩 蕌 蕐 蕐 雚 歡	joy; glad; to welcome
			fùn　　　　　　huān

止　Section

1555 **	止	丨 丄 止 止	to stop
			jí　　　　　　zhǐ
1556 **	正	一 丅 下 正 正	[1] upright, [1] positive, [1] proper, [1] in progress, [1] correct; [2] January
			[1] jīng; [2] jīng　　　　[1] zhèng; [2] zhēng
1557 **	此	止 此 此	this, the
			chí　　　　　　cǐ
1558 **	步	止 步 步 步	to walk; footstep
			bouh　　　　　　bù
1559 *	歧	止 止 止 岐 歧	forked, diverging
			keìh　　　　　　qí
1560 **	武	一 二 亖 武 武	military
			móuh　　　　　　wǔ
1561 *	歪	一 丆 才 不 歪 歪	awry, slanting
			wàai　　　　　　wāi
1562 **	歲	止 些 些 虍 虍 虍 歲 歲 歲 歲	year, age
			seui　　　　　　sùi

1563 **	歷	一 厂 厂 厂 厈 床 麻 歷	to experience; history; past; clearly
			lihk 　　　　　 *lì*

1564 **	歸	＇ ｆ ｐ ｐ 自 皀 皀 皀 皀 皀 歸 歸 歸 歸	to return, go back, send back, belong to
			gwài 　　　　　 *gūi*

歹　　Section

1565 *	歹	一 丁 歹 歹	bad, wicked
			daái 　　　　　 *dǎi*

1566 **	死	歹 歹 死	to die; dead
			séi 　　　　　 *sǐ*

1567 *	殆	歹 歼 死 死 殆 殆	perilous; almost
			tóih 　　　　　 *dái*

1568 *	殊	歹 歼 死 殊 殊	different, distinguished, special
			syùh 　　　　　 *shū*

1569 *	殘	歹 歼 残 残 残 残	to ruin; cruel
			chaàhn 　　　　　 *cán*

1570 *	殖	歹 歼 歼 殖 殖 殖 殖 殖	to produce, grow
			jihk 　　　　　 *zhí*

1571 *	殞	歹 歹 殞 殞 殞 殞 殞 殞 殞	to die, perish
			wáhn 　　　　　 *yǔn*

1572 *	殲	歹 歼 殲 殲 殲 殲 殲 殲 殲 殲 殲	to destroy, exterminate
			chìm 　　　　　 *jiān*

殳　　Section

1573 **	段	＇ ｆ ｆ ｆ 钅 釢 釕 段 段	section, paragraph
			dyuhn 　　　　　 *duàn*

№	字	筆順	意味・読み
1574 *	殷	ノ ｊ ｆ ｆ ｆ 身 殷	abundant, earnest, dark red *yàn* *yīn*
1575 **	殺	メ 二 乎 杀 杀 殺	to kill *saat* *shā*
1576 *	殼	一 十 士 声 吉 吉 声 壳 殼	shell *hok* *ké*
1577 *	毀	ノ ｆ ｆ ｆ ｆ 臼 臼 臼 臼 毀	to ruin, destroy, slander *wái* *huǐ*
1578 *	殿	コ コ 尸 尸 尸 屏 屏 屏 殿	palace, temple *dihn* *dian*
1579 *	毆	一 匚 匚 匚 匝 區 區 毆	to bear, strike *ngàu* *ōu*
1580 *	毅	、 一 亡 立 产 亨 青 豪 毅	fortitude; firm *ngaih* *yi`*

毋 Section

№	字	筆順	意味・読み
1581 **	母	し 幻 母 母 母	mother *móuh* *mǔ*
1582 ***	每	ノ 广 每	each, every *múih* *měi*
1583 **	毒	一 十 主 毒	poison, drug; to poison *duhk* *dú*

比 Section

№	字	筆順	意味・読み
1584 ***	比	Ｉ 片 上 比 比	to compare, sort; than *béi* *bǐ*

		毛 Section	

		毛 Section	
1585 ***	毛	ノ ニ 二 毛	hair, feather; small
			mòuh　　　máo
1586 *	毫	、 亠 亠 宀 古 亠 高 毫	dime; trifling
			hòuh　　　háo
1587 *	毯	毛 毛 毛' 毛` 毯 毯	rug, carpet
			táam　　　tǎn
1588 *	氈	、 亠 亠 宀 向 向 向 亶 亶 亶 亶 亶 氈	rug, carpet
			jìn　　　zhǎn

		氏 Section	
1589 *	氏	ノ 𠂆 ⺪ 氏	family surname
			sih　　　shì
1590 ***	民	⊃ ⊐ 民	people, citizens
			màhn　　　mín

		气 Section	
1591 *	氛	ノ ニ 气 气 气 氛 氛 氛	atmosphere
			fàn　　　fēn
1592 *	氧	气 气 氫 氧	oxygen
			yéuhng　　　yǎng
1593 ***	氣	气 气 気 氣 氣	air, atmosphere, gas, weather
			hei　　　qì
1594 *	氫	气 气 氫 氫 氫 氫	hydrogen
			hìng　　　qīng

| 1595 * | 氯 | 气 气 气 氧 氧 氧 氯 | chlorine |
| | | | luhk lü |

水　Section

| 1596 *** | 水 | ↓ 기 氺 水 | water |
| | | | seúi shǔi |

| 1597 ** | 永 | ⁊ 永 | eternal, everlasting, perpetual |
| | | | wíhng yǒng |

| 1598 ** | 求 | 一 寸 寸 求 求 求 | to beg, inquire, request |
| | | | kàuh qíu |

| 1599 * | 汁 | ⁚ 氵 氵 汁 | juice |
| | | | jàp zhí |

| 1600 * | 氾 | 氵 氿 氾 | flooding |
| | | | faahn fàn |

| 1601 * | 汝 | 氵 氵 汝 汝 | you |
| | | | yúh rǔ |

| 1602 * | 污 | 氵 氵 氵 污 | dirty; to stain |
| | | | wù wú |

| 1603 ** | 汗 | 氵 氵 汗 | perspiration, sweat |
| | | | hohn hàn |

| 1604 ** | 江 | 氵 氵 汀 江 | river |
| | | | gòng jiāng |

| 1605 * | 池 | 氵 氵 池 池 | pool, tank, pond |
| | | | chìh chí |

| 1606 * | 汞 | 一 丅 工 汞 | mercury, quicksilver |
| | | | hung gǒng |

1607 *	汽	シ シ 汐 汽	steam, vapor, gas hei　　　qì
1608 *	沙	シ シ 沙 沙 沙	sand sà　　　shā
1609 *	沖	シ 氵 汩 沖 沖	to shoot out, rush at, infuse chùng　　chōng
1610 *	洶	シ 氿 汹 洶 洶	surging, tumultuous hùng　　xiōng
1611 *	沃	シ 氵 沪 汗 沃	fertile; to irrigate yùk　　　wò
1612 ***	沒	シ 氵 沙 没 沒	[1] to drown, [1] sink; [2] don't have, [2] not yet [1][2] muht;　[1] mò; [2] méi
1613 **	決	シ 氿 汧 决 決	to determine, decide; certainly kyut　　jué
1614 *	沐	シ 氵 汁 沐 沐	to clean, bathe muhk　　mù
1615 *	汪	シ 氵 汗 汗 汪	vast and calm as the sea; barking of a dog wòng　　wāng
1616 *	汰	シ 氵 汁 汏 汰	excessive; to take out less useful ones taai　　tài
1617 *	沉	シ 氵 沪 沪 沉	to sink, drown chàhm　　chén
1618 *	沫	シ 氵 汒 沫 沫	foam, suds, bubbles muht　　mò
1619 *	泉	ノ 亻 白 白 泉	fountain, spring chyùhn　　quán

1620 *	沸	シ シ シ 沪 沸	boiling
			fai　　　　　　　fèi
1621 *	泛	シ シ シ 江 汐 泛	to float; unrealistic
			faan　　　　　　fàn
1622 **	油	シ シ 汩 油 油 油	oil, grease
			yàuh　　　　　　yóu
1623 **	波	シ シ 汩 沖 波 波	waves
			bò　　　　　　　bō
1624 ***	法	シ シ 汁 注 法 法	laws, constitution, method; France; French
			faat　　　　　　fǎ
1625 *	沿	シ シ 汛 沪 沿 沿	along
			yùhn　　　　　　yán
1626 **	治	シ シ 氿 浍 治 治	to govern, manage, punish, cure
			jih　　　　　　　zhì
1627 **	注	シ シ 汇 汁 注	to pour into, concentrate
			jyu　　　　　　　zhù
1628 *	沾	シ シ 汁 汁 沾 沾	to moisten, touch, contact
			jìm　　　　　　　zhān
1629 *	泳	シ シ 汀 泳	to swim; swimming
			wihng　　　　　yǒng
1630 ***	河	シ シ 沪 河 河 河	river, canal
			hòh　　　　　　hé
1631 *	泡	シ シ 沟 泡 泡 泡	[1] foam, [1] suds, [1] bubbles, [2] pus
			[1] póuh; [2] paau　　[1][2] pào
1632 **	況	シ シ 汩 沪 沪 況	condition; furthermore
			fong　　　　　　kuàng

1633 **	泥	シ氵江沪沪泥	mud, soil; muddy	
			nàih	nì
1634 *	泰	三手夫夫秦秦 秦泰	peaceful, comfortable, large	
			taai	tài
1635 *	沫	シ氵汁沫	small light	
			muih	mèi
1636 *	泣	シ氵沪沪泣	to weep	
			yàp	qì
1637 *	沽	シ氵汁汁沽 沽	to sell, buy	
			gu	gū
1638 *	洞	シ氵汩汩洞 洞洞	hole, cave, opening	
			duhng	dòng
1639 ***	活	シ氵汗汗汗 活活	to live; living, lively, active	
			wuht	huó
1640 *	洒	シ氵沂沔洒 洒	to sprinkle; charming	
			sá	sǎ
1641 **	洗	シ氵汁泩泩 泩洗	to wash, cleanse, baptize	
			sái	xǐ
1642 **	洋	シ氵洋洋	ocean; foreign, vast	
			yeùhng	yáng
1643 *	柒	シ氵汕汕泩 柒	seven	
			chàt	qī
1644 *	洽	シ氵沿沿洽 洽洽	to be in harmony with, discuss	
			hàp	qià
1645 *	津	シ氵沪沪洼 津	to moisten; saliva, allowance, grant	
			jeùn	jīn

No.	Char	Strokes	Meaning / Readings
1646 *	洩	シ シ 汁 汩 泄 泄	to leak, divulge *sit*　　　*xiè*
1647 *	洲	シ シ 汁 洲 洲	continent *jàu*　　　*zhōu*
1648 *	洪	シ シ 汁 汫 泄 洪	vast, great *hùhng*　　　*hóng*
1649 **	派	シ シ 氵 沪 沉 派 派	group, faction; to appoint *paai*　　　*pài*
1650 **	流	シ シ 広 注 法 济 济 流	to flow; current, class *làuh*　　　*liú*
1651 **	消	シ シ 丬 沙 沂 消 消	to dissolve, digest, eliminate, consume *siù*　　　*xiāo*
1652 *	涉	シ シ 汁 汁 沙 涉 洗 涉 涉	to wade, become involved in *sit*　　　*shè*
1653 ***	海	シ シ 汇 汇 汻 沟 海 海	sea, marine *hói*　　　*hǎi*
1654 *	浪	シ シ 汾 沪 泹 沪 浪 浪	waves *lohng*　　　*làng*
1655 *	浮	シ シ 氵 浮 浮 浮	to float, drift *faùh*　　　*fú*
1656 *	浦	シ シ 汁 汁 沽 浦 浦	river bank *póu*　　　*pǔ*
1657 *	涕	シ シ 沙 泮 洋 涕 涕	tears, mucous *tai*　　　*ti`*
1658 *	浸	シ シ 沪 沪 沪 浔 浸 浸	to soak, immerse *jam*　　　*jìn*

1659 *	浩	シ シ 汁 汁 洸 浩 浩	vast, great
			houh　　　　　　hào
1660 *	浴	シ シ 汐 汾 浴 浴	to bathe
			yuhk　　　　　　yù
1661 *	涎	シ シ 汁 汇 沃 诞 涎 涎 涎	saliva
			yìhn　　　　　　xián
1662 *	凄	シ シ 汽 汽 淒 淒 淒 淒 淒	cold, miserable, sorrowful, desolate
			chài　　　　　　qī
1663 **	深	シ シ 汈 汈 汉 汈 浑 深	deep, late, profound
			sàm　　　　　　shēn
1664 *	淡	シ シ 沪 沙 沙 淡	light color, slack season, indifferent
			daahm　　　　　dàn
1665 **	清	シ シ 汁 泔 渚 清 清	pure, clear; to clear
			chìng　　　　　qīng
1666 *	淘	シ シ 沟 沟 淘 淘 淘 淘	to wash
			tòuh　　　　　　táo
1667 **	混	シ シ 汜 汨 湦 湦 混 混	[1] mixed, [2] muddy, [2] turbid; [1] to mix, [1] idle
			[1][2] wahn　　　[1] hùn; [2] hún
1668 **	淨	シ シ 沙 浮 浮 浄 淨	clean, net amount, net weight
			jihng　　　　　jìng
1669 *	淮	シ シ 沣 沣 汋 汋 汼 淮	a large river in China
			wàaih　　　　　huái
1670 *	淹	シ シ 汁 冼 沆 淹 淹 淹 淹	to immerse, be flooded, drown
			yìm　　　　　　yān
1671 *	淫	シ シ 沙 沙 淫 淫 淫	obscene; to commit adultery
			yàhm　　　　　yín

1672 *	液	シ シ シ゛ 汀 汀 泸 泧 液 液 液	liquid, fluid	
			yihk	ye`
1673 **	淺	シ シ゛ シ゜ 浅 浅 浅 淺	shallow, light, easy, simple	
			chín	qiǎn
1674 **	涼	シ シ゛ 汁 汁 汴 泞 涼 涼	¹ cool, ² to cool off	
			¹ ² leùhng	¹ liáng; ² liàng
1675 *	淋	シ シ゛ 汁 沐 沐 淋	to pour on, shower	
			làhm	lín
1676 *	涯	シ シ゛ 汇 汇 汇 涯 涯	shore, limit	
			ngàaih	yá
1677 *	添	シ シ゛ 汗 沗 沗 添 添 添	to add to, increase	
			tìm	tiān
1678 *	淑	シ シ゛ 汁 汁 沽 淑 淑	virtuous, pure	
			suhk	shū
1679 *	淚	シ シ゛ 汴 汸 汸 汸 泿 淚 淚	tears	
			leuih	leì
1680 *	港	シ シ゛ 汢 沣 洪 洪 洣 港 港	port, harbor, Hong Kong	
			góng	gǎng
1681 *	渾	シ シ゛ 汇 汇 汇 渭 渭 渭 渾	turbid, muddy	
			wahn	hún
1682 *	湊	シ 江 沪 浃 浃 湊 湊 湊	to gather, collect	
			chau	coù
1683 *	渠	シ シ゛ 汇 沰 沰 渠 渠 渠 渠	ditch, gutter, drain	
			keùih	qú
1684 *	渺	シ シ゛ 沠 泪 泪 沠 沠 渺 渺	small, tiny	
			miúh	miǎo

1685 *	渡	シ ジ 浐 沪 沪 泸 沪 渟 渡 渡	to cross the sea *douh*　　*dù*
1686 **	游	シ ジ 汸 汸 游 游 游 游 游	to swim, travel *yàuh*　　*yóu*
1687 ***	湖	シ シ 汁 汁 沽 沽 沽 湖 湖 湖	lake *wùh*　　*hú*
1688 *	渣	シ 氵 汁 沐 沐 渣 渣 渣 渣	sediment, dregs *jà*　　*zhā*
1689 *	渦	シ 氵 汈 沪 沪 渦 渦 渦 渦 渦	whirlpool *wò*　　*wò*
1690 *	湧	シ 氵 氵 氵 沪 沪 涌 涌 涌 湧	to gust, spout, flow rapidly *yúng*　　*yǒng*
1691 *	測	シ 氵 汩 汩 泪 測 測 測	to estimate, measure *chàk*　　*cè*
1692 *	渴	シ 氵 氵 汩 汩 渇 渇 湯 渴	thirsty; to long for *hot*　　*kě*
1693 *	湯	シ 氵 汩 汩 沪 沪 湯 湯	soup *tòng*　　*tāng*
1694 **	減	シ 氵 氵 汇 沪 沶 湐 減 減 減	to reduce, decrease, subtract *gáam*　　*jiǎn*
1695 **	溫	(溫) シ 氵 氵 汩 泪 泪 渇 溫 溫	warm, mild; to warm, review *wàn*　　*wēn*
1696 *	滙	シ 氵 汇 汇 沤 泟 泟 泟 滙	to remit *wuih*　　*hùi*
1697 *	滋	シ 氵 汁 汁 汁 汁 滋 滋 滋	to sprout; taste *jī*　　*zī*

1698 **	滅	氵 氵 氵 沪 沪 沥 沥 減 滅 滅	to extinguish, destroy, exterminate	miht	miè
1699 *	溺	氵 氵 氵 沪 沔 溺	to drown, indulge in	nihk	nì
1700 *	滑	氵 氵 氵 沪 沪 沪 滑 滑 滑 滑	slippery, smooth, funny; to slip, ski	waaht	huá
1701 *	溶	氵 氵 氵 沪 浐 浐 浐 溶 溶	to dissolve	yùhng	róng
1702 *	溜	氵 氵 氵 沪 沟 沟 沟 淄 溜	to glide, skate, slide; slippery	lauh	liū
1703 *	源	氵 氵 氵 沪 沪 沥 沥 沥 源 源	fountain, source	yùhn	yuán
1704 *	溝	氵 氵 氵 沪 泄 洪 洪 溝 溝 溝	ditch, gutter	kàu	gōu
1705 *	溢	氵 氵 氵 汷 汷 洪 溢 溢 溢	to overflow; excessive	yaht	yì
1706 *	溪	氵 氵 氵 沪 淫 淫 溪 溪 溪	stream	kài	xī
1707 *	準	氵 氵 氵 沪 沪 沪 淮 淮 準	standard; accurate; to get ready	jéun	zhǔn
1708 *	滓	氵 氵 氵 沪 沪 沪 滓 滓 滓	sediment, dregs	jí	zǐ
1709 *	溉	氵 氵 氵 泊 泊 泊 洹 洹 溉 溉 溉	to irrigate	koi	gài
1710 **	演	氵 氵 氵 沪 沪 沪 淙 淙 演 演 演	to perform, act	yín	yǎn

1711 *	漠	シ ジ ゾ ゾ 浐 浐 浐 浐 浐 漠 漠	desert; indifferent	
			mohk	mò
1712 *	滯	シ ジ 汁 汫 浨 浨 洲 泄 滯 滯	to detain	
			jaih	zhì
1713 *	漬	シ ジ 汁 洼 泩 凊 凊	to soak, stain	
			jik	zì
1714 *	漂	シ ジ ゾ 沪 沔 沔 漂 漂 漂	[1] to drift, [1] float, [2] bleach	
			[1] piu; [2] piu	[1] piāo; [2] piǎo
1715 *	漲	シ ジ 汙 汚 汚 浉 浉 涱 涱 漲 漲	[1] to expand, [1] swell, [2] rise	
			[1] [2] jeung	[1] zhàng; [2] zhǎng
1716 *	漁	シ ジ 汐 汍 泊 泊 淢 淢 漁	to fish	
			yùh	yú
1717 *	滲	シ ジ 汐 泫 浍 浍 浍 滲	to soak through	
			sam	shèn
1718 *	漸	シ ジ 汀 沔 泹 泹 泹 渲 渲 渐 渐	gradually	
			jihm	jiàn
1719 *	滴	シ ジ 汐 泩 泝 泝 济 商 滴 滴 滴	drops; to drip	
			dihk	dī
1720 *	漆	シ ジ 汁 沐 泆 泆 泆 漆 漆 漆	to paint	
			chat	qī
1721 **	滿	シ ジ 汁 汗 泄 泄 浩 浩 浂 満 満 満	full, satisfied	
			múhn	mǎn
1722 **	漢	シ ジ 汀 泩 泩 泩 浩 浩 漟 漟 漢 漢	Chinese, Han dynasty, good fellow	
			hon	hàn
1723 *	漏	シ ジ 汀 沪 沪 沪 漏 漏 漏 漏	to leak, leave out	
			lauh	lòu

No.	Character	Strokes	Definition	Cantonese	Mandarin
1724 *	漱	シ シ 汀 沪 沪 泙 涑 涑 漱 漱 漱	to rinse	sau	shù
1725 *	漫	シ シ 沪 沪 沮 沪 湯 湯 湨 漫 漫	[1] to overflow, [1] flood; [2] limitless	[1][2] maahn	[1] màn; [2] mán
1726 *	漿	ㄐ ㄐ ㄐ ㄐ 爿 牀 牀 牀 將 將 將 漿	fluid, thick fluid	jeùng	jiāng
1727 *	滾	シ シ 沪 泫 泫 浐 浐 滻 滚 滚 滚	to roll about, boil, order someone to go away	gwán	gǔn
1728 *	潑	シ シ 沪 沪 潑 潑 潑 潑 潑 潑 潑	to splash	put	pō
1729 *	潛	シ シ 汇 沪 汱 浧 涔 潜 潛 潛	to dive, hide; secretly	chìhm	qián
1730 *	潤	シ 氵 沪 沪 沪 淠 潤 潤 潤 潤 潤	lubricated; to moisten, enrich	yuhn	rùn
1731 *	澎	シ シ 沪 洁 洁 洁 洁 漕 漕 澎	noise of rushing waters	pàahng	pēng
1732 *	澈	シ シ 汇 泔 泔 泞 济 清 清 澈 澈 澈	clear; to understand	chit	chè
1733 *	潔	シ 汇 注 潔 潔 潔 潔 潔 潔 潔 潔	clean, pure	git	jié
1734 *	澇	シ シ 沙 沙 泬 泬 淞 潲 澇 澇	flood	loùh	lào
1735 *	潦	シ シ 沪 沪 泲 泺 淶 澇 澇 澇 潦	[1] rain falling heavily; [2] unsuccessful in life, [2] neglectful	[1] lóuh; [2] liùh	[1] lǎo; [2] liǎo
1736 *	潰	シ シ 沪 沪 沪 泄 泄 漕 漕 漕 潰	to overflow the banks; ulcer	kúi	kùi

1737 *	澆	シ ミ ミニ ジニ ミ泛 シ澆 シ澆 シ澆 澆	to pour hiù	jiāo
1738 *	澄	シ ミ ミ ジン ミ バ バ 澄 澄 澄 澄 澄	clear; to clarify chìhng	chéng
1739 *	潮	シ シ シ シ 沽 沽 沽 沽 沽 潮 潮 潮	tide, current; moist chìuh	cháo
1740 *	濁	シ シ シ 浔 浔 浔 浔 浔 浔 濁 濁	muddy juhk	zhuó
1741 *	激	シ シ シ 泊 泊 沖 沖 滂 滂 激 激 激	to excite, stimulate gik	jī
1742 *	濃	シ シ シ シ 油 油 濃 濃 濃 濃	thick, rich, dense nùhng	nóng
1743 *	澳	シ シ シ 汩 汩 沟 沟 潤 澳 澳 澳	dock, Macao ou	aò
1744 *	澡	シ シ シ シ 渦 渦 渦 澡 澡 澡	to bathe; bath chou	zăo
1745 *	澤	シ シ シ シ シ シ シ 澤 澤 澤 澤	marsh jaahk	zé
1746 *	濕	シ シ シ シ シ シ 濕 濕 濕 濕	wet, damp sàp	shī
1747 *	澀	シ シ シ シ シ シ 澀 澀 澀	rough, harsh, acrid sik, gip	sè
1748 *	濫	シ シ シ 泣 泣 泣 滥 滥 滥 滥 濫 濫	to overflow, abuse laahm	laǹ
1749 **	濟	シ シ シ シ 沖 沖 沖 済 済 済 済 済	to help jai	jì

1750 *	濱	シ ジ ジ 泞 渀 渀 渀 渀 渀 渀 濱 濱 濱 濱	shore
			bàn　　　　　bīn
1751 *	瀉	シ ジ ゾ 泸 泸 泸 泸 洞 涵 涵 泻 瀉 瀉	to purge; diarrhea
			se　　　　　xiè
1752 *	瀑	シ ジ 广 氾 沪 沪 渥 渥 渥 渠 渠 湨 瀑 瀑	waterfall
			buhk　　　　　pù
1753 *	瀋	シ ジ ゾ 泞 泲 泌 泌 渁 渁 渁 濬 濬 瀋	juice (other than fruit)
			sám　　　　　shěn
1754 *	濾	シ ジ 汁 泸 泸 泸 泸 泸 瀌 瀌 瀌 濾 濾 濾	to strain, filter
			leuih　　　　　lù
1755 *	灌	シ ジ ジ 汫 ジ 澝 澝 澝 澝 灌 灌 灌	to irrigate, pour into
			gun　　　　　guàn
1756 *	灘	シ ジ ジ 泮 泄 洪 洪 漢 漢 漢 灘 灘 灘 灘 灘	beach, shore
			taàn　　　　　tān
1757 *	灑	シ ジ 汩 沰 沰 溮 溮 溮 溮 溮 溮 灑 灑 灑 灑	to sprinkle
			sá　　　　　sǎ
1758 *	灣	シ ジ ゾ 沱 泞 泞 湾 湾 灣 灣 灣 灣 灣 灣	bay
			wàan　　　　　wān

火　Section

1759 ***	火	丶 丷 少 火	fire
			fó　　　　　huǒ
1760 **	灰	一 ナ 灰	gray color, ashes
			fùi　　　　　hūi
1761 **	災	巛 災	disaster, misfortune
			jòi　　　　　zāi

1762 *	灼	火 灯 灼 灼	to burn; clear, distinct, bright
			cheuk　　　　　　　zhuó
1763 *	灶	火 灯 灶 灶	stove, furnace
			jou　　　　　　　　zaò
1764 *	灸	ノ ク 久 灸	acupuncture
			gau　　　　　　　　jiǔ
1765 *	炊	火 灯 炌 炊 炊	to cook
			cheùi　　　　　　　chūi
1766 *	炒	火 灯 灶 炒 炒	to pan fry
			chaáu　　　　　　　chǎo
1767 *	炎	火 炎	flame, blaze; hot
			yìhm　　　　　　　yán
1768 *	炕	火 灯 灯 灯 炕	to toast; brick oven; dry
			kong　　　　　　　kàng
1769 *	炳	火 灯 炌 炳 炳 炳	bright, luminous
			bíng　　　　　　　bǐng
1770 *	炬	火 灯 灯 炉 炬 炬	torch
			geuih　　　　　　　jù
1771 *	炮	火 灯 炌 炝 炮 炮	[1] cannon, [1] gun; [2] to roast, [2] bake
			[1] paau; [2] baau　　[1] pào; [2] paó
1772 *	炸	火 灯 炌 炸 炸	[1] to explode, [2] deep fry
			[1][2] ja　　　　[1] zhà; [2] zhá
1773 *	炭	一 山 山 岸 岸 炭	charcoal
			taan　　　　　　　tàn
1774 **	烟	火 灯 炉 烟 烟 烟 烟	smoke, tobacco, cigarette
			yìn　　　　　　　　yán

1775 *	烘	火 灯 灯 炒 炒 烘 烘	to roast, dry by the fire
			hung　　　　　　hōng
1776 *	烤	火 灯 灯 灯 炷 烤 烤 烤	to toast, roast
			haàu　　　　　　kǎo
1777 *	烝	乛 了 丞 丞 丞 丞 丞	vapor
			jìng　　　　　　zhēng
1778 *	烙	火 灯 灯 灯 灯 烙 烙 烙	to brand; brand
			lohk　　　　　　laò
1779 *	烏	ノ イ 竹 白 白 烏 烏	black, dark
			wù　　　　　　　wū
1780 **	烈	一 丆 歹 歹 列 列 烈	fierce; fiery
			liht　　　　　　liè
1781 *	焉	一 丁 下 正 正 正 焉 焉	[1] how can, [1] how, [1] why, [2] ending word
			[1] yìn; [2] yìhn　　[1][2] yān
1782 *	烹	丶 亠 亠 亠 言 亨 亨 烹	to cook
			paàng　　　　　pēng
1783 *	焊	火 灯 灯 焊 焊 焊 焊	to weld
			hohn　　　　　　hàn
1784 *	焦	ノ イ 竹 竹 竹 隹 焦	scorched; anxious
			jiù　　　　　　jiāo
1785 **	無	ノ 仁 仁 無 無 無	none, without
			mòuh　　　　　wú
1786 ***	然	ノ 夕 夕 夕 夕 然 然 然 然	then, but, however
			yìhn　　　　　rán
1787 *	焰	火 灯 灯 灯 灯 焰 焰 焰 焰	flame
			yihm　　　　　yàn

1788 *	焚	一 十 オ オ 木 林 焚	to burn *fàhn*　　　　　　*fén*
1789 **	照	l 冂 冂 日 日 日 日ʳ 日ᵖ 日ᵖ 昭 昭 照	to shine at, follow, aim at, photograph; photograph *jiu*　　　　　　*zhào*
1790 *	煮	+ 土 耂 耂 者 者 者 者 煮	to cook *jyú*　　　　　　*zhǔ*
1791 *	煲	ノ イ 亻 亻 亻 仁 仴 保 煲	to boil *bòu*　　　　　　*bāo*
1792 *	煎	⺍ 丷 丷 亣 亣 前 煎	to fry in small amount of oil *jìn*　　　　　　*jiān*
1793 **	煤	火 灯 灶 灶 灿 灿 烘 煤 煤	coal, charcoal *mùih*　　　　　　*méi*
1794 *	煩	火 灯 灯 灯 炉 煩 煩 煩	troubled, annoyed *faàhn*　　　　　　*fán*
1795 *	煉	火 灯 灯 炬 炬 炬 煉 煉	to refine, smelt *lihn*　　　　　　*liàn*
1796 *	熄	火 火 灯 炉 炉 炉 炉 熄 熄 熄	to extinguish *sìk*　　　　　　*xī*
1797 *	熔	火 火 灯 炉 炉 炉 烧 熔 熔	to smelt *yùhng*　　　　　　*róng*
1798 *	熊	ㄥ ㄙ 亇 育 育 能 能 熊	bear *hùhng*　　　　　　*xióng*
1799 *	熏	ノ ㇒ 千 占 向 向 車 重 熏	[1] to smoke, [2] fumigate [1] [2] *fàn*　　　[1] *xūn*; [2] *xùn*
1800 *	熬	一 十 土 吉 圭 耂 耂 耂 敖 敖 熬	[1] to cook something for a long time, [1] endure, [2] feel depressed [1] [2] *ngòuh*　　　[1] *áo*; [2] *āo*

1801 **	熱	一 十 土 チ 夫 幸 刼 執 執 熱	hot, zealous, in style; heat	
			yiht	rè
1802 **	熟	、 亠 亠 亠 古 亨 亨 亨 享 孰 孰 孰 熟	cooked, ripe, familiar with	
			suhk	shú; shóu
1803 *	熨	一 コ 尸 戸 尿 尉 尉 尉 熨	[1] to iron; [1] iron; [2] pressed (clothing)	
			[1] wahn; [2] wàt	[1] yùn; [2] yù
1804 *	燙	シ ジ ゙ 沪 沪 湡 沪 湯 湯 燙	boiling hot; to warm up, burn, iron	
			tong	tàng
1805 *	燃	火 火 灯 灯 灯 灯 燃 燃 燃 燃	to light a fire	
			yìhn	ràn
1806 **	燒	火 炉 炉 炉 炘 烧 燒 燒 燒	to burn, cook, roast; fever	
			siù	shāo
1807 *	燐	火 灯 灯 炒 炒 烂 烊 炸 烊 燒 燐	phosphorus	
			leùhn	lín
1808 *	燉	火 灯 灯 灯 炖 炖 焞 焞 焞 燉 燉	to stew	
			dahn	dùn
1809 *	燕	、 十 廿 廿 芷 芷 芷 苙 莊 菰 菰 燕	swallow	
			yin	yàn
1810 **	燈	火 灯 灯 炉 烂 烂 熔 熔 燈 燈	lamp, light	
			dàng	dēng
1811 *	燦	火 火 灯 灯 炉 炉 烂 烟 燦 燦 煙 燦	brilliant, glittering	
			chaan	càn
1812 *	燭	火 灯 灯 烟 烟 烟 烟 焗 焗 煴 燭 燭 燭	candle	
			jùk	zhú
1813 **	營	火 炊 炊 炌 焱 焱 營 營 營	camp, battalion, nutrition; to manage	
			yìhng	yíng

1814 *	燬	火 犬 炉 炉 炉 炉 烟 烟 烜 煜 煜 燬 燬 燬	to destroy by fire *wái*　　　　*huǐ*
1815 *	燥	火 犬 炉 炉 炉 焊 焐 焊 燥	dry *chou*　　　　*zào*
1816 *	爆	火 犬 炉 炉 炉 炉 焊 焊 煜 焊 煤 爆 爆	to explode, burst *baau*　　　　*bào*
1817 *	爐	火 炉 炉 炉 炉 炉 熕 熕 熐 熐 熛 熛 熛 爐	stove, furnace *loùh*　　　　*lú*
1818 **	爛	火 灯 灯 炉 炉 炉 炉 炉 燜 熌 熌 熌 爛 爛	rotten, spoiled, broken *laahn*　　　　*làn*
		爪　Section	
1819 *	爪	ノ ㇅ 爪 爪	claws *jaáu*　　　　*zhǎo*
1820 *	爬	爪 爬 爬 爬 爬	to crawl, climb *pàh*　　　　*pá*
1821 **	爭	ノ ㇇ 乌 乌 乌 爭	to strive, quarrel, fight for *jàng*　　　　*zhēng*
1822 ***	爲	(為) ㇀ ノ 尸 戶 為 為	[1] to do, [1] be; [2] why; [2] for, [2] because of [1] *wàih;* [2] *waih*　　　[1] *wéi;* [2] *wèi*
1823 *	爵	⺊ ⺊ 乌 甶 甾 甾 甾 甾 甾 甾 甾 甾 爵 爵	nobility *jeuk*　　　　*jué*
		父　Section	
1824 **	父	㇀ ㇇ ㇒ 父	father *fuh*　　　　*fù*

1825 **	爸	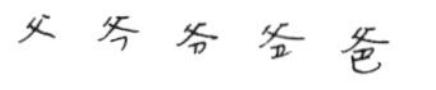	father	*bà*	*bà*
1826 *	爹		father	*dè*	*diē*
1827 *	爺		father, grandfather, father's father	*yèh*	*yé*
		爻 Section			
1828 *	爽	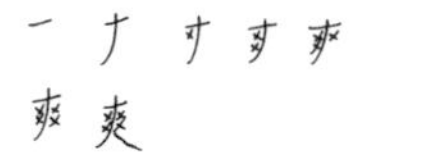	refreshed, comfortable, straightforward	*sóng*	*shuǎng*
1829 *	爾	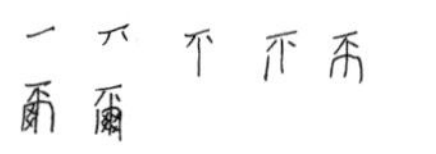	you	*yúh*	*ěr*
		爿 Section			
1830 **	牀	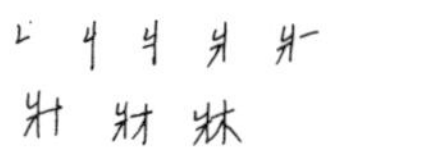	bed	*chòhng*	*chuáng*
1831 *	牆	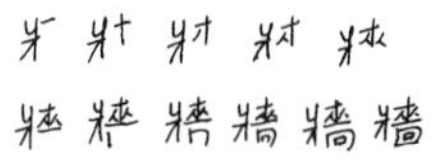	wall	*cheùhng*	*qiáng*
		片 Section			
1832 **	片		[1] slice, [1] piece, [1] card, [2] photo, [2] movie, [2] record	[1] *pin;* [2] *pín*	[1] *piàn;* [2] *piān*
1833 ***	版	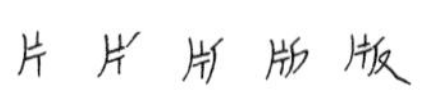	printing plate, edition, copyright	*baán*	*bǎn*
1834 *	牌	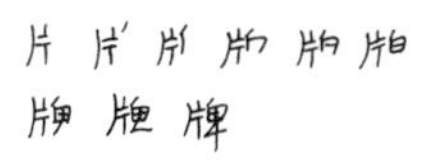	sign, trademark, playing cards, license	*pàaih*	*pái*

	牙	Section	

1835 **	牙	一 匚 牙 牙	tooth *ngàh* *yá*

	牛	Section	

1836 ***	牛	丿 丿 二 牛	cow, ox *ngàuh* *niú*
1837 *	牢	丶 丶 宀 宇	prison, firmly *loùh* *láo*
1838 *	牧	丿 牛 牛 牛 牛 牥 牧	to tend, shepherd, priest *muhk* *mù*
1839 **	物	牛 牜 牞 物	article, object, thing, substance *maht* *wù*
1840 *	牲	牛 牜 牲 牲 牲	cattle, animal, poultry *sàng* *shēng*
1841 **	特	牛 牛 牛 牛 牲 特 特	special; purposely *dahk* *tè*
1842 *	牽	丶 二 玄 玄 玄 牽 牽	to pull, drag *hìn* *qiān*
1843 *	犁	丿 二 千 禾 利 利 犁	plow; to plow *làih* *lí*
1844 *	犢	牛 牛 牜 牲 牲 犢 犢 犢 犢 犢 犢 犢	calf, heifer *suhk* *dú*
1845 *	犧	牛 牜 牜 牲 犧 犧 犧 犧 犧 犧 犧 犧	to sacrifice *hèi* *xī*

	犬　Section		
1846 *	犬	一 ナ 大 犬	dog *hyún*　　　*quǎn*
1847 **	犯	ノ 犭 犭 犭 犯	to violate, offend; criminal *faahn*　　　*fàn*
1848 **	狀	犭 犭 犺 狀 狀	form, shape, appearance *johng*　　　*zhuàng*
1849 *	狂	犭 犭 犴 狂	mad, crazy, violent *kòhng*　　　*kuáng*
1850 **	狗	犭 犭 犳 犳 狗 狗	dog *gáu*　　　*gǒu*
1851 *	狐	犭 犭 犭 狐 狐 狐	fox *wùh*　　　*hú*
1852 *	狠	犭 犭 犭 犭 犯 犯 狠	cruel, hard-hearted *hán*　　　*hěn*
1853 *	狡	犭 犭 犷 狡 狡 狡	sneaky, cunning *gaáu*　　　*jiǎo*
1854 *	狼	犭 犭 犳 犷 狼 狼 狼 狼	wolf, cruel, awkward *lòhng*　　　*láng*
1855 *	狹	犭 犭 狆 犿 犿 狹 狹	narrow *hahp*　　　*xiá*
1856 *	猛	犭 犭 犳 犴 犴 猛 猛 猛	brave, fierce *máahng*　　　*měng*
1857 *	猜	犭 犭 犺 狂 猜 猜 猜	to guess, doubt *chàai*　　　*cāi*

1858 *	猴	犭 犭′ 犭″ 犭犭 犭犭′ 犭犭″ 犭犭 犭犭 犭犭 猴	monkey	
			haùh	hóu
1859 *	猶	犭 犭′ 犭″ 犭犭 犭犭 犭犭 犭犭 犭犭 猶	like, undecided; still; Jew	
			yàuh	yóu
1860 *	猿	犭 犭′ 犭⁺ 犭⁻ 犭⁻ 犭 犭 犭 猿 猿 猿	ape	
			yùhn	yuán
1861 *	獅	犭 犭′ 犭 犭 犭 犭 犭 獅 獅 獅	lion	
			sī	shī
1862 *	猾	犭 犭′ 犭 犭 犭 犭 犭 猾 猾 猾 猾	sneaky, cunning	
			waaht	huá
1863 *	獄	犭 犭′ 犭 犴 狺 狺 狺 狺 獄 獄 獄	prison, jail	
			yuhk	yù
1864 **	獨	犭 犭′ 犭 犭 犭 犭 犭 獨 獨 獨 獨 獨	single, only, alone	
			duhk	dú
1865 *	獲	犭 犭′ 犭 犭 犭 犭 犭 狟 狟 獲 獲 獲	to obtain, catch	
			wohk	huò
1866 *	獵	犭 犭 犭 犭 犭 犭 犭 獵 獵 獵	to hunt	
			lihp	liè
1867 *	獸	丶 亠 吅 吅 吅 甲 甲 單 留 單 獸 獸	beast, wild animal	
			sau	shòu
1868 *	獻	丶 广 广 户 庐 虍 虍 虐 虐 虔 虜 膚 膚 膚 膚 獻	to offer, present	
			hin	xiàn
	玄　Section			
1869 *	玄	丶 亠 亡 玄 玄	black, dark, profound	
			yìhn	xuán

1870 *	率	玄 玄 玄 率 率	[1] to lead; [1] pretty, [1] straightforward; [2] rate, [2] ratio
			[1] syùt; [2] lyuht　　　[1] shuài; [2] lǜ

	王　Section

1871 **	王	一 丁 千 王	king, ruler
			wòhng　　　　　wáng

1872 *	玉	王 玉	jade
			yuhk　　　　　yù

1873 *	玫	王 玗 玒 玫 玫	rose
			mùih　　　　　méi

1874 **	玩	王 玕 玕 玩	[1] to play, [1] be amused with; [2] antique
			[1] wuhn; [2] wún　　[1][2] wán

1875 *	玻	王 玕 玒 玻 玻 玻	glass
			bò　　　　　　bō

1876 *	珍	王 玕 玪 珍	precious
			jàn　　　　　zhēn

1877 *	珠	王 玕 玪 珔 珠 珠	pearl, bead
			jyù　　　　　zhū

1878 **	班	王 玉 玨 班	class, grade
			baàn　　　　bān

1879 ***	現	王 玔 玑 玥 珇 現 現	to appear; now, at present
			yihn　　　　xiàn

1880 **	球	王 玕 玗 玽 球 球 球 球	ball, globe, sphere
			kaùh　　　　qiú

1881 **	理	王 玑 玕 珇 珇 珇 理 理	to manage; reason, science, theory
			léih　　　　lǐ

1882 *	琴	王 珏 珐 瑇 瑇 琴	lute, organ, piano
			kàhm qín
1883 *	瑞	王 珏 珄 珄 珄 珳 瑞 瑞	good omen, auspicious
			seuih rùi
1884 *	瑰	王 珏 珏 玧 珀 珀 玥 瑰 瑰 瑰	¹ rose; ² precious
			¹ gwai; ² gwài ¹ ² gūi
1885 *	瑣	王 珏 玧 珜 珘 琑 瑣	trifling
			só sǒ
1886 *	璃	王 王 玙 珳 琂 琺 璃 璃 璃	glass
			lèi lí
1887 *	環	玊 玧 珂 珅 珚 珲 環 環 環 環 環 環	ring, circle; to surround
			wàahn huán
1888 *	璧	一 コ ア ア 启 启 启 启 础 辟 辟 璧 璧	piece of jade
			bìk bì

瓜   Section

1889 **	瓜	丿 丨 几 瓜 瓜	melon, squash
			gwà guā
1890 *	瓣	丶 一 ᅩ 立 辛 瓡 瓣	petals of a flower
			faàn bàn

瓦   Section

1891 *	瓦	一 工 瓦 瓦	tile, earthenware
			ngáh wǎ
1892 *	瓷	丶 冫 沙 汸 次 瓷	porcelain, china
			chìh cí

| 1893 * | 瓶 | ｀ ｀ 兰 并 瓶 | bottle, jug

pìhng   *píng* |

| | 甘   Section |

1894 *	甘	丨 十 卄 甘 甘	sweet; voluntary *gàm* *gān*
1895 ***	甚	丨 十 卄 甘 其 其 甚	[1] very; [2] how, [2] why [1][2] *sàhm* [1] *shèn;* [2] *shén*
1896 *	甜	｀ ㇒ 千 舌 舌 甜	sweet *tìhm* *tián*

| | 生   Section |

1897 ***	生	ノ ㇒ 牛 生	to give birth, be born, happen, live; life; raw *sàng* *shēng*
1898 **	產	｀ 亠 文 产 产 產	to give birth, produce; property *cháan* *chǎn*
1899 *	甥	生 牛 钓 甥 甥 甥 甥 甥	nephew, niece *sàng* *shēng*

| | 用   Section |

| 1900 *** | 用 | 丿 几 月 用 | to use, spend; effect, expense

yuhng   *yòng* |

| | 田   Section |

| 1901 *** | 田 | 丶 冂 日 田 田 | field, land

tìhn   *tián* |

1902 ***	由	日 由 由	reason; from, by; to allow
			yàuh · yóu
1903 *	甲	日 日 甲	first; fingernails
			gaap · jiǎ
1904 *	申	日 日 申	to express, extend
			sàn · shēn
1905 ***	男	田 甼 男	male; man, son
			naàhm · nán
1906 **	界	田 罗 界 界	boundary, border
			gaai · jiè
1907 *	畏	田 田 畀 畏 畏	to fear, dread
			wai · wèi
1908 **	留	丿 丨 ﾉ 化 丣 留	to remain, stay, keep, reserve
			làuh · liú
1909 *	畝	丶 亠 亩 亩 畝 畝	a Chinese acre
			máuh · mǔ
1910 *	畜	丶 亠 玄 玄 玄 畜	[1] animal; [2] to raise or feed animals
			[1] [2] chùk · [1] chù; [2] xù
1911 *	畢	田 甲 里 界 里 異 畢	to finish; entire
			bàt · bì
1912 **	略	田 田 町 畋 畔 略 略 略	plan, outline, summary; briefly
			leuhk · lüè
1913 *	番	丿 丷 丷 半 釆 番	foreign; time, turn
			faàn · fān
1914 *	異	田 甲 里 界 里 異	different, strange, special
			yih · yì

1915 ***	畫	⁻ ⁼ ⁼ ⁼ ⁼ 畫 畫 畫	¹ to plan, ¹ draw, ¹ divide; ² picture, ¹ stroke ¹ waahk; ² wá　　　¹ ² huà
1916 ***	當	⼁ ⼩ ⼩ ⼩ ⼩ ⼩ 尚 當	¹ to bear, ¹ take place; ¹ should; ² suitable; ² when ¹ dòng; ² dong　　¹ dāng; ² dàng
1917 *	彊	⁻ ⁻ 弓 弓 弓 弹 彊 彊 彊	boundary, limit gèung　　　jiāng
1918 *	疊	田 畕 畾 畾 畾 畾 畾 疊	to pile up, fold dihp　　　dié

疋　Section

1919 *	疋	⁻ ⁻ ⼅ 疋 疋	piece (for cloth) pàt　　　pǐ
1920 *	疏	⁻ ⼅ ⼅ 疋 正 正 正 疋 疋 疋 疏 疏	thin, sparse, careless; distance sò　　　shū
1921 **	疑	⁻ ⼂ ⼂ ⼂ 矣 矣 矣 矣 疑 疑 疑 疑 疑	to doubt, suspect yìh　　　yí

疒　Section

1922 *	疙	⼂ ⁻ 广 疒 疒 疒 疙	pimple gaht　　　gē
1923 *	疫	疒 疒 疒 疫 疫	disease yihk　　　yì
1924 *	症	疒 疒 疒 疒 症 症	sickness jing　　　zhèng
1925 *	疹	疒 疒 疒 疹	rash, measles chán　　　zhěn

1926 *	疾	疒 疒 疟 疾 疾	sickness *jaht* *jí*
1927 ***	病	疒 疒 疒 疜 病 病	sick; sickness *bihng* *bìng*
1928 *	疼	疒 疒 疒 疼 疼	pain; to love *tàhng* *téng*
1929 *	疲	疒 疒 疒 疒 疲 疲	tired, exhausted *pèih* *pí*
1930 *	痕	疒 疒 疒 疒 痕 痕 痕	scar, mark, trace *hàhn* *hén*
1931 *	痊	疒 疒 疒 疒 痊 痊	cured, recovered *chyùhn* *quán*
1932 **	痛	疒 疒 疒 疒 痏 痛 痛	pain, ache; extremely *tung* *tòng*
1933 *	痘	疒 疒 疒 痀 痘 痘	smallpox, chickenpox *dauh* *dòu*
1934 *	痣	疒 疒 疒 疜 疢 疢 痣 痣	mole *ji* *zhì*
1935 *	痢	疒 疒 疒 疒 痢 痢 痢	dysentery *leih* *lì*
1936 *	痰	疒 疒 疒 疢 痰	phlegm *taàhm* *tán*
1937 *	痳	疒 疒 疒 疒 痳 痳	numbness, paralysis *màh* *má*
1938 *	痹	(痺) 疒 疒 疒 疒 疒 痹 痹 痹 痹	paralysis *bei* *bì*

1939 *	瘋	广 疒 疒 疯 疯 疯 疯 疯 瘋 瘋	insane; leprosy	
			fùng	fēng
1940 *	瘦	广 疒 疒 疒 疒 疖 瘐 瘦 瘦	thin, lean	
			sau	shòu
1941 *	瘩	广 广 广 疒 疒 疢 疢 瘩 瘩	pimple	
			daap	da
1942 *	瘤	广 广 疒 疒 疒 疯 疯 瘤 瘤 瘤	tumor	
			laùh	liú
1943 *	瘡	广 广 疒 疒 疹 疹 疹 瘡 瘡 瘡 瘡	scab	
			chòng	chuáng
1944 *	瘟	(瘟) 广 广 疒 疒 疒 疒 瘟 瘟 瘟 瘟	plague, epidemic	
			wàn	wēn
1945 *	療	广 疒 疒 疒 疒 疹 疹 瘩 瘩 瘩 瘩 療	to cure, heal	
			liùh	liáo
1946 *	癌	广 广 疒 疒 疗 痁 癌 癌 癌	cancer	
			ngaàhm	ái
1947 *	癆	广 广 广 疒 疒 疹 疹 瘄 瘄 癆	tuberculosis	
			loùh	láo
1948 *	癢	广 疒 疒 疒 疒 痒 痒 痒 瘩 瘩 瘩 癢 癢	itch; itching	
			yéuhng	yǎng
1949 *	癮	广 疒 疒 疒 疒 疒 疯 疯 瘾 瘾 癮 癮 癮 癮	habit, craving	
			yáhn	yǐn
癶 Section				
1950 **	登	丁 ヲ ヲ゛ 癶 癶 癶 癶 啓 啓 登	to go up, record, register	
			dàng	dēng

| 1951 ** | 發 | ㄱ ㄱ ㄌ 癶 癶 発 発 発 發 發 發 | to sprout, send out, start, issue

faat　　　　*fā* |

白　Section

1952 ***	白	ノ ィ ⼁ 白 白	white, bright, clear *baahk*　　　　*bái*
1953 ***	百	一 百	hundred; numerous *baak*　　　　*bǎi*
1954 *	皂	白 皀 皂	soap; black *jouh*　　　　*zaò*
1955 ***	的	白 白′ 的 的	[1] goal; [1] apparent, [2] certain; [3] possessive pronoun [1][2][3] *dìk*　　　[1] *dì;* [2] *dí;* [3] *de*
1956 *	皆	⺊ ㇀ 比 比 皆	all, altogether *gaài*　　　　*jiē*
1957 *	皇	白 皀 皁 皇	emperor *wòhng*　　　　*huáng*
1958 *	皓	白 白′ 白ˊ 皓 皓 皓 皓 皓	bright *houh*　　　　*haò*

皮　Section

| 1959 ** | 皮 | ㄱ ㄏ 皮 皮 皮 | skin, leather, fur, peel

pèih　　　　*pí* |
| 1960 * | 皺 | ノ ㄅ ㄅ 匂 芻 芻 皺 | to wrinkle; wrinkle

jau　　　　*zhoù* |

四　Section

1961 *	皿	丶 冂 皿 皿	utensil *míhng*　　　*mǐn*
1962 *	盂	二 于 盂	spittoon *yùh*　　　*yú*
1963 *	盅	丶 冂 口 中 盅	small covered cup *jùng*　　　*zhōng*
1964 *	盆	丿 八 今 分 盆	basin, tub *pùhn*　　　*pén*
1965 *	盈	乃 乃 孕 孕 盈	full, excessive; to overflow *yìhng*　　　*yíng*
1966 **	益	丷 丷 共 益	benefit, advantage *yik*　　　*yì*
1967 *	盒	丿 人 人 今 合 合 盒	box, case *hahp*　　　*hé*
1968 **	盛	一 厂 厉 成 成 成 盛	[1] flourishing, [1] prosperous; [2] to contain [1][2] *sihng*　　[1] *shèng;* [2] *chéng*
1969 *	盜	冫 冫 氵 汷 次 盜	to rob; robber *douh*　　　*dào*
1970 *	盟	丨 冂 日 日 旳 明 明 盟	[1] treaty, [1] oath; [2] to swear [1][2] *màhng*　　[1] *méng;* [2] *míng*
1971 *	盞	一 弋 戈 戋 戔 盞	small cup, measure word for lamps *jaán*　　　*zhǎn*
1972 *	監	一 丁 丏 片 臣 卧 卧 臤 監	to supervise; prison *gaàm*　　　*jiān*
1973 **	盡	乛 ⺈ ⺕ 큭 盡 聿 盡	to exhaust, finish; extreme; all *jeuhn*　　　*jìn*

1974 *	盤	ノ イ 力 弁 舟 舟 舟 舟 般 般 盤	tray, plate *pùhn* 　　　　　　 *pán*

目　Section

1975 ***	目	丨 冂 月 目	eye; to see *muhk* 　　　　　　 *mù*
1976 *	盲	` 二 亡 盲	blind *maàhng* 　　　　 *máng*
1977 ***	直	一 十 盲 直	straight, vertical, straightforward; directly *jihk* 　　　　　　 *zhí*
1978 **	相	一 十 才 木 相	mutual, reciprocal; looks, appearance *seùng; seung* 　　 *xiāng; xiàng*
1979 *	盾	ノ ｆ 厂 斥 盾	shield *teúhn* 　　　　　 *dùn*
1980 *	盼	目 目ˊ 目ˋ 盼 盼	to hope for *paan* 　　　　　 *pàn*
1981 ***	省	⺌ 小 少 省	[1] province; [1] to spare, [1] save, [2] visit, [2] understand [1] *sáang;* [2] *síng* 　 [1] *shěng;* [2] *xǐng*
1982 ***	看	ノ 三 手 看	[1] to see, [1] watch, [1] visit, [1] predict, [2] look after [1] *hon;* [2] *hòn* 　 [1] *kàn;* [2] *kān*
1983 *	眉	⼁ ⼁ ⼝ 尸 眉	eyebrows *mèih* 　　　　　 *méi*
1984 *	眠	目 目ｆ 目ｆ 眠 眠 眠	to sleep, lie down *mihn* 　　　　　 *mián*
1985 ***	眞	一 匕 旨 直 眞	real, sincere, true *jàn* 　　　　　 *zhēn*

1986 **	眼	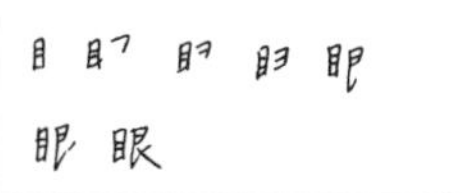	eye, hole *ngáahn*	*yǎn*
1987 *	眷		to be fond of; family, relatives *gyun*	*juàn*
1988 **	衆		crowd; many *jung*	*zhòng*
1989 **	着	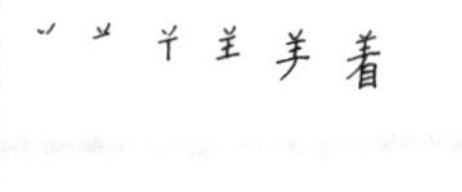	[1] to wear (clothes), [2] lay hands on; [3] anxious; [4] present participle [1] *jeuk;* [2 3 4] *jeuhk*	[1 2] *zhuó;* [3] *zhāo;* [4] *zhe*
1990 *	睛	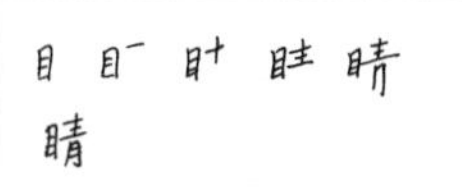	eyeball *jìng*	*jīng*
1991 *	睜	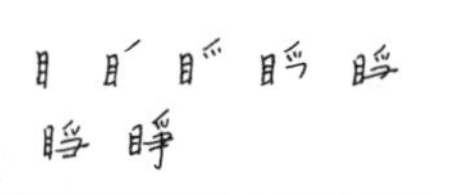	to open the eyes *jàng*	*zhēng*
1992 **	睡	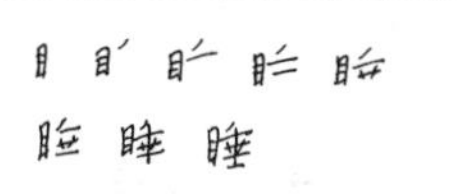	to sleep *seuih*	*shuì*
1993 *	督	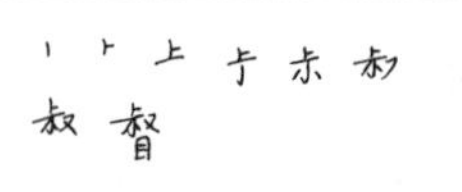	to urge, supervise *dùk*	*dū*
1994 *	瞄	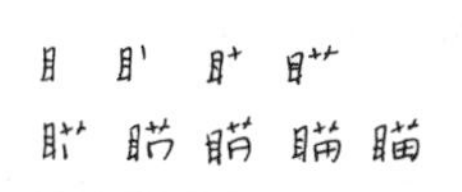	to aim at *miùh*	*miáo*
1995 *	瞎	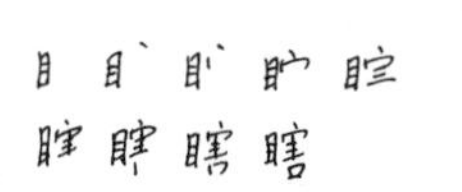	blind; blindly, carelessly *got*	*xiā*
1996 *	瞌	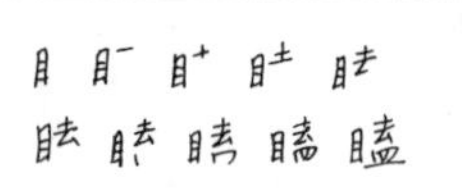	to nap, doze *hahp*	*kē*
1997 *	瞞	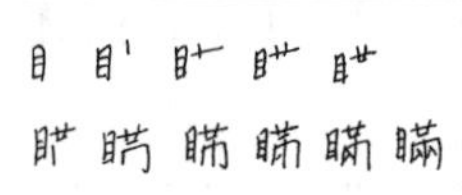	to hide, conceal the truth *mùhn*	*mán*
1998 *	瞬	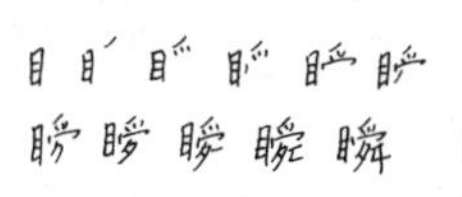	wink, an instant *seun*	*shùn*

1999 *	瞥	丨 小 尚 尚 肖 肖 尚' 肖㣺 肖㣺 敝 敝 瞥	to peep; glimpse
			pit *piē*
2000 *	瞧	目 目 肌 肌' 肝 肝 雎 瞧	to peep, look
			chiùh *qiáo*
2001 *	瞭	目 目' 肟 胅 肤 肤 睞 睠 睠 睹 瞭 瞭	[1] to understand, [2] look from a distance
			[1] *liúh;* [2] *liùh* [1] *liǎo;* [2] *liào*
2002 *	瞪	目 目' 肝 肝' 肤 肤 瞪 睽 睞 瞪 瞪	to stare, gaze, look at angrily
			dahng *dèng*
2003 *	瞻	目 目' 肳 旷 旷 脐 脐 瞻 瞻 瞻 瞻 瞻	to look up
			jìm *zhān*

	矛 Section

2004 *	矛	㇇ ㇇ 子 予 矛	spear
			maàuh *máo*

	矢 Section

2005 *	矢	丿 ㇇ 午 矢	arrow, manure
			chí *shǐ*
2006 *	矣	㇏ ㇺ 矣	final article
			yíh *yǐ*
2007 ***	知	矢 矢 知 知	to know; knowledge
			jì *zhī*
2008 *	矩	矢 矢 知 矩 矩 矩	ruler (for drawing); policy, rule
			geúi *jǔ*
2009 ***	短	矢 矢 矢 知 知 短 短	to lack; short, temporary, brief; shortcoming
			dyún *duǎn*

2010 *	矮	矢 矢´ 矢ˇ 矢ⁿ 矢ⁿ 矮 矮 矮	short, low
			ngái *ǎi*
2011 *	矯	矢 矢´ 矢ˇ 矢ⁿ 矢ⁿ 矫 矫 矫 矫 矯 矯	to straighten, correct, pretend; strong
			giú *jiǎo*

石　　Section

2012 **	石	一 丁 丆 石 石	rock, stone
			sehk *shí*
2013 *	砌	石 石´ 石ˇ 砌 砌 砌	to build, pave
			chai *qì*
2014 *	砍	石 石´ 砂 砂 砍	to chop, cut down
			hám *kǎn*
2015 **	砲	石 石´ 砂 砂 砲 砲	cannon, gun
			paau *pào*
2016 **	破	石 石´ 砂 砰 破 破	to break, destroy
			po *pò*
2017 ***	研	石 石´ 砰 研	to grind, study, research
			yìhn *yán*
2018 **	硬	石 石´ 砂 硭 硬 硬 硬 硬	hard, firm, stiff
			ngaahng *yìng*
2019 *	碗	石 石´ 砂 砂 砂 砂 碗 碗 碗	bowl
			wún *wǎn*
2020 **	碎	石 石´ 砂 砂 砕 砕 碎 碎	to break into pieces; fragment
			seui *suì*
2021 *	碉	石 石´ 砂 硐 硐 硐 硐 碉 碉	stone house
			diù *diāo*

2022 **	碰	石 石ˋ 石广 石扩 石碰 石碰	to meet, run into, collide with
			pung · pèng
2023 *	碑	石 石ˊ 石叨 石㓉 石白 石白 碑 碑 碑	monument
			bēi · bēi
2024 *	碟	石 石 石十 石廿 石世 石世 碟 碟 碟	dish, saucer
			dihp · dié
2025 **	確	石 石 石厂 石石 砗 砗 砗 砗 確	certainly, actually
			kok · què
2026 *	碼	石 石 石厂 石F 石厈 碼 碼	number, one yard, wharf
			máh · mǎ
2027 *	磁	石 石 石丷 砳 砝 磁 磁	magnetic; chinaware, magnet
			chìh · cí
2028 *	磅	石 石 石亠 砳 砳 砳 砳 磅 碲 磅	pound
			bohng · bàng
2029 **	磨	ˋ 亠 广 广 庐 床 麻 磨	[1] to grind, [1] polish, [1] practice; [2] millstone
			[1][2] mòh · [1] mó; [2] mò
2030 *	磚	石 石 石石 砳 砳 砳 砳 砳 磚 磚	brick
			jyùn · zhuān
2031 *	礎	石 石 石廾 砳 石林 石梵 砳 砳 砳 礎	foundation, base
			chó · chǔ
2032 **	礙	石 砳 砳 砳 砳 砳 砳 砳 砳 砳 砳 砳 礙 礙	to obstruct, hinder
			ngoih · ài
2033 *	礦	石 石 石广 砳 砳 砳 砳 砳 砳 砳 砳 砳 砳 礦	mine, mineral
			kong · kuàng

示 Section

2034 **	示	二 丁 示	to show, proclaim; announcement
			sih shì
2035 *	祁	丶 ㇇ 才 ネ ネ' ネβ 祁	large; gently
			kèih qí
2036 ***	社	ネ ネ' 一 社 社	association, society
			séh shè
2037 *	祈	ネ ネ' 祈 祈 祈	to pray, implore
			kèih qí
2038 **	祖	ネ ネ' 初 袒 祖	ancestor
			jóu zǔ
2039 **	神	ネ ネ' 初 祁 袒 神	God, spirit, energy; mysterious
			sàhn shén
2040 *	祕	ネ ネ' 祕 祕 祕 祕	[1] secret, [1] mysterious; [1] secretary, [2] constipation
			[1][2] bei [1] mì; [2] bì
2041 **	祝	ネ ネ' 祀 祝 祝 祝	to bless, congratulate
			jùk zhù
2042 ***	票	一 ㇒ 覀 西 西 覀 栗 票	ticket, coupon, bill
			piu piaò
2043 *	祥	ネ ネ' 祥 祥	luck, good omen
			cheùhng xiáng
2044 *	祭	ノ ク タ ㇆ 夕' 夕〵 奴 奴 祭 祭	to offer a sacrifice
			jai jì
2045 *	禁	一 十 木 林 禁 禁 禁	to avoid, stop, prohibit, prevent
			gam jìn
2046 *	祿	ネ ネ' 祊 袒 袢 袢 祿 祿	prosperity
			luhk lù

2047 **	福	示 礻 衦 衦 衦 福 祸 祸 褔 福	fortune, benefits; lucky
			fùk *fú*
2048 **	禍	示 礻 衦 祸 祸 祸 祸 禍 禍 禍	misfortune, disaster
			woh *huò*
2049 *	禦	㇒ 彳 彳' 行 行 徏 徍 御 御 禦	to resist; enemy
			yuh *yù*
2050 **	禮	示 礻 衦 衦 神 神 神 禮 禮 禮 禮 禮 禮	ceremony, manner, gift, politeness
			láih *lǐ*
2051 *	禱	示 礻 社 社 禱 禱 禱 禱 禱 禱 禱 禱 禱	to pray
			tóu *daǒ*

内 Section

2052 *	禽	㇒ 人 人 仐 仐 含 含 禽 禽 禽 禽	birds, poultry, animal
			kàhm *qín*

禾 Section

2053 *	禾	㇒ 二 千 禾 禾	crops, grain
			wòh *hé*
2054 *	禿	禾 禿 禿	bare, bald, hairless
			tùk *tū*
2055 **	私	禾 私 私	private, selfish; secretly
			sì *sī*
2056 *	秀	禾 秀 秀	pretty, graceful, elegant
			sau *xiù*
2057 **	秋	禾 禾 秋' 秋 秋	autumn, fall
			chàu *qiū*

2058 *	秒	禾 利 利 秒 秒	a second of time	
			miuh	*miǎo*
2059 ***	科	禾 禾 利 科	course, class, studies, science	
			fò	*kē*
2060 *	秧	禾 利 利 利 秧 秧	seedling, rice shoot	
			yeùng	*yāng*
2061 **	租	禾 利 利 和 租	rent; to rent, lease	
			jòu	*zū*
2062 *	秤	禾 利 利 利 秤	¹ scale, ² steelyard	
			¹ *chìng;* ² *pìhng*	¹ *chèng;* ² *píng*
2063 *	秩	禾 利 利 秒 秩	order, sequence	
			diht	*zhì*
2064 *	移	禾 利 利 移 移	to move	
			yìh	*yí*
2065 *	稀	禾 利 利 移 稀 稀 稀	thin, sparse, loose, scattered	
			hèi	*xī*
2066 *	稍	禾 利 利 利 稍 稍	a little bit, slightly	
			saáu	*shāo*
2067 *	税	禾 利 利 税 税 税 税	tax, duty	
			seui	*shùi*
2068 *	稈	禾 利 利 和 稈 稈	straw, stalk	
			gón	*gǎn*
2069 **	程	禾 禾 利 和 利 稆 程	measure, journey, procedure, standard, degree	
			chìhng	*chéng*
2070 *	稚	禾 利 利 利 利 稚 稚	young, immature, childish	
			jih	*zhì*

2071 **	種	禾 禾 禾 秄 秄 稆 稆 稆 種 [1] seed, [1] race, [1] type; [2] to plant [1] júng; [2] jung [1] zhǒng; [2] zhòng
2072 *	穀	一 十 士 吉 声 声 吉 壹 索 禾 彀 穀 穀 grain gùk gǔ
2073 **	稱	禾 禾 禾 秆 秤 秤 稱 稱 [1] to weigh, [2] address someone, [3] fit; [4] suitable [1] [3] ching; [2] chìng; [4] chan [1] [2] chèng; [3] chèng; [4] chèn
2074 *	稿	禾 禾 禾 科 秆 秆 秆 稿 稿 draft, manuscript góu gǎo
2075 *	稽	禾 禾 秒 秒 秒 秒 稭 稭 稽 稽 稽 to examine kài jī
2076 *	稻	禾 禾 禾 秒 秒 秒 秒 稻 稻 稻 paddy, rice douh dào
2077 *	穎	㇉ 匕 呆 呆 郛 釦 頴 頴 頴 頴 clever, eminent wihng yǐng
2078 **	積	禾 禾 秆 秄 秳 秳 秳 秸 積 to store up, accumulate jìk jī
2079 *	穗	禾 禾 禾 秆 稆 秱 稙 稙 稙 穗 穗 grain, wheat, spike, elegant seuih sùi
2080 *	穩	禾 秇 稆 秿 秿 秱 秱 穏 穏 穏 穩 穩 secure, stable wán wěn
2081 *	穫	禾 禾 秄 秄 秚 秚 秝 秚 秚 稚 穫 穫 to harvest; harvest wohk hùo
	穴 Section	
2082 *	穴	㇔ 八 宀 宀 穴 cave, hole yuht yué

2083 *** 究	穴 穴 究	to study, investigate; after all gau　　　　　　jiù
2084 ** 空	穴 空 空 空	¹ empty, ² vacant; ¹ space, ¹ sky, ² free time ¹ ² hùng　　　　¹ kōng; ² kòng
2085 ** 穿	穴 空 空 穿 穿	to go through, pierce, wear chyùn　　　　chuān
2086 * 突	穴 空 穸 突 突	suddenly, abruptly; to protrude daht　　　　　tú
2087 * 窄	穴 穴 空 窄 窄	narrow jaak　　　　　zhǎi
2088 * 窒	穴 空 空 空 窒 窒 窒	to smother, stop jaht　　　　　zhì
2089 ** 窗	穴 空 空 窎 窎 窗 窗	window cheùng　　　chuāng
2090 * 窩	穴 穴 空 窎 窎 窎 窩 窩 窩 窩	nest, den wò　　　　　　wō
2091 * 窪	穴 窊 空 空 空 窪	hollow; swamp wà　　　　　　wā
2092 ** 窮	穴 穴 穴 窎 穹 穹 窮 窮 窮	poor; extremely kùhng　　　qióng
2093 * 窯	穴 空 穸 穸 穸 空 窯 窯 窯 窯	kiln yiùh　　　　　yáo
2094 * 窺	穴 空 空 穼 窥 窥 窥 窺 窺 窺	to spy, watch kwài　　　　　kúi
2095 * 竅	穴 空 窎 窎 窎 窎 窎 窎 窎 窎 窎 竅	opening, hole kiu　　　　　　qiào

2096 *	竄	穴 穴 穴 突 突 窏 窏 窏 窏 窏 竄 竄	to escape
			chyún　　　*cuàn*
2097 *	竊	穴 穴 穴 宰 宲 宲 穷 穷 穷 穷 窃 竊 竊 竊 竊	to steal; thief
			sit　　　*qiè*

立 Section

2098 **	立	丶 二 六 立	to stand, establish; immediate
			lahp　　　*lì*
2099 ***	站	立 刘 站 站 站 站	to stand; station
			jaahm　　　*zhàn*
2100 **	竟	立 产 音 音 音 竟 竟	actually, after all, finally
			gíng　　　*jìng*
2101 **	章	立 产 音 音 音 章 章	essay, chapter, rule, seal
			jeùng　　　*zhǎng*
2102 **	童	立 产 音 音 音 童 童	child
			tùhng　　　*tóng*
2103 *	端	立 立' 站 站 站 站 站 端 端	straight; beginning, reason, end; to hold
			dyùn　　　*duān*
2104 *	競	立 产 音 音 竞 竞 竞 競	to compete, strive
			gihng　　　*jìng*

竹 Section

2105 *	竹	ノ ト ケ ケ 竹 竹	bamboo
			jùk　　　*zhú*
2106 *	竿	亡 址 竹 竿	pole, rod, stick
			gòn　　　*gān*

2107 **	笑	竹 竹 竺 竺 笑	to smile, laugh
			siu xiào
2108 ***	第	竹 竺 笃 笃 笃 笰 笰	order, sequence, class
			daih dì
2109 *	笛	竹 竺 竹 笘 笛 笛	flute, fife
			dehk dí
2110 *	符	竹 竹 竹 竹 符 符	symbol, mark; to agree with, coincide
			fùh fú
2111 *	笨	竹 竺 竿 笋 笨 笨	clumsy, stupid
			bahn bèn
2112 **	答	竹 竺 竺 竺 竺 答 答	¹ to reply, ¹ answer, ² promise
			¹ ² daap ¹ dá; ² dā
2113 ***	筆	竹 竺 竺 竺 筆 筆 筆	pen, pencil, brush
			bàt bǐ
2114 ***	等	竹 竺 竺 竺 笘 等 等	class, rank, grade; equal to; to wait
			dáng děng
2115 *	筐	竹 竺 竺 竺 筐 筐	basket
			hòng kuāng
2116 *	筋	竹 竹 竹 筋 筋 筋	tendons, muscles
			gàn jīn
2117 *	筒	竹 竹 筒 筒 筒 筒	pipe, tube
			túng tǒng
2118 *	筍	竹 竹 竺 笋 筍 筍 筍	bamboo shoots
			séun sǔn
2119 *	策	竹 竺 竺 筆 策 策	plan, scheme
			chaak cè

2120 *	筷	竹 竹 竹 竹 竹 竹 侠 筷	chopsticks
			faai	kuài

2121 *	筵	竹 竹 竹 竹 竹 延 延 筵	banquet, feast
			yìhn	yán

2122 **	管	竹 竹 竹 竹 竹 竹 管 管	pipe, tube; to manage, control
			gwún	guǎn

2123 **	算	竹 竹 竹 筲 筲 筲 算	to calculate, complete, plan
			syun	suàn

2124 *	箋	竹 竹 爰 箋 箋 箋 箋	note, note-paper.
			jin	jiān

2125 *	箏	竹 竹 竹 筥 笸 箏 箏	kite
			jàng	zhēng

2126 **	節	(節) 竹 竹 竹 筥 筥 筥 節 節	node, joint, knot, chapter, festival
			jit	jié

2127 *	箭	竹 竹 竹 箭 筲 箭	arrow
			jin	jiàn

2128 *	箱	竹 竹 竹 竹 箱 箱 箱	chest, box
			sèung	xiāng

2129 *	範	竹 竹 竹 筥 筥 筥 範 範 範	pattern, model, scope
			faahn	fàn

2130 **	篇	竹 竹 筥 筥 筥 筥 篇 篇 篇	chapter, page
			pìn	piān

2131 *	築	竹 竹 竹 筥 筑 筑 築 築 築	to construct
			jùk	zhù

2132 *	篤	竹 竹 筥 筥 筥 篤 篤	sincere, honest, earnest
			dùk	dǔ

2133 *	篷	艹 艹 竻 竻 篷 篷 篷 篷 篷 篷	awning, sail	
			fùhng	péng
2134 ***	簡	艹 竹 竻 竻 竻 竻 筲 筲 筲 簡 簡 簡 簡	paper, letter; simple	
			gáan	jiǎn
2135 *	簧	艹 竹 竺 竺 笁 笁 笁 笁 笁 笁 笁 簧	reed, spring	
			wòhng	huáng
2136 *	簫	艹 竻 竺 笁 竿 竿 笨 笨 笨 簫 簫 簫 簫	flute	
			siù	xiāo
2137 *	簿	艹 竻 竻 笘 笘 笘 笘 笘 簿 簿 簿 簿	book, account book	
			bouh	bù
2138 *	簽	艹 竻 失 竻 笘 笘 笘 笘 簽 簽	to sign; label	
			chìm	qiān
2139 *	簾	艹 艹 竺 竻 竻 笘 笘 簾 簾 簾 簾	curtain, screen	
			lìhm	lián
2140 *	籃	艹 竻 竺 竻 竻 竻 笘 笘 笘 籃 籃	basket, hamper	
			laàhm	lán
2141 *	籌	竺 竺 笀 竿 竿 笨 笨 笨 笨 笨 籌 籌 籌 籌	tally, poker chip; to devise, plan, prepare	
			chàuh	chóu
2142 *	籍	艹 竺 竿 笨 籵 籵 籵 籍 籍 籍 籍	book, one's native town	
			jihk	jí
2143 *	籤	艹 艹 笀 笘 笘 笆 笨 笨 簽 簽 籤 籤 籤	slip of bamboo, label	
			chìm	qiān
2144 *	籠	艹 竻 竺 竻 竻 笨 笨 笨 笨 笨 籠 籠 籠	cage	
			lùhng	lóng
		米　　Section		

2145 **	米	丶 丶 ニ 半 半 米	uncooked rice
			maíh · · · · · · · · · mǐ
2146 **	粉	半 米 米ハ 粉 粉	flour, powder
			fán · · · · · · · · · fěn
2147 *	粒	米 米 米ヽ 粒 粒	particle, measure word for small pieces
			làp · · · · · · · · · lì
2148 *	粘	米 米ヽ 料 料 粘 粘	a type of rice
			jìm · · · · · · · · · zhān
2149 **	粗	米 料 粗 粗 粗	rough, crude, coarse, bulky
			chòu · · · · · · · · · cū
2150 *	粟	一 厂 亐 西 西 粟	corn, grain
			sùk · · · · · · · · · sù
2151 *	粧	米 米 料 粁 粧 粧 粧	to dress up, beautify
			jòng · · · · · · · · · zhuāng
2152 *	粥	フ フ 弓 弜 粥	rice gruel
			jùk · · · · · · · · · zhōu
2153 *	粵	丶 亻 门 向 甪 粵 粵	Canton
			yuht · · · · · · · · · yùe
2154 **	精	米 米 料 粧 精 精 精	refined, fine, accurate, shrewd; semen, spirit
			jìng · · · · · · · · · jīng
2155 *	粽	米 米 米 粉 粉 粽 粽	rice dumpling wrapped in leaves
			júng · · · · · · · · · zòng
2156 *	粹	米 米 米 粋 粋 粋 粹 粹	unmixed, pure
			seuih · · · · · · · · · cùi
2157 *	糊	米 米 料 料 粘 粘 糊 糊 糊	[2] thick liquid; [1] to paste, [2] fool, [3] block
			[1][2][3] wùh · · · [1] hú; [2] hù; [3] hū

2158 *	糕	米 米′ 米″ 籵 糕 糕	cake, pastry
			gòu — gāo
2159 **	糖	米 米 米′ 籵 粐 粐 粐 粐 糖 糖 糖	sugar, candy
			tòhng — táng
2160 *	糟	米 米′ 米″ 米″ 粐 糟 糟 糟 糟 糟 糟	sediment, dregs
			jòu — zāo
2161 *	糠	米 米′ 米′ 粐 粐 粐 粐 粐 粐 糠 糠 糠	chaff, bran
			hòng — kāng
2162 *	糞	米 米 粠 粠 粠 粠 黄 黄 黄 黄 糞	manure
			fan — fèn
2163 **	糧	米 米′ 米′ 米″ 粐 粐 糧 糧 糧	food, provisions
			leùhng — liáng
2164 *	糯	米 米′ 米″ 粐 粐 粐 糯 糯 糯 糯 糯 糯	glutinous rice
			noh — nùo

糸   Section

2165 *	系	丿 幺 幺 幺 系 系	system, connection, college major
			haih — xì
2166 *	糾	幺 幺 糸 糾 糾	to correct, tangle, involve, gather
			dáu — jiū
2167 **	紅	糸 糸 紅 紅	red
			hùhng — hóng
2168 *	紀	糸 糸 紀 紀	to record; annals, age
			géi — jì
2169 **	約	糸 糾 約 約	to restrain, make an appointment; appointment, lease; approximately
			yeuk — yūe

2170 *	紉	糸 糿 紉 紉	to sew; thread
			yahn 　　　　　 *rèn*
2171 *	紐	糸 糿 紂 紐 紐	button, knot
			naú 　　　　　 *niǔ*
2172 *	納	糸 糺 糽 納 納	to receive, take, accept, give to, pay
			naahp 　　　　　 *nà*
2173 *	紋	糸 糸 紆 紋 紋	lines, stripes
			màhn 　　　　　 *wén*
2174 **	級	糸 糿 級 級	step, grade, rank
			kàp 　　　　　 *jí*
2175 *	紗	糸 糺 紗 紗	gauze
			sà 　　　　　 *shā*
2176 *	紡	糸 糸 紆 紡 紡	to spin cloth
			fóng 　　　　　 *fǎng*
2177 *	紛	糸 糸 紛 紛 紛	disorderly; many
			fàn 　　　　　 *fēn*
2178 *	素	一 十 主 素	plain, simple
			sou 　　　　　 *sù*
2179 **	紙	糸 糸 紙 紙 紙	paper
			jí 　　　　　 *zhǐ*
2180 *	純	糸 糸 紅 純 純	pure, unmixed, sincere
			seùhn 　　　　　 *chún*
2181 *	索	一 十 牛 击 索	rope; to look for, ask for
			sok 　　　　　 *suǒ*
2182 *	紮	一 十 木 札 紮	[1] to stay at, [2] fasten, [2] tie; [2] measure word for bundles
			[1] [2] *jaat*; 　 [1] *zhā*; [2] *zā*

2183 **	組	糸 糸l 糸l 絹 組	to organize; section, group *jóu* 　　　　　　 *zǔ*
2184 **	細	糸 糸 細 絹 細 細	small, fine *sai* 　　　　　　 *xì*
2185 *	累	ˋ ⼝ ⼞ 田 田 累	[1] to accumulate, [2] involve; [2] tired [1] *leúih;* [2] *leuih* 　 [1] *lěi;* [2] *lèi*
2186 ***	紹	糸 糸l 糸l 糸刀 紹 紹	to continue, introduce *siuh* 　　　　　　 *shào*
2187 **	終	糸 糸l 糸l 紋 終	entire; end; to die, close; finally *jùng* 　　　　　　 *zhōng*
2188 *	紫	ˋ ⼘ ⼮ 止 此 此 紫	purple *jí* 　　　　　　 *zǐ*
2189 **	統	糸 糸 紂 紵 統 紗 統	to rule; total, entire; statistics *túng* 　　　　　　 *tǒng*
2190 ***	給	糸 糸l 糸l 給 給 給 給	[1] to supply, [2] give; [2] for [1][2] *kàp* 　 [1] *jǐ;* [2] *gěi*
2191 **	絶	糸 糸l 糸l 絡 絡 絶 絶	to break off; extremely, absolutely *jyuht* 　　　　　　 *jué*
2192 **	結	糸 糸 針 結 結 結 結	[1] to tie a knot; [1] knot; [2] durable, [2] strong [1][2] *git* 　 [1] *jié;* [2] *jiē*
2193 *	絡	糸 糸l 紂 紋 絡 絡 絡	vein, blood vessels; to connect *lok* 　　　　　　 *luò*
2194 **	絲	糸 絲	silk *sì* 　　　　　　 *sī*
2195 *	絨	糸 糸l 紅 絨 絨 絨 絨	wool *yùhng* 　　　　　　 *róng*

2196 *	綏	糸 糹 紅 綏 綏 綏	peaceful
			seùi　　　　　　súi
2197 *	綁	糸 糹 紳 綁 綁 綁	to tie
			bóng　　　　　băng
2198 ***	經	糸 糹 緬 經 經 經	classics; to manage, already
			gìng　　　　　jīng
2199 *	綿	糸 糹 糺 紗 紿 紿 綿 綿 綿	cotton, soft
			mìhn　　　　　mían
2200 *	網	糸 糹 約 網 網 網 網 網	net, web, network
			móhng　　　　wăng
2201 *	維	糸 糹 糺 紗 紵 維	to maintain
			wàih　　　　　wéi
2202 *	綱	糸 糹 約 網 網 網 綱 綱 綱	principles, outline, laws
			gòng　　　　　gāng
2203 *	綢	糸 糹 紂 綢 綢 綢 綢 綢 綢 綢	thick silk
			chàuh　　　　chóu
2204 *	綽	糸 糹 糺 紵 紵 綰 綰 綽 綽	ample, spacious; nickname
			cheuk　　　　chuò
2205 *	綠	糸 糹 糸 紁 紵 紵 綠 綠 綠 綠	green
			luhk　　　　　lǜ
2206 **	緊	一 十 厂 厅 王 手 臣 臤 臤 緊	tight, urgent, tense
			gán　　　　　jǐn
2207 **	綫	糸 糹 紁 綫 綫 綫 綫	thread, yarn, line
			sin　　　　　xiàn
2208 **	編	糸 糹 糼 紵 紗 紵 絹 絹 編 編	to compose, arrange, compile
			pìn　　　　　biān

2209 *	緒	纟 纠 纤 纴 纵 纵 绪 绪 绪 緒	beginning, clue		
			seúih	*xù*
2210 *	締	纟 纟' 纤 纩 纩 纴 綿 締 締	to join		
			dai	*dì*
2211 *	緩	纟 纟' 纴 纴 綬 綬 綬 緩	slow; to delay		
			wuhn	*huǎn*
2212 *	緝	糸 纟 纠 纫 纫 絆 絆 絹 緝	to arrest, catch		
			chàp	*jī*
2213 **	練	糸 糸 纴 纴 緉 緉 緉 練 練	to practice		
			lihn	*liàn*
2214 *	緣	糸 糸' 糸 糸 糸 糸 繇 繇 緣	reason, fate, edge		
			yùhn	*yuán*
2215 *	縛	糸 纟 纤 纤 綿 綿 綿 縛 縛 縛	to fasten, tie up		
			bok	*fù*
2216 *	縫	糸 糸' 糸 緂 緂 緂 緂 縫 縫	to sew; gap		
			fùhng	*féng*
2217 ***	縣	丨 冂 日 目 且 旦 県 県 縣	county, district		
			yuhn	*xiàn*
2218 *	緻	糸 糸 絅 絅 絅 絟 緅 緅 緻 緻	delicate, elegant		
			ji	*zhì*
2219 **	總	糸 糸' 糸 糸 絪 絪 緫 緫 總 總	total, chief; all		
			júng	*zǒng*
2220 *	縱	糸 糸 糸 糸 絆 絆 絆 縱 縱 縱	[1] to allow, [1] indulge; [2] vertical		
			[1] *jung;* [2] *jùng*	[1] [2] *zòng*
2221 *	縮	糸 糸' 糸 糸 絡 絡 綂 綂 縮 縮 縮	[1] to draw back, [1] shrink, [1] reduce, [2] to be frugal		
			[1] [2] *sùk*	[1] *suō;* [2] *sù*

2222 **	績	糸 糸 糸 糺 結 績 績 績 績	merit
			jik 　　　　　　　*jī*
2223 *	繁	ノ ト 广 攵 毎 毎 毎 敏 敏 敏 繁	numerous, complicated, annoying
			faàhn 　　　　　*fán*
2224 *	繞	糸 糸 糸 結 結 結 結 繞 繞 繞	to surround, bypass
			yiú 　　　　　　*raò*
2225 **	織	糸 糸 糸 紅 紂 結 結 結 結 織 織 織	to weave
			jik 　　　　　　*zhī*
2226 *	繩	糸 糸 糸 紅 紀 紀 紲 絕 繩 繩 繩 繩	string, rope, cord
			sìhng 　　　　*shéng*
2227 *	繡	糸 糸 糸 結 絆 結 結 結 結 結 結 繡 繡 繡 繡	to embroider
			sau 　　　　　　*xiù*
2228 *	繫	一 厂 百 百 百 亘 車 軎 軎 軤 軤 穀 繫 繫	[1] to be in touch, [2] tie, [2] fasten
			[1] [2] *haih* 　　　[1] *xì*; [2] *jì*
2229 *	繳	糸 糸 糸 紗 紗 紗 絈 絈 絈 絈 繞 繞 繳 繳	to pay
			giú 　　　　　　*jiǎo*
2230 *	繪	糸 糸 糸 糸 給 給 給 給 繪 繪 繪 繪 繪	to draw
			kúi 　　　　　　*huì*
2231 *	繼	糸 糸 糸 絲 絲 絲 絲 繼 繼	to continue, adopt, succeed
			gai 　　　　　　*jì*
2232 **	續	糸 糸 糸 結 結 結 結 續 續 續 續 續	to continue
			juhk 　　　　　*xù*
2233 *	纏	糸 糸 糸 紅 紅 紅 紅 紂 紲 紵 纏 纏 纏 纏 纏	to bind, entwine, bother
			chìhn 　　　　　*chán*

缶　　Section

2234 *	缸	ノ ヽ 上 午 缶 缶 缶 缸 缸	jar, earthen vessel
			gòng gāng
2235 **	缺	缶 缶 缶 缺 缺 缺	to lack, be short of; defect, weakness
			kyut quē
2236 *	罐	缶 缶 缶 缶 缶 缶 缶 缶 缶 缶 缶 罐	a can
			gwun guàn

网   Section

2237 *	罕	ヽ 宀 冖 罕 罕 罕	scarce, rare
			hón hǎn
2238 **	罪	ヽ 宀 罒 罒 罪 罪 罪 罪	crime, guilt; to offend
			jeuih zùi
2239 *	罩	罒 罒 罒 罩 罩 罩 罩 罩 罩	shade, cover
			jaau zhào
2240 *	置	罒 罒 罒 罒 罟 置 置 置	to put, place, establish, buy
			ji zhì
2241 *	罰	罒 罒 罚 罚 罚 罚 罚 罰 罰 罰	to punish; penalty
			faht fá
2242 *	署	罒 罒 罒 罒 罜 署 署 署	public court; to sign
			chyúh shǔ
2243 **	罵	罒 罒 罜 罜 罵 罵	to scold
			mah mà
2244 *	罷	罒 罒 罟 罟 罟 罷 罷 罷 罷	to cease
			bah bà
2245 *	羅	罒 罒 罜 罜 罜 罜 罜 罜 羅 羅	net, gauze
			lòh luó

	羊 Section		
2246 **	羊	⸍ 芏 羊	lamb, goat, sheep *yeùhng*　　　　*yáng*
2247 ***	美	⸍ ⸗ ⸱ 芏 兰 美 美	beautiful, pretty; United States of America *méih*　　　　*měi*
2248 *	羔	羊 羔	lamb *goù*　　　　*gaō*
2249 *	羞	羊 羊 美 羞 羞 羞	good food; ashamed, shy *saù*　　　　*xiū*
2250 **	羣	⎡ ⎡ ⸗ 尹 尹 君 君 羣	group, herd *kwàhn*　　　　*qún*
2251 **	義	芏 羊 差 羊 羔 義 義 義	righteousness, meaning *yih*　　　　*yì*
2252 *	羨	兰 羊 差 羡 羡 羨	to admire *sihn*　　　　*xiàn*
2253 *	羹	兰 羔 羣 羹	thick soup *gàng*　　　　*gēng*
	羽 Section		
2254 *	羽	⎂ 习 羽	feathers, wings, birds *yúh*　　　　*yǔ*
2255 *	翁	⼋ 公 公 翁	father, husband's father, old man, father-in-law *yùng*　　　　*wēng*
2256 *	翅	一 ⼗ 尹 支 翅	wings, fins *chi*　　　　*chì*

2257 *	翌	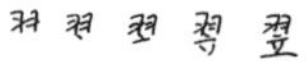	the next (for day or year)	*yihk*	*yì*
2258 **	習	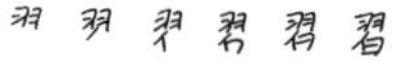	to learn, practice; habit, custom	*jaahp*	*xí*
2259 *	翔		to soar, hover	*cheùhng*	*xiáng*
2260 *	翼		wing, flank of an army	*yihk*	*yì*
2261 **	翻	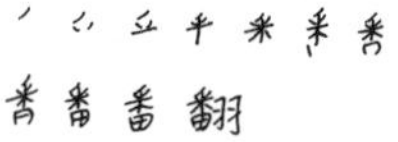	to turn over, reverse	*faàn*	*fān*
2262 *	耀		to shine on; brilliant	*yiuh*	*yào*

老 Section

2263 ***	老	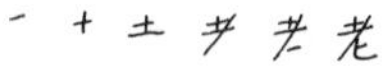	old, aged, experienced, overcooked	*loúh*	*laǒ*
2264 ***	考		to examine, test	*háau*	*kaǒ*
2265 ***	者	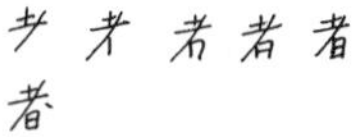	person	*jé*	*zhě*

而 Section

2266 **	而		yet, moreover	*yìh*	*ér*
2267 **	耐	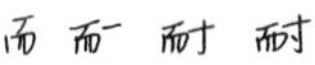	to endure; long time	*noih*	*nài*

| 2268 * | 耍 | 而 耍 耍 耍 | to play, tease, gamble

sá   shuǎ |

耒   Section

2269 *	耙	三 丰 耒 耒 耒 耙 耙 耙	rake pàh pá
2270 *	耕	耒 耒 耒 耕 耕	to plough, cultivate gaàng gēng
2271 *	耗	耒 耒 耗 耗	to spend, waste; news, rat hou haò
2272 *	耢	耒 耒 耒 耢 耢 耢 耢 耢 耢 耢	to pull weeds and cultivate soil póhng pǎng
2273 *	耩	耒 耒 耒 耕 耕 耕 耩 耩 耩 耩	to spread seed and fertilizer by machine kau jiǎng

耳   Section

2274 **	耳	一 丁 丌 耳 耳	ear, handle yíh ěr
2275 *	耿	耳 耳 耳 耿 耿	straightforward, bright gáng gěng
2276 *	聆	耳 耳 耴 聆 聆 聆 聆	to listen, pay attention to lihng líng
2277 *	聊	耳 耳 耳 耶 耶耳 聊	to depend on, chat liùh liáo
2278 *	聖	耳 耳 耵 耵 耵 聖 聖 聖	holy, sage sing shèng

2279 *	聘	耳 耴 耴 耵 聊 聃 聘 聘	to employ, engage, invite ping　　　　pìn
2280 *	聚	耳 耴 取 取 聚 聚 聚 聚	to gather, collect jeuih　　　　jù
2281 **	聞	｜ ｜’ 門 門 門 門 門 門 門 聞	to hear, smell; news, knowledge; famous màhn　　　　wén
2282 *	聯	耳 耵 耴 聅 聯 聯 聯 聯 聯 聯	to unite; alliance lyùhn　　　　lián
2283 **	聲	一 十 士 士 吉 吉 吉 声 声 声 声 殸 殸 聲	sound, reputation sìng　　　　shēng
2284 *	聰	耳 耵 取 耺 耸 聰 聰 聰 聰 聰 聰	wise, clever chùng　　　　cōng
2285 **	職	耳 耴 耴 耵 耺 聅 職 職 職 職 職	duty, position, occupation jik　　　　zhí
2286 **	聽	耳 耴 耵 耴 耳 聑 聑 聑 聽 聽 聽 聽 聽 聽	[1] to hear, [1] listen to, [1] obey, [1] wait, [2] let [1] tìng; [2] ting　　　　[1] [2] tīng
2287 *	聾	` 亠 亠 立 产 育 育 育 育 龍 龍 龍 聾	deaf lùhng　　　　lóng

| | 聿 Section | |

2288 *	肆	一 丁 F 丟 丟 丟 丟 丟 丟 髟 肆 肆	profligate; store si　　　　sì
2289 *	肄	一 匕 匕 匕 匕 㠯 肄	to learn yih　　　　yì
2290 *	肅	肀 肃 肃 肃 肅 肅 肅 肅 肅	solemn, reverential sùk　　　　sù

		肉 Section	
2291 **	肉	丨 冂 内 内 肉	meat, flesh *yuhk* *roù*
2292 *	肌	丿 刀 月 刖 肌	flesh, muscle *gèi* *jī*
2293 *	肘	月 月一 肘 肘	elbow *jaáu* *zhoǔ*
2294 *	肛	月 月一 肛 肛	anus *gòng* *gāng*
2295 *	肝	月 肝一 肝	liver *gòn* *gān*
2296 *	肚	月 月一 肚 肚	[1] belly, [1] abdomen, [2] animal's stomach [1] [2] *tóuh* [1] *dù;* [2] *dǔ*
2297 **	股	月 月丿 肌 股 股	thigh, share of stock *gú* *gǔ*
2298 *	肴	乂 丷 肀 肴	cooked food *ngaàuh* *yaó*
2299 **	肥	月 肌 肌 肥 肥	fat, fertile *fèih* *feí*
2300 **	肯	丨 ⺊ ⺊ 止 肯	to consent to, be willing *háng* *kěn*
2301 **	育	丶 亠 云 育	to bear children, nourish *yuhk* *yù*
2302 *	肪	月 月丶 肪 肪 肪	fat, grease *fòng* *fáng*

2303 *	肢	月 刖一 肚 肢 肢	limbs		
			ji		zhī
2304 *	肺	月 刖一 肺 肺	lungs		
			fai		fèi
2305 *	肩	、 ン ラ 尸 肩	shoulders		
			gin		jiān
2306 **	胡	一 十 才 古 古 胡	random, casual		
			wùh		hú
2307 *	胎	月 肜 肜 肜 胎 胎	embryo, womb		
			tòi		tāi
2308 *	胞	月 肜 肜 肜 胞 胞	placenta		
			baàu		bāo
2309 **	背	一 ニ キ 北 北 背	[1] back; [1] to turn against, [2] carry on the back		
			[1] [2] bui		[1] bèi; [2] bēi
2310 *	胖	月 肜' 肸 胖	plump		
			buhn		pàng
2311 *	胃	、 ワ 曰 田 田 胃	stomach		
			waih		wèi
2312 *	脊	ノ 人 火 火 脊	backbone, ridge		
			jek		jǐ
2313 ***	能	ム ム 育 育 育 能 能	ability, energy; to be able to		
			nàhng		néng
2314 *	脈	月 肜' 肜 肵 肵 肵 脈	pulse, veins		
			mahk		mài
2315 *	脆	月 月' 肜 肜 肜 肜 脆	fragile, crisp		
			cheui		cùi

2316 *	胳	月 肜 肜 脓 胶 胳 胳	armpit	
			gaak	gē
2317 *	胸	月 肜 肜 胸 胸	chest, breast, bosom	
			hùng	xiōng
2318 *	脂	月 肜 肜 胪 脂 脂 脂	fat, grease	
			jì	zhī
2319 *	脅	宀 力 力 劦 脅	rib; to coerce	
			hip	xié
2320 *	脖	月 肜 肜 肜 胪 胯 脖 脖	neck	
			buht	bó
2321 *	脛	月 肜 肟 脬 脛 脛	shin	
			ging	jìng
2322 **	脫	月 肜 肜 脬 脫 脫 脫	to undress, take off, slip away	
			tyut	tuō
2323 **	脚	月 肜 肜 肚 肚 月去 胠 脚	foot	
			geuk	jiǎo
2324 *	脾	月 肜 肜 肜 胂 胂 脾 胂 脾	spleen, temper	
			pèih	pí
2325 *	腑	月 肜 肜 肟 肟 肜 脧 脒 腑	viscera	
			fú	fǔ
2326 *	腎	一 丁 丌 丣 丣 臣 臤 臤 腎	kidney	
			sahn	shèn
2327 *	腐	丶 亠 广 广 庐 府 府 腐	rotten, spoiled, decayed	
			fuh	fǔ
2328 *	腕	月 肜 肜 肟 脘 脘 脘 脘 腕	wrist	
			wún	wǎn

2329 *	脹	月 月´ 肝 腒 腒 腒 脹 脹	bloated; to puff, swell, inflate
			jeung　　　　　　zhàng
2330 *	腔	月 月` 月广 肸 肸 腔 腔 腔 腔	cavity, tune, tone
			hòng　　　　　　qiāng
2331 *	腰	月 月´ 肟 肟 腰 腰 腰 腰 腰	waist, loins
			yiù　　　　　　yāo
2332 **	腦	月 肶 肶 脺 脺 腦 腦	brain
			nóuh　　　　　　nǎo
2333 *	腹	月 月´ 肟 肟 肟 肟 肟 肟 腹 腹	abdomen, belly
			fùk　　　　　　fù
2334 *	腫	月 月´ 肟 肟 肟 肸 肸 腄 腫	to swell
			júng　　　　　　zhǒng
2335 *	腸	月 月´ 肛 朋 朋 朋 腸 腸 腸	bowels, intestines
			chéung　　　　　　cháng
2336 *	腥	月 月´ 肘 肘 胆 胆 胆 腥 腥	fishy smell
			sìng　　　　　　xīng
2337 *	腿	月 月´ 月³ 月³ 肥 肥 肥 腿 腿	leg, thigh
			téui　　　　　　tuǐ
2338 *	膊	月 月´ 肘 肘 肺 膊 膊 膊 膊	upper arm, shoulder
			bok　　　　　　bó
2339 *	膀	月 月´ 肟 肟 肸 肸 肸 膀 膀	[1] arm, [2] bladder
			[1] bóng; [2] pòhng　　　[1] bǎng; [2] páng
2340 *	膏	` 亠 六 古 古 高 高 膏	fat, ointment, plaster
			gòu　　　　　　gāo
2341 *	膠	月 肥 肥 肥 胛 胛 腏 膠	glue, plastic, rubber
			gàau　　　　　　jiāo

2342 *	膝	月 月⁻ 月⁺ 胙 胅 胘 脐 膝 膝 膝	knee
			sàt xī
2343 *	膚	⼀ ⼀ ⼐ 广 卢 虍 虍 虐 庐 庐 膚 膚 膚	skin; superficial
			fù fū
2344 *	膩	月 月⁻ 肝 肝 肵 脂 脂 膩 膩 膩	oily, greasy
			leih nì
2345 *	膨	月 月⁻ 月⁺ 月⁺ 肰 脏 脖 膪 膨 膨	expanded, swollen
			paàhng péng
2346 *	膽	月 月' 月° 胪 胪 胪 脒 脒 脥 脥 膠 膽 膽 膽	gall bladder; courage
			daàm dǎn
2347 *	臂	⼁ ⼂ 尸 尽 启 启 启 启 辟 辟 臂	fore-arm
			bei bì
2348 *	臉	月 月⼃ 胪 胪 胎 胎 胎 胎 臉 臉	face, cheeks
			lihm liǎn
2349 *	臍	月 月' 月⁻ 月⁻ 胪 脐 脐 脐 脐 脐 膌 臍 臍	navel
			chih qí
2350 *	臘	月 月ᵞ 月ᵞ 月ᵞ 膟 膟 膣 膣 膣 臘	dried meat
			laahp là
2351 *	臟	月 月' 肬 脏 肝 肝 胪 脏 脏 脏 脏 脏 膒 膐 臟 臟	viscera
			johng zàng

臣 Section

2352 *	臣	⼀ ⼂ 厅 臣 臣 臣	statesman
			sàhn chén
2353 *	臥	臣 臤 臥	to lie down, sleep
			ngoh wò

2354 **	臨	臣 臣 臣 臣 臣 臣 臣 臨	approaching; to imitate writing, face
			làhm lín

自 Section

2355 **	自	ノ イ 自 自 自	self; natural; since, from
			jih zì

2356 **	臭	自 自 臭 臭 臭	foul smell
			chau chòu

至 Section

2357 **	至	一 工 云 互 至 至	to, until; extreme, best
			ji zhì

2358 *	致	至 到 致 致 致	to cause, give, show, reach
			ji zhì

2359 *	臺	一 十 士 吉 吉 吉 高 臺	stage, platform
			tòih tái

臼 Section

2360 *	舅	ノ イ ヒ ヒヨ ヒヨ 臼 臼 臼 舅 舅 舅 舅	mother's brother, uncle
			káuh jiù

2361 **	與	ノ イ ヒ ヒ ヒ ヒ 的 的 的 與 與	with, and; to give
			yúh yǔ

2362 **	興	ノ イ ヒ 白 的 的 的 的 的 的 興 興	[1] to thrive, [1] prosper; [1] in style, [2] happy; [2] interest
			[1] hìng; [2] hing [1] xīng; [2] xìng

2363 **	舉	ノ イ ヒ ヒ ヒ 的 的 的 的 的 與 與 舉 舉	to elevate; motion; whole
			geúi jǔ

2364 **	舊	丶 ー 丷 艹 扩 扩 花 桙 萑 舊	old, ancient
			gauh jiù

舌   Section

2365 *	舌	丿 ー 千 千 舌 舌	tongue
			sit shé
2366 *	舍	丿 人 合 全 令 舍 舍	residence, cottage
			se shè
2367 *	舒	舍 舍 舒 舒 舒	to spread; comfortable
			syù shū

舛   Section

2368 *	舞	丿 ㇒ 仁 ㅤ 無 無 舞 舞 舞 舞 舞 舞	to dance, flourish; dance
			móuh wǔ

舟   Section

2369 *	舟	丿 ㇒ 力 丹 舟 舟	boat, ship
			jàu zhōu
2370 *	航	舟 舟 舟 航 航	to sail, navigate
			hòhng háng
2371 **	般	舟 舟 船 船 般	type, affair
			bùn bān
2372 ***	船	舟 舟 船 船 船 船	boat, ship
			syùhn chuán
2373 *	舵	舟 舟 舟 船 船 舵	helm, rudder
			tòh duò

2374 *	舶	舟 舟ˊ 舟 舟 舟 舟 舟	ship, vessel
			paak　　　　　　bó

2375 *	艇	舟 舟ˊ 舟 舟 舟ˇ 舟 舟 舟	boat, barge
			téhng　　　　　tǐng

2376 *	艙	舟 舟ˊ 舟 舟 舟 舟 舟 舟 舟 舟	cabin on a ship
			chòng　　　　　cāng

2377 *	艦	舟 舟ˊ 舟 舟 舟 舟 舟 舟 舟 舟 舟 舟 艦	battleship
			laahm　　　　　jiàn

艮 Section

2378 **	良	、 ㄱ ㅋ ㅋ 艮 艮 良	good, virtuous
			leùhng　　　　liáng

2379 *	艱	、 十 艹 艹 艹 芟 芟 菫 菫 菫 菫 艱 艱 艱	difficult, distressing
			gaàn　　　　　jiān

色 Section

2380 **	色	⁄ ㄅ ㄅ ㄅ 多 色	color, lust
			sìk　　　　　　sè

艸 Section

2381 *	芋	、 十 艹 艼 芋	taro
			wuh　　　　　yù

2382 *	芒	艹 艹 艹 芒	[1] sharp point of grass, [2] mango
			[1] mòhng; [2] mòng　　　[1] [2] máng

2383 **	花	艹 艹 艹 花 花	flower, blossom
			fà　　　　　　huā

2384 *	芬	丷 艹 芩 芬	fragrance fàn fēn
2385 *	芳	丷 艹 芝 芳 芳	fragrance fòng fāng
2386 *	芙	丷 艹 芋 芙	hibiscus fùh fú
2387 *	芥	丷 艹 芥 芥	[1] mustard greens, [2] broccoli [1] [2] gaai [1] jiè; [2] gài
2388 *	芽	丷 艹 芒 芽 芽	shoot, sprout, bud ngàh yá
2389 *	茄	丷 艹 芀 茄 茄 茄	eggplant, tomato ké qié
2390 ***	英	丷 艹 芒 芇 荁 英	heroic, graceful, English; England yìng yīng
2391 *	茂	丷 艹 芦 芪 茂 茂	exuberant, flourishing mauh mào
2392 *	苗	丷 艹 芕 苗 苗 苗	sprout, shoot, bud miùh miáo
2393 *	苔	丷 艹 丛 苔 苔 苔	moss tòih tái
2394 *	茅	丷 艹 芼 芼 茅	reeds màuh máo
2395 **	苦	丷 艹 芢 苦 苦 苦	bitter, grievous fú kǔ
2396 *	苟	丷 艹 芍 苟 苟	careless; if gáu gǒu

2397 **	若	艹 芏 芋 芉 若 若	if, as if	
			yeuhk	ruò
2398 *	苛	艹 芏 芷 芷 苦 苛	harsh, cruel	
			hò	kē
2399 **	茶	艹 艻 苂 苶 苶 茶	tea	
			chàh	chá
2400 **	荒	艹 艹 芒 芒 芒 荒	wild, barren	
			fòng	huāng
2401 *	茫	艹 汒 沙 泟 茫	vast, vague	
			mòhng	máng
2402 *	茲	艹 苂 茲 茲 茲	this, now	
			jì	zī
2403 *	荆	艹 芏 荆 荆 荆	bramble, thorn	
			gìng	jīng
2404 *	茸	艹 芏 芦 芽 茸 茸	deer's horn	
			yùhng	róng
2405 *	荔	艹 艻 艻 荔 荔	lichee	
			laih	lì
2406 **	草	艹 艹 芦 芦 苩 莒 草	grass, straw; careless	
			chóu	cǎo
2407 *	莊	艹 芏 芣 芣 芣 芲 荓 莊	solemn; village	
			jòng	zhuāng
2408 *	莫	艹 芏 苩 苩 莒 荁 莫	do not, not	
			mohk	mò
2409 *	莖	艹 芏 茲 茲 茎 莖	stem of a plant	
			gìng	jīng

2410 *	荷	艹 艹 艻 荶 荷 荷 荷 荷	lotus, water lily	
			hòh	hé
2411 ***	華	艹 艹 苎 苈 苹 苹 華	China; Chinese, brilliant, elegant	
			wàh	huá
2412 *	菇	艹 艺 艿 艿 女 女 奵 奵 菇 菇	mushroom	
			gù	gū
2413 *	萃	艹 艹 芐 芐 茓 茓 萃	collection, crowd	
			seuih	cùi
2414 *	菊	艹 艹 芍 芍 筍 苖 菊	chrysanthemum	
			gùk	jú
2415 *	菌	艹 芇 芇 芮 芮 菛 菛 菌	fungus, bacteria, mold	
			kwán	jūn
2416 *	菩	艹 艹 艼 芳 芲 苙 菩 菩	Bodhisattva	
			pòuh	pú
2417 **	菜	艹 艹 艻 芯 苹 芩 芽 菜	vegetables, food	
			choi	cài
2418 *	萎	艹 艹 芝 芊 芉 荗 荗 萎	to wither, decay	
			wái	wěi
2419 *	萍	艹 芐 芳 荋 萢 萍	duckweed; drifting	
			pìhng	píng
2420 ***	萬	艹 芇 芍 苗 苗 苗 萬 萬 萬 萬	ten thousand, numerous	
			maahn	wàn
2421 **	落	艹 芐 茓 茫 荗 莈 落 落	to fall, drop	
			lohk	luò
2422 *	著	艹 艹 芏 芏 芖 荖 著 著 著 著	conspicuous, famous; to write books	
			jyu	zhù

2423 *	董	⺾ ⺌ ⺬ ⺲ 芑 苔 苔 葷 董	to direct, govern; director dúng　　　dǒng
2424 *	葬	⺾ 世 少 歺 歺 芗 苑 莚 葬	to bury jong　　　zàng
2425 *	葱	⺾ ⺾ 芍 苟 苟 蒟 葱 葱 葱	onion chùng　　　cōng
2426 *	葛	⺾ 艹 茍 苷 苜 苩 莴 莴 葛 葛	arrow root got　　　gé
2427 **	葉	⺾ ⺼ 艹 苷 苷 苩 茈 茟 葉	leaf, page yihp　　　yè
2428 *	葡	⺾ 艿 芍 芍 苟 荀 葡 葡 葡	grape pòuh　　　pú
2429 *	葦	⺾ ⺌ 苳 苬 荦 苹 莟 莟 葦	reed wáih　　　wěi
2430 *	蒜	⺾ 兰 芓 茱 蒜	garlic syun　　　suàn
2431 *	蒙	⺾ ⺌ 兰 芦 茔 荸 荸 蒙 蒙	to cover, conceal, deceive mùhng　　　méng
2432 *	蒞	⺾ 荮 荮 荮 茘 荶 莅 蒞	to attend leih　　　lì
2433 *	蓄	⺾ 艾 兰 苎 苎 荖 荖 蒿 蒿 蓄 蓄	to save chùk　　　xù
2434 *	蒸	⺾ 艿 茅 芧 茅 茏 荥 蒸	steam; to steam jìng　　　zhēng
2435 *	蒼	⺾ ⺌ 犬 苂 苂 苓 苓 荅 苍 苍 蒼 蒼	dark blue, dark green, azure chòng　　　cāng

2436 *	蓉	艹 艹 艿 莩 莈 荄 荄 荄 蓉 蓉	hibiscus
			yùhng　　　　róng
2437 **	蓋	艹 艹 艾 苎 苎 苎 荖 荖 蓋 蓋	to cover, build, stamp; lid
			goi　　　　gài
2438 *	蓮	艹 艹 芢 苪 苜 苜 苩 萆 萆 蓮 蓮	lotus, water lily
			lìhn　　　　lián
2439 *	蔓	艹 艹 艿 苩 苩 苩 萬 萬 萬 蔓 蔓	to creep; vines
			maahn　　　　màn
2440 *	蔭	艹 艹 艿 於 於 於 菸 蓜 蓜 蔭 蔭 蔭	shade; shady; to protect
			yàm　　　　yìn
2441 *	蔣	艹 艹 艹 艹 茾 茾 茾 茾 蔣 蔣 蔣	a last name
			jéung　　　　jiǎng
2442 *	蔬	艹 艿 艿 芽 芽 荘 荘 荘 荘 荘 蔬 蔬	vegetables, greens
			sò　　　　shū
2443 *	蔽	艹 艹 莎 莎 芇 甫 萳 萳 蔽 蔽 蔽	to cover, conceal
			bai　　　　bì
2444 *	蕉	艹 艹 艻 花 花 荏 萑 蕉	banana
			jiù　　　　jiāo
2445 *	蕩	艹 艻 艻 荡 荡 荡 蓮 蓮 蕩	to clean, move, rock
			dohng　　　　dàng
2446 *	薑	艹 艹 芢 苧 苩 菖 菖 葍 葍 薑 薑	ginger
			geùng　　　　jiāng
2447 **	薄	艹 艿 苪 苪 芗 芗 萡 薄 薄 薄 薄	[1] thin, [2] weak, [2] feeble; [3] Mentholatum
			[1][2][3] bohk　　　　[1] baó; [2] bó; [3] bò
2448 *	薪	艹 艹 艺 芐 莁 莘 薪 薪 薪 薪	firewood, salary
			sàn　　　　xīn

No.	Character	Stroke order	Meaning / Readings
2449 *	蕭	艹 艹 艹 萝 芦 芹 蕭 蕭 蕭 蕭 蕭 蕭 蕭 蕭	depression; lonely siù · xiāo
2450 *	薦	艹 艹 兰 疒 萨 萨 蓙 薦 薦 薦	to recommend, introduce jin · jiàn
2451 *	藍	艹 艹 艹 芐 芐 芐 荁 茛 蓝 蓝 蓝 藍 藍	blue laahm · lán
2452 **	藏	艹 兰 疒 芹 芹 芦 芦 莎 莎 莊 莊 藏 藏 藏	[1] to hide, [1] conceal, [1] store; [2] treasure [1] chòhng; [2] johng · [1] cáng; [2] zàng
2453 *	薯	艹 芍 芇 苗 苗 萆 萆 萝 萆 薯 薯 薯 薯	potato, sweet potato syùh · shǔ
2454 *	薩	艹 艹 艹 萨 萨 萨 萨 薩 萨 萨 萨 萨 薩 薩 薩	Bodhisattva saat · sà
2455 *	藐	艹 艹 艾 芳 芴 莪 莪 藐 藐 藐 藐 藐 藐	petty; to view with contempt míuh · miǎo
2456 *	藉	艹 兰 芏 莱 莱 莱 莱 藉 藉 藉 藉 藉 藉	excuse; to rely on jihk · jiè
2457 *	藝	艹 兰 艹 艼 芺 藝 蓺 蓺 埶 藝 藝 藝	skill, art ngaih · yì
2458 *	藤	艹 疒 芦 芦 芦 胪 萨 脒 藤 藤 藤	vines tàhng · téng
2459 **	藥	艹 芍 芦 芍 莒 茸 苩 箔 菭 薌 鐮 鏗 藥	medicine, drugs yeuhk · yào
2460 *	藕	艹 芏 萊 莉 莉 莉 莉 藕 藕 藕 藕	lotus root ngáuh · ǒu
2461	蘇	艹 艹 艹 艻 芍 芐 苒 芭 蒐 蒹 蔛 蔛 蘇	to revive sòu · sū

2462 *	藹	(strokes)	kind, loving	ngói	ǎi
2463 *	蘋	(strokes)	apple	pìhng	píng
2464 *	蘭	(strokes)	orchid	laàhn	lán

虍　Section

2465 *	虎	(strokes)	tiger	fú	hǔ
2466 *	虐	(strokes)	to torture; cruel	yeuhk	nüè
2467 *	虔	(strokes)	sincere, pious	kìhn	qián
2468 **	處	(strokes)	[2] place, [1] office; [2] to live, [2] manage; [1] chyu; [2] chýu; [1] chù; [2] chǔ		
2469 *	虛	(strokes)	unreal, humble, empty	heùi	xū
2470 *	虜	(strokes)	to capture; prisoner of war	lóuh	lǔ
2471 ***	號	(strokes)	name, size, sign, number	houh	hào
2472 **	虧	(strokes)	to lose; fortunately; deficit	kwài	kūi

虫　Section

№	字	筆順	意味 / 読み
2473 *	虱	乀 乁 乁 乬 乬 乬 乬 乬	louse *sàt* shī
2474 *	虹	丶 冖 口 中 虫 虫 虫一 虹丁 虹	rainbow *hùhng* hóng
2475 *	蚜	虫 虫一 虫丆 蚜 蚜	aphid *ngàh* yá
2476 *	蚊	虫 虫一 虫丆 蚊 蚊	mosquito *màn* wén
2477 *	蚌	虫 虫三 蚌	clam *póhng* bàng
2478 *	蚤	刁 又 叉 蚤	flea *jóu* zǎo
2479 *	蛀	虫 虫丶 虫亠 蛀丁 蛀	moth-eaten, decayed *jyu* zhù
2480 *	蛇	虫 虫丶 虫宀 蛇宀 蛇宀 蛇	snake, serpent *sèh* shé
2481 **	蛋	一 丅 丆 丕 疋 蛋	egg *daán* dàn
2482 *	蛛	虫 虫丶 虫丆 蚌 蛛 蛛	spider *jyù* zhū
2483 *	蛙	虫 虫丶 虫圭 蛙圭 蛙	frog *wà* wā
2484 *	蜆	虫 虫刂 蚬刂 蚬目 蚬目 蜆 蜆	small clam *hín* xiǎn
2485 *	蛾	虫 虫一 虫一 蛾 蛾 蛾 蛾 蛾	moth *ngòh* é

2486 *	蜂	虫 虫′ 虬 蚁 蜂 蜂	bee, wasp	
			fùng	fēng
2487 *	蛻	虫 虫″ 虮 蚧 蚧 蛻 蛻	to shed skin	
			teui	tùi
2488 *	蜢	虫 虫″ 虮 蚄 蚄 蛞 蜢 蜢	grasshopper	
			máahng	měng
2489 *	蜜	丶 宀 宀 宓 宓 宓 宓 蜜	honey, nectar	
			maht	mì
2490 *	蝠	虫 虫′ 虮 蚄 蚄 蝠 蝠 蝠 蝠	bat	
			fùk	fú
2491 *	蝸	虫 虫′ 虰 蚄 蜎 蜎 蝸 蝸 蝸	snail	
			wò	wō
2492 *	蝶	虫 虫一 蚪 蚌 蚁 蚁 蝶 蝶 蝶 蝶	butterfly	
			dihp	dié
2493 *	蝟	虫 虫′ 虰 蚄 蚄 蚄 蝟 蝟 蝟	hedgehog	
			wai	wèi
2494 *	蝗	虫 虫′ 虰 蚄 蚄 蛑 蛑 蜳 蝗	locust	
			wòhng	huáng
2495 *	蝦	虫 虫″ 虰 蚄 蚄 蚄 蚄 蝦	shrimp, prawn	
			hà	xiā
2496 *	螢	丶 丷 ⺌ 大 炊 炊 炊 炊 螢 螢 螢	firefly	
			yìhng	yíng
2497 *	融	一 冖 冃 冐 鬲 鬲 鬲 鬲 融	to melt, dissolve	
			yùhng	róng
2498 *	螺	虫 虫′ 虰 蚄 蜎 蜎 蜎 螺 螺 螺 螺	conch	
			lòh	luó

2499 *	蟀	虫 虫 虫 虫 虾 蚊 蛠 蛠 蟀 蟀	cricket sùt	shuài
2500 *	蟄	一 十 土 吉 幸 刲 軌 軌 蟄	to hibernate jaht, jihk	zhé
2501 *	蟒	虫 虫 虫 虫 蚱 蚱 蛱 蟒 蟒 蟒	python móhng	mǎng
2502 *	蟬	虫 虫 虫 虫 虫 蚴 蝍 蝸 蟬 蟬	cicada sìhm	chán
2503 **	蟲	虫 蚰 蟲	insect, worm chùhng	chóng
2504 *	蟹	` ⺈ ⺈ 甪 甪 角 角 解 解 解 蟹	crab háih	xiè
2505 *	蠅	虫 虫 虫 虷 虵 蚆 蛆 蛆 蝇 蝇 蠅 蠅	fly; small yìhng	yíng
2506 *	蟻	虫 虫 虫 虫 蚝 蛘 蛘 蟒 蟒 蟻 蟻 蟻	ant; many, small ngáih	yǐ
2507 *	蠔	虫 虫 虫 虫 蛄 蛴 蛴 蠔 蠔 蠔 蠔 蠔 蠔	oyster hòuh	háo
2508 *	蠟	虫 虫 蚧 蚧 蝐 蝐 蝟 蝟 蠟 蠟 蠟	wax laahp	là
2509 *	蠢	三 ⺸ 夫 夫 春 春 春 蠢 蠢	stupid, foolish chéun	chǔn
2510 *	蠶	一 ⺆ 尸 兂 兂 兓 朁 朁 朁 蠶 蠶 蠶	silkworm chàahm	cán
2511 *	蠻	` ⺀ 言 言 言 信 絔 絃 絲 縊 縊 蠻	barbarous, unreasonable màahn	mán

血　Section

2512 **	血	丶 丨 彳 血 血	blood *hyut*　　　　*xuè*

行　Section

2513 **	行	彳 彳 彳 行	[1] to walk, [1] do; [1] may; [2] behavior, [3] occupation, [3] row, [3] line [1] *hàhng;* [2] *hahng;* [3] *hòhng* [1] *xíng;* [2] *xìng;* [3] *háng*
2514 *	衍	彳 衫 衫 衍	to extend, spread *yín*　　　　*yǎn*
2515 **	術	彳 宀 什 杧 杧 杧 術	skill, method, way, art *seuht*　　　　*shù*
2516 ***	街	彳 彳 什 往 往 街	street, avenue *gàai*　　　　*jiē*
2517 **	衝	彳 彳 衫 杧 杧 衎 衎 衕 衝	[1] to rush against, [2] nap; [1] impulse, [2] drive [1] *chùng;* [2] *chung* [1] *chōng;* [2] *chòng*
2518 **	衛	彳 彳 衫 衫 德 德 德 德 德 德 衛	to protect, guard *waih*　　　　*wèi*
2519 *	衡	彳 彳 衫 衫 衍 衍 衎 衎 衎 衡 衡 衡 衡	to weigh, compare; balance *hàhng*　　　　*héng*

衣　Section

2520 **	衣	丶 亠 ㇆ 才 衣 衣	clothes, garments *yì*　　　　*yī*
2521 ***	表	一 十 圭 表	to show; surface, meter, table, cousin *bíu*　　　　*biǎo*

2522 *	衫	、ヲ衤衤衫	shirt, clothes
			saàm　　　　　shān
2523 *	衰	、一广产卞衣 衰衰	to decline; fading
			seùi　　　　　shuāi
2524 *	衷	一冖冂中東	conscience, sincerity
			chùng　　　　zhōng
2525 *	被	衤衤初衫被 被	[1] bedding, [1] quilt; [2] by
			[1] péih; [2] beih　　[1][2] bèi
2526 *	袖	衤衤衤衪袖 袖	sleeve
			jauh　　　　　xiù
2527 *	袍	衤衤初衪袍 袍	gown, robe
			pòuh　　　　　páo
2528 *	袋	ノイ化代代袋	bag, pocket, measure word for things in bags
			doih　　　　　dài
2529 *	裁	一十士表栽 裁裁	to cut (garments), decide
			chòih　　　　cái
2530 *	裂	一厂歹列列裂	to crack, split
			liht　　　　　liè
2531 *	袱	衤衤衬衬衬袂 袱袱	luggage in a sack
			fuhk　　　　　fú
2532 **	裝	╰丬爿爿壯壯 壯裝	clothing, luggage; to pack, pretend, equip
			jōng　　　　zhuāng
2533 *	裔	衣衣齐裔裔 裔裔裔	offspring, descendant
			yeuih　　　　yì
2534 ***	裏	、一广产言盲 盲审重裏	inside, inner
			léuih　　　　lǐ

2535 *	裙	衤 衤 衤 衤 衵 裙 裙 裙	skirt, dress
			kwàhn　　　　qún
2536 **	補	衤 衤 衤 衻 補 補 補	to repair, make up, mend
			bóu　　　　bǔ
2537 *	裕	衤 衤 衻 衿 裕 裕	wealthy, abundant
			yuh　　　　yù
2538 *	裘	一 寸 寸 求 求 裘	fur garments
			kaùh　　　　qiú
2539 *	裸	衤 衤 衤 衵 衵 裡 裸 裸	naked, unclothed
			ló　　　　luǒ
2540 *	裹	丶 亠 亠 宀 宀 宣 宣 裹 裹 裹	to wrap, bundle up
			gwó　　　　guǒ
2541 *	褂	衤 衤 衤 衦 褂 褂 褂	Chinese coat
			gwá　　　　guà
2542 *	裨	衤 衤 衤 衦 衵 衵 裨 裨 裨	benefit, advantage
			beì　　　　bì
2543 *	製	ノ ﾉ 二 午 告 制 制 製	to make, manufacture
			jai　　　　zhì
2544 *	裳	丨 丷 丷 屮 当 当 常 裳	clothes
			seùhng　　　　shang
2545 *	複	衤 衤 衦 衦 衦 衦 複 複 複 複	complex, compound, duplicate, double; to review
			fùk　　　　fù
2546 *	褪	衤 衤 衤 衤 衵 衵 褪 褪 褪 褪 褪	to take off, fade
			tan　　　　tùn
2547 *	褲	衤 衤 衤 衦 衦 衦 褲 褲 褲 褲 褲	pants, trousers
			fu　　　　kù

2548 *	褥	衤 衤̄ 衤̇ 衤̇ 衤̇ 衤̇ 衤̇ 衤̇ 褥 褥	mattress, cushion
			yuhk　　　　　　　rù
2549 *	襖	衤 衤́ 衤̇ 衤̇ 衤̇ 衤̇ 衤̇ 衤̇ 衤̇ 襖	Chinese jacket
			óu　　　　　　　ào
2550 *	襤	衤 衤 衤̇ 衤̇ 衤̇ 衤̇ 衤̇ 衤̇ 衤̇ 襤	ragged, torn
			laàhm　　　　　　lán
2551 *	襪	衤 衤 衤̇ 衤̇ 衤̇ 衤̇ 衤̇ 衤̇ 襪 襪	socks, stockings
			maht　　　　　　wà
2552 *	襯	衤 衤 衤̇ 衤̇ 衤̇ 衤̇ 衤̇ 衤̇ 衤̇ 襯	to put a layer under a layer, give to charity
			chan　　　　　　chèn
2553 *	襲	亠 亠 亠 产 产 育 肯 肯 肯 龍 龍 襲	to attack; suit of clothes
			jaahp　　　　　　xí

西　Section

2554 ***	西	一 厂 门 西 西	west; western
			sài　　　　　　　xī
2555 ***	要	西 要 要 要	[1] to ask for, [1] want, [1] need, [2] claim, [2] threaten; [1] should; [1] important; [1] if
			[1] yiu; [2] yiù　　　[1] yào; [2] yāo
2556 *	覆	西 覀 覂 覂 覂 覂 覈 覆 覆 覆 覆 覆	to cover, reply
			fùk　　　　　　　fù

見　Section

2557 ***	見	丨 冂 月 目 貝 見	to see, visit; opinion
			gin　　　　　　　jiàn
2558 **	規	二 キ 夫 規	regulation, rule
			kwài　　　　　　guī

2559 *	覓	⺊ ⺌ 覓	to look for mihk · · · · · · · · · · · mì
2560 *	視	⺀ ⺁ ⺙ 礻 視	to see, look at, watch sih · · · · · · · · · · · shì
2561 **	親	⺀ 亠 立 辛 亲 親	[1] parent, [1] relatives, [2] relatives by marriage; [1] to love, [1] kiss [1] chàn; [2] chan · · · [1] qīn; [2] qìng
2562 **	覺	⺅ 旧 𦥑 臼 爲 爲 爲 覺	[1] to feel, [1] discover; [2] nap, [2] sleep [1] gok; [2] gau · · · [1] jué; [2] jiào
2563 *	覽	一 丁 石 王 手 臣 臣 臣 臨 臨 臨 覽	to view, look around laáhm · · · · · · · · · · lán
2564 **	觀	⺀ 十 艹 苎 芦 苫 苩 茈 荳 華 莑 藿 觀	to observe, look; sight gwùn · · · · · · · · · · guān

角   Section

2565 ***	角	⺊ ⺆ 广 角 角 角 角	horn, angle, corner, dime; to wrestle gok · · · · · · · · · · jiǎo
2566 **	解	角 角 𤣩 𧢲 𤭖 解	to untie, release, explain, understand gaai · · · · · · · · · · jiě
2567 *	觸	角 𧢲 𧣒 𧣛 𧣮 𧣲 𧤃 𧤕 𧤦 觸 觸	to touch; touched jùk · · · · · · · · · · chù

言   Section

| 2568 *** | 言 | ⺀ 亠 亖 言 言
言 | to speak; words, speech

yìhn · · · · · · · · · · yán |
| 2569 * | 訂 | 言 訁 訂 | to engage, subscribe, order

dihng · · · · · · · · · · dìng |

2570 **	計	言 訂 計	to calculate, plan; plan *gai*　　　　*jì*
2571 *	訃	言 訂 訃	announcement of death *fuh*　　　　*fù*
2572 **	記	言 訂 訂 記	to remember, record; mark *gei*　　　　*jì*
2573 **	討	言 訂 討 討	to beg, ask for *tóu*　　　　*taǒ*
2574 *	訊	言 訂 訊 訊	to investigate; trial, message *seun*　　　　*xùn*
2575 *	託	言 訂 訐 託	to entrust *tok*　　　　*tuō*
2576 **	訓	言 訓	to advise, instruct *fan*　　　　*xùn*
2577 **	設	言 訂 訂 訅 設	to set up, establish, plan *chit*　　　　*shè*
2578 *	訝	言 訂 訐 訝 訝	surprised *ngah*　　　　*yà*
2579 **	許	言 訂 訐 許	to promise, consent, allow; many, much *héui*　　　　*xǔ*
2580 *	訛	言 訂 訐 訐' 訛	false *ngòh*　　　　*é*
2581 *	訟	言 訟 訟 訟	dispute, lawsuit *juhng*　　　　*sòng*
2582 *	訣	言 訂 訐 訣 訣	method *kyut*　　　　*jué*

2583 *	訪	言 言` 訂 訂 訪	to inquire, visit fóng fǎng
2584 *	詞	言 訂 訶 訶 詞 詞	compound word, phrase chìh cí
2585 *	評	言 言 訶 訂 評	to criticize, judge, appraise pìhng píng
2586 *	詆	言 訂 訂 訴 詆 詆	to defame, slander dái di ˇ
2587 ***	訴	言 訂 訂 訴 訴 訴	to tell, inform sou sù
2588 *	註	言 言 訂 計 註	to remark, register; explanation jyu zhù
2589 *	詐	言 訂 訝 訝 詐	to deceive, cheat; false ja zhà
2590 *	詠	言 言 訶 詠 詠 詠	to chant, sing, hum wihng yǒng
2591 *	診	言 言 訡 診	to diagnose, examine chán zhěn
2592 *	詛	言 訂 訋 詛 詛	to curse jó zǔ
2593 *	詩	言 言 計 註 詿 詩 詩	poem, poetry si` shī
2594 ***	試	言 言 訐 訐 試 試 試	to test, try, attempt si shì
2595 *	詳	言 訂 詳 詳	in detail cheùhng xiáng

2596 *	詫	言 言 訁 訁 訐 訏 訛	to be surprised, amazed	
			cha	chà
2597 *	誇	言 訁 訏 訡 訡 誇	to boast, praise, exaggerate	
			kwà	kuā
2598 *	詭	言 訁 訂 訏 訏 詝 詭	cunning; trick	
			gwái	gúi
2599 ***	話	言 訁 訐 訐 訐 話 話	to say; language, conversation, words	
			wah	hùa
2600 ***	該	言 言 訁 訐 該 該 該	should; that	
			gòi	gāi
2601 *	詢	言 訁 訋 訋 詢 詢 詢	to inquire, interrogate	
			seùn	xún
2602 *	詣	言 言 訁 訐 訐 詣 詣	to go to, reach	
			ngaih	yì`
2603 **	誠	言 訁 訐 訹 誠 誠 誠	sincere, honest	
			sìhng	chéng
2604 **	認	言 訁 訒 認 認 認 認	to acknowledge, recognize, know, confess	
			yihng	rèn
2605 ***	說	言 訁 訋 訜 訜 說 說	[1] to speak, [1] tell, [1] say, [2] persuade	
			[1] syut; [2] seui	[1] shūo; [2] shùi`
2606 ***	語	言 訁 訐 訐 訐 語 語 語	language, speech, words	
			yúh	yǔ
2607 *	誓	一 ナ オ 扩 扩 扩 折 誓	to swear; oath, vow	
			saih	shì`
2608 *	誣	言 言 訂 訐 訐 誣 誣	to make a false accusation	
			moùh	wú

2609 *	誡	言 計 許 許 誡 誡 誡	to prohibit; commandment gaai jiè
2610 **	誤	言 言 訂 記 誤 誤 誤 誤	mistake; mistaken; to delay mh wù
2611 *	誦	言 言 訂 訂 誦 誦 誦	to recite, praise juhng sòng
2612 *	誨	言 言 訏 訏 誨 誨 誨	to teach fui hùi
2613 *	誌	言 言 計 計 誌 誌 誌 誌	record, mark; to show ji zhì
2614 *	誘	言 言 訂 訽 誄 誘 誘	to teach, allure, induce yáuh yòu
2615 *	誕	言 言 訂 訂 訢 誕 誕 誕 誕	to boast, give birth to; birthday daan dàn
2616 ***	誰	言 言 訃 訃 訐 訐 誰	who, whom seuih shéi / shúi
2617 ***	請	言 言 計 計 請 請 請	to ask sincerely, invite; please chíng qǐng
2618 *	諒	言 言 計 訂 訶 諒 諒 諒	to forgive, excuse, pardon leuhng liàng
2619 **	調	言 訂 訂 訶 調 調 調 調 調	[1] to mix, [1] adjust, [1] fix, [1] tease, [2] move, [2] switch; [2] tune [1] tiùh; [2] diuh [1] tiáo; [2] diào
2620 ***	課	言 訂 訂 記 記 記 課 課 課	lesson, tax; to tax fo kè
2621 **	論	言 訂 訃 訥 訥 訥 諭 論 論	[1] to debate, [1] discuss, [1] criticize; [2] one of the Four Books [1] leuhn; [2] leuhn [1] lùn; [2] lún

2622 ***	談	言 言 訓 討 談 談	to chat; conversation, discussion	
			taàhm	tán
2623 *	誹	言 訓 訓 誹 誹	to defame, slander	
			féi	fěi
2624 *	誼	言 言 訂 訮 訮 訥 誼 誼	friendship	
			yìh	yì
2625 *	諂	言 言 訂 訋 訋 訧 訧 訧 諂	to flatter, butter up	
			chím	chǎn
2626 *	諾	言 言 訂 訣 訣 訝 訝 諾 諾	to promise; promise	
			lok	nuò
2627 *	諜	言 訂 訂 訍 訕 訕 訕 諜 諜	spy	
			dihp	dié
2628 *	謂	言 訂 訂 謂 謂 謂 謂 謂 謂	to say, call	
			waih	wèi
2629 *	諧	言 言 訧 訧 訧 訧 訧 諧 諧	harmonious; joke	
			haàih	xié
2630 *	謀	言 訂 計 詿 詿 詿 詿 謀 謀	to plan, plot; plan, scheme	
			màuh	móu
2631 *	諸	言 言 訂 諸 諸 諸 諸 諸 諸	every, all	
			jyù	zhū
2632 *	諷	言 訂 訊 訊 訊 諷 諷 諷 諷 諷	to ridicule; satire	
			fung	fěng
2633 *	諺	言 言 訂 諺 諺 諺 諺	proverb	
			yihn	yàn
2634 *	謎	言 言 訂 訧 謎 謎 謎 謎	riddle, puzzle	
			màih	mí

2635 *	謙	humble, modest		
		hìm		qiān
2636 **	謝	to thank, wither		
		jeh		xiè
2637 **	講	to speak, tell, say		
		góng		jiǎng
2638 *	謠	rumor, street song		
		yiuh		yáo
2639 *	謄	to copy, transcribe		
		tàhng		téng
2640 *	謗	to slander		
		bong		bàng
2641 *	謊	lie		
		fòng		huǎng
2642 *	謬	false		
		mauh		miù
2643 *	謹	careful, respectful		
		gán		jǐn
2644 *	證	evidence, identification; to prove		
		jing		zhèng
2645 *	譜	genealogy, a piece of music		
		póu		pǔ
2646 *	譏	to ridicule, satirize		
		gèi		jī
2647 **	識	to know, recognize; knowledge		
		sìk		shí

2648 *	譯	言 訁 訳 謬 謬 謬 譯 譯 課 譯 譯	to translate, interpret yihk　　　　yì
2649 *	議	言 訁 訏 訐 詳 詳 誁 譁 譁 議 議 議	to discuss, negotiate, consult yíh　　　　yì
2650 *	譬	一 コ ア ア 启 启 启 启 启 启 辟 譬	for instance pei　　　　pì
2651 **	警	' 十 艹 艹 苟 苟 苟 苟 苟 敬 敬 警	to caution, warn; alert; warning, policeman ging　　　　jǐng
2652 *	譽	' ト ト ト ド ド 钌 臼 臼 與 與 與 譽	to praise; reputation yuh　　　　yù
2653 **	護	言 訁 訁 訐 訏 詳 詳 誁 誰 護 護 護	to guard, protect wuh　　　　hù
2654 **	讀	言 訁 訐 詩 誹 讀 誚 誚 誚 請 請 讀 讀	to read, study duhk　　　　dú
2655 **	變	言 信 纩 綜 結 絲 絲 戀 戀 戀 變 變	to change, transform; change bin　　　　biàn
2656 **	讓	言 訁 訂 訝 討 誧 誧 誧 誧 譁 讓 讓 讓	to yield, give away, allow, cause yeuhng　　　　ràng
2657 *	讚	言 訁 訁 許 詩 詩 誅 讖 許 讚 讚 讚 讚 讚	to praise, eulogize jaan　　　　zàn
		谷　Section	
2658 *	谷	八 父 仒 仒 谷 谷 谷	valley, ravine gùk　　　　gǔ
		豆　　Section	

2659 **	豆	一 厂 厅 戸 豆 豆	beans, peas
			dauh — dòu
2660 *	豈	丨 山 山 豈	how
			héi — qǐ
2661 *	豉	豆 豆 虹 豉 豉	salted beans
			sih — chǐ
2662 *	豎	一 丁 丒 ェ 于 臣 臤 臤 豎	to erect; vertical
			syuh — shù
2663 **	豐	丨 彐 彗 ㅃ 耕 蚩 蚩 豐	abundant, fruitful
			fung — fēng
2664 *	豔	豐 豐 豐 豐 豐土 豐去 豐去 豐嘉 豐嘉 豔	charming, pretty
			yihm — yàn

| | 豕 Section | | |

2665 *	象	丿 夕 甶 甶 甶 甶 多 兜 兜 象 象 象	elephant, figure, phenomenon
			jeuhng — xiàng
2666 *	豪	丶 亠 亠 六 言 亯 亯 豪 豪	superior, brave, luxurious
			hòuh — háo
2667 **	豬	豕 豕 豕 豺 豺 豬 豬 豬 豬 豬	pig
			jyù — zhū

| | 豸 Section | | |

2668 *	豹	丿 丬 豸 豸 豹 豹 豹	leopard, panther
			paau — bào
2669 *	貂	豸 豸 豸 豹 貂 貂	sable, mink
			diu — diāo

| 2670 * | 貌 | 豸 豸 豸 豹 豹 豹 豹 豹 貌 貌 | outlook, complexion, manner

maauh　　　　　*mào* |
| 2671 * | 貓 | 豸 豸 豸 豸 豹 豹 豹 貓 貓 貓 | cat

maàu　　　　　*māo* |

貝　Section

2672 *	貝	丨 冂 冃 目 貝	shell, money *bui*　　　　　*bèi*
2673 *	貞	丨 卜 貞	virtuous, pure *jing*　　　　　*zhēn*
2674 **	負	丿 ⺈ 負	to lose, bear, carry; negative, ungrateful *fuh*　　　　　*fù*
2675 *	貢	一 丅 工 貢	to pay tribute *gung*　　　　　*gòng*
2676 **	財	貝 貝 財 財 財	property, wealth *chòih*　　　　　*cái*
2677 *	貧	丿 八 今 分 貧	poor, needy *pàhn*　　　　　*pín*
2678 **	責	一 十 主 責	responsibility; to blame, punish *jaak*　　　　　*zé*
2679 *	貪	丿 人 人 今 貪	greedy *tàam*　　　　　*tān*
2680 **	貨	丿 亻 亻 化 貨	goods, merchandise *fo*　　　　　*huò*
2681 *	販	貝 貝 販 販 販	to sell, trade; peddler *faán*　　　　　*fàn*

2682 *	貫	ㄥ ㄉ 毋 毋 貫	continuing; to penetrate
			gwun guàn
2683 *	賀	ㄅ ㄉ 加 加 加 賀	to congratulate
			hoh hè
2684 ***	貴	丶 ㄇ 口 中 虫 貴	noble, expensive, precious
			gwai gùi
2685 *	貼	貝 貝 貼 貼 貼 貼	to paste up, stick; near
			tip tiē
2686 ***	買	丶 ㄇ 罒 四 買	to buy, purchase
			maáih mǎi
2687 **	費	ㄱ ㄹ 弓 弗 費	fee, expense; to waste, spend
			fai fèi
2688 *	貿	ノ ㇐ ㇀ ㄠ 卯 貿	to trade
			mauh màu
2689 *	貸	ノ イ 仁 代 代 貸	to lend with interest
			taai dài
2690 *	貳	一 二 弍 貳 貳 貳	two
			yih èr
2691 *	貶	貝 貝 貶 貶 貶 貶	to devalue, degrade
			bín biǎn
2692 *	貯	貝 貝 貯 貯 貯 貯	to store up, save
			chyúh zhù
2693 **	資	冫 冫 汷 汷 次 資	capital, wealth, talent, expense, qualification
			jì zī
2694 *	賈	一 ㇐ 襾 襾 賈	[1] merchant, [2] a last name; [1] to trade, [1] cause
			[1] gú; [2] gá [1] gǔ; [2] jiǎ

2695 *	賊	貝 貝一 貝一 貝二 賊 賊 賊	thief, pickpocket	chaahk _ zéi
2696 *	賄	貝 貝一 貝一 貝一 賄 賄	wealth; to bribe	kúi _ huì
2697 *	賓	丶 丷 宀 宀 宀 宀 宀 賓	guest, visitor	ban _ bīn
2698 *	賒	貝 貝 貝 賒 賒 賒	to buy or sell on credit	se _ shē
2699 *	賦	貝 貝一 貝一 貝一 賦 賦 賦 賦	to levy, give; talent	fu _ fù
2700 ***	賣	一 十 土 士 吉 高 賣 賣	to sell	maaih _ mài
2701 *	賠	貝 貝 貝一 賠 賠 賠 賠 賠	to compensate, lose, apologize	puìh _ péi
2702 *	賜	貝 貝 貝一 貝月 貝月 貝月 賜 賜	to give, bestow	chi _ cì
2703 *	賞	丨 丷 丷 ⺍ 尚 尚 賞 賞	to reward, enjoy, appreciate	seúng _ shǎng
2704 *	賢	一 T 丆 五 ẞ 臣 臤 賢	virtuous, kind, judicious	yìhn _ xián
2705 *	賬	貝 貝 貝一 賬 賬 賬 賬 賬	account, debt	jeung _ zhàng
2706 *	質	丿 亻 千 斤 斦 質	substance, quality	jat _ zhì
2707 *	賤	貝 貝 貝一 賤 賤 賤	low, without value	jihn _ jiàn

2708 *	賭	貝 貝ˊ 貝ˇ 貝ˇ 財 財 賭 賭 賭 賭	to gamble, bet *dóu*　　　　　*dǔ*
2709 *	賴	一 ㇋ ㇒ 日 束 束 敕 敕 賴 賴	to rely on, deny, blame *laaih*　　　　*lài*
2710 *	購	貝 貝ˈ 貝ˇ 貝ˇ 購 購 購 購 購 購	to buy, purchase *kau*　　　　　*gòu*
2711 *	賺	貝 貝ˇ 貝ˇ 貝ˇ 賺 賺 賺 賺	to earn, gain *jaahn*　　　　*zhuàn*
2712 **	賽	㇒ ㇜ ㇕ 宀 宀 宗 宇 寀 寀 賽	to race; match *choi*　　　　　*sài*
2713 *	贈	貝 貝ˇ 貝ˇ 賸 賸 賸 賸 贈 贈 贈	to give a gift, bestow *jahng*　　　　*zèng*
2714 **	贊	㇒ ㇜ ㇓ 生 先 先 先先 贊	to assist, praise *jaan*　　　　　*zàn*
2715 *	贍	貝 貝ˈ 貝ˇ 賘 賘 賘 賘 賗 贍 贍 贍 贍 贍	to support, provide for *sihn*　　　　*shàn*
2716 *	贖	貝 貝ˈ 貝ˇ 賈 賈ˇ 賣 賣 賣 贖	to redeem *suhk*　　　　*shú*
	赤　Section		
2717 *	赤	一 十 士 尹 赤 赤	red, naked *chek*　　　　*chì*
2718 *	赦	赤 赤ˇ 赤ˇ 赦 赦	to forgive *se*　　　　　*shè*
	走　Section		

2719 ***	走	一 十 土 キ キ 走 走	to walk, run, go, leave jáu / zǒu
2720 *	赴	走 赴 赴	to attend, go to fuh / fù
2721 *	赳	走 赳 赳	brave dáu / jiū
2722 **	起	走 起 起 起	to rise, start héi / qǐ
2723 *	超	走 起 起 起 超 超	to exceed, excel chìu / chāo
2724 **	越	走 起 赴 越 越 越	to surpass, exceed yuht / yuè
2725 *	趁	走 起 赴 趁	to take advantage of an opportunity chan / chèn
2726 **	趕	走 起 起 起 起 趕 趕	to chase, get rid of, hurry gón / gǎn
2727 *	趙	走 起 赳 赴 趙 趙	to return something to its owner; a surname jiuh / zhào
2728 **	趣	走 走 起 起 趄 趣 趣 趣	interest; interesting, amusing cheui / qù
2729 *	趟	走 起 起 趄 趄 趟 趟 趟	a time, round tong / tàng
2730 *	趨	走 走 起 起 起 趨 趨	tendency, trend; to hasten cheui / qū

足 Section

2731 **	足	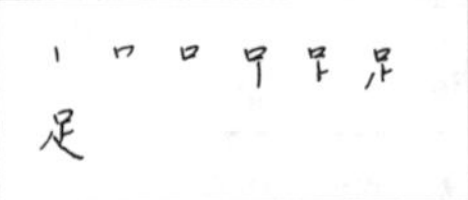	foot, leg; enough, satisfied *jùk* *zú*	
2732 *	趾		toe *jí* *zhǐ*	
2733 *	跋	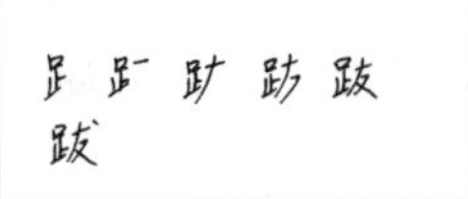	to walk with difficulty *baht* *bá*	
2734 *	跌	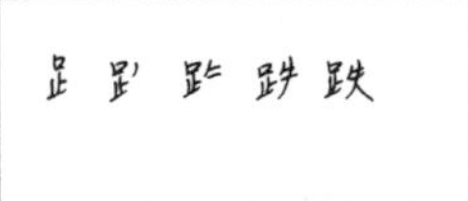	to fall, stumble *dit* *diē*	
2735 *	距	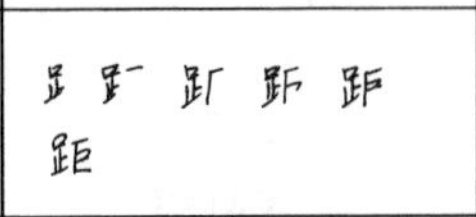	distance from *keúih* *jù*	
2736 ***	跑		to run, leak *paáu* *pǎo*	
2737 *	跛	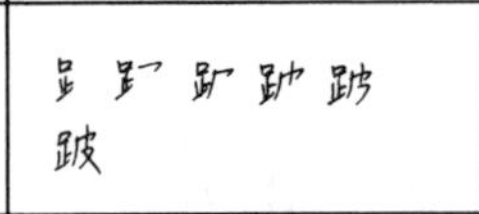	lame, crippled *bài* *bǒ*	
2738 **	跳	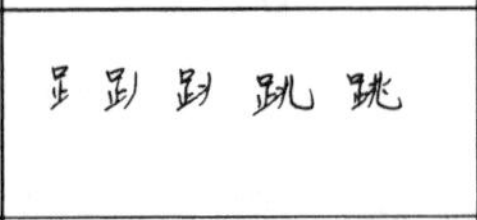	to jump, leap *tiu* *tiào*	
2739 ***	路	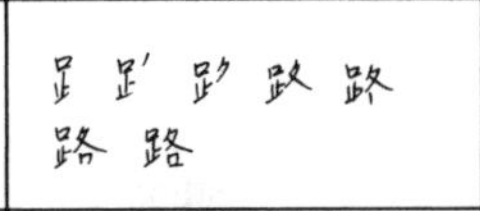	road, path, way *louh* *lù*	
2740 ***	跟		heel; to follow; and *gàn* *gēn*	
2741 *	跨		to bestride, carry in the elbow *kwà* *kuà*	
2742 *	跪	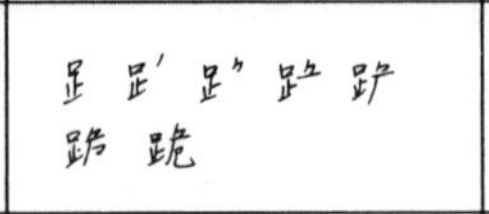	to kneel *gwaih* *guì*	
2743 *	踢	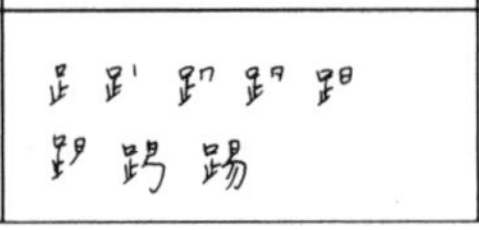	to kick *tek* *tī*	

2744 *	踐	足 足ˊ 践 践 践 踐	to tramp, tread on
			chíhn *jiàn*
2745 *	踏	足 足ˌ 趵 趵 趺 趻 跿 踏 踏	to step upon, tramp, tread on
			daahp *tà*
2746 *	踹	足 足ˊ 趾 趾 跐 趴 跐 踹 踹	to kick, ruin, tread on
			cháai *chuài*
2747 *	踴	足 足ˊ 趵 趵 趵 踊 踊 踊 踴	zealous, enthusiastic
			yúng *yǒng*
2748 *	踱	足 足ˋ 距 趵 趵 趷 跊 跊 踱 踱	to stroll
			dohk *dúo*
2749 *	蹄	足 足ˋ 足 趵 趵 趵 蹄 蹄	hoof
			taìh *tí*
2750 *	蹈	足 足ˊ 趵 趵 趵 趵 趵 蹈 蹈	to tread on, jump into
			douh *dǎo*
2751 *	蹤	足 足ˊ 趵 趵 趵 趵 趵 跊 蹤 蹤	trace, footprint
			jùng *zōng*
2752 *	蹲	足 足ˊ 趵 趵 趵 趵 跻 蹅 蹅 蹲 蹲 蹲	to squat down, crouch
			dèun *dūn*
2753 *	躁	足 足ˋ 趵 趵 跟 跟 跲 踤 踤 躁	short-tempered
			chòu *zào*
2754 *	躍	足 足ˊ 趵 趵 趵 趵 趵 趵 趵 躍	to leap, jump
			yeuk *yuè*
2755 *	躡	足 足ˊ 趵 跞 跞 趵 跞 躡 躡	to walk on tiptoes
			nihp *nièˋ*

身 Section

2756 **	身	ノ イ 勹 勹 身 身	body sàn · shēn
2757 *	躬	身 躬 躬 躬	to bow; personally gùng · gōng
2758 *	躭	身 躬 身 躬 躭	to delay, hinder daàm · dān
2759 *	躲	身 躬 躬 躬 躲 躲	to hide, avoid dó · duǒ
2760 *	躺	身 躬 躬 躬 躬 躬 躬 躺	to lie flat tóng · tǎng
2761 *	軀	身 躬 軀 軀 軀 軀 軀 軀	body, trunk keùi · qū

車 Section

2762 ***	車	一 一 一 一 一 車	vehicle, car, cart; to sew with a sewing machine chè · chē
2763 *	軌	車 軌 軌	rail, track gwái · guǐ
2764 **	軍	丶 冖 軍	army gwàn · jūn
2765 **	軟	車 軟 軟 軟 軟	soft, weak yúhn · ruǎn
2766 *	軸	車 軸 軸 軸 軸 軸	axis juhk · zhóu
2767 **	較	車 軟 軟 較 較	to compare; in comparison gaau · jiào

2768 *	載	一 十 土 吉 載 載 載	¹ to contain; ¹ record, ² year
			¹ joi; ² joi ¹ zài; ² zai
2769 **	輕	車 車 斬 輕 輕 輕	light, frivolous
			hìng qīng
2770 *	輔	車 車 車 斬 斬 輔 輔	to assist
			fuh fǔ
2771 **	輪	車 車 斬 斬 斬 輪 輪	wheel, turn; to rotate
			leùhn lún
2772 *	輛	車 車 斬 斬 斬 斬 輛 輛 輛	measure word for vehicles
			leuhng liàng
2773 *	輝	丨 ⺌ ⺌ 少 光 光 光 輝	brightness; splendid
			fài huī
2774 *	輩	丨 才 扎 非 輩	generation
			bui bei
2775 *	輸	車 車 斬 斬 斬 斬 斬 輸	to transport, lose
			syù shū
2776 *	輯	車 車 車 斬 斬 斬 斬 輯 輯	to compile
			chàp jí
2777 *	輾	車 車 斬 斬 斬 斬 斬 斬 輾 輾 輾	to roll over, turn over
			jín zhǎn
2778 **	轉	車 車 車 斬 斬 斬 斬 斬 斬 轉 轉 轉	¹ to rotate, ¹ roll, ² turn
			¹ jyún; ² jyun ¹ zhuǎn; ² zhuàn
2779 *	轍	車 車 車 斬 斬 斬 斬 斬 斬 斬 斬 斬 轍	track of a wheel
			chit zhé
2780 *	轎	車 車 斬 斬 斬 斬 斬 斬 斬 轎 轎	sedan chair
			giù jiào

| 2781 * | 轟 | 車　車　轟 | to bomb, blow up; vigorous |
| | | | *gwàng* 　　　　　*hōng* |

| | 辛　Section | | |

| 2782 ** | 辛 | 、　一　亠　立　辛 | grievous, distressing |
| | | | *sàn* 　　　　　*xīn* |

| 2783 * | 辣 | 辛　辛　刺　刺　刺　辣　辣 | spicy hot |
| | | | *laaht* 　　　　　*là* |

| 2784 * | 辨 | 辛　辛　刔　辨 | to distinguish, identify |
| | | | *bihn* 　　　　　*biàn* |

| 2785 ** | 辦 | 辛　刔　刔　辦 | to manage |
| | | | *baahn* 　　　　　*bàn* |

| 2786 ** | 辭 | 一　爫　爫　爫　爭　爭　爭　爭　辭 | statement; to depart, refuse, resign |
| | | | *chìh* 　　　　　*cí* |

| 2787 * | 辯 | 辛　辛　辝　辝　辝　辝　辯 | to debate, argue, dispute |
| | | | *bihn* 　　　　　*biàn* |

| | 辰　Section | | |

| 2788 * | 辰 | 三　厂　戶　辰　辰 | time of the day |
| | | | *sàhn* 　　　　　*chén* |

| 2789 * | 辱 | 辰　辰　辱　辱 | to disgrace, insult |
| | | | *yuhk* 　　　　　*rù* |

| 2790 ** | 農 | 丶　冖　曰　曲　曲　農 | agriculture |
| | | | *nùhng* 　　　　　*nóng* |

| | 辵　Section | | |

2791 *	迅	㇒ 几 凡 凡 汛 迅	quick, swift seun · xùn
2792 *	迄	㇒ 乀 乞 迄	until, up to ngaht · qì
2793 *	巡	巛 巡	to patrol chèuhn · xún
2794 *	返	㇒ 厂 反 反 返	to return fáan · fǎn
2795 ***	近	㇒ 厂 斤 斤 近	near, close; to approach gahn · jìn
2796 **	迎	㇒ 匚 卬 卬 迎	to welcome, receive; towards yìhng · yíng
2797 **	迫	㇒ 亻 白 白 白 迫	to compel, coerce; imminent bik · pò
2798 *	述	一 十 才 木 术 述	to state, describe seuht · shù
2799 **	逃	㇒ 扌 兆 兆 逃	to escape, flee tòuh · táo
2800 *	迴	丨 冂 回 回 回 迴	circular, revolving, crooked, winding wùih · huí
2801 **	退	㇕ ㇕ ㇕ ㇠ 艮 艮 退	to retreat, withdraw teui · tùi
2802 **	迷	丷 丷 米 米 迷	to get lost, delude; superstitious màih · mí
2803 *	逆	丷 丷 屰 屰 屰 逆	to rebel, oppose yihk · nì

2804 **	追	丿 亻 户 户 𠂤 追	to chase, pursue, follow, overtake *jèui* *zhuī*
2805 *	迹	丶 亠 亣 亦 迹	trace *jìk* *jī*
2806 **	送	丷 兰 关 关 送	to give a gift, send, deliver *sung* *sòng*
2807 **	通	㇇ マ 乛 乃 甬 甬 通	to go through, pass, notify, communicate *tùng* *tōng*
2808 *	逐	一 丆 丂 豕 豕 豕 逐	to chase, expel; one by one *juhk* *zhú*
2809 ***	連	一 丆 冂 百 百 亘 車 連	to join, connect; continuous *lìhn* *lián*
2810 ***	這	丶 亠 亠 亖 言 言 這	[1] this, [2] this one [1] [2] *jéh* [1] *zhè;* [2] *zhèi*
2811 *	途	丿 人 亼 全 余 途	road, passage *tòuh* *tú*
2812 *	逝	一 寸 才 扩 扩 扩 折 逝	to die, pass away *saih* *shì*
2813 *	逗	一 丆 冂 戸 豆 豆 逗	to remain, loiter, tease *dauh* *dòu*
2814 **	造	丿 𠂉 ⺧ 生 牛 告 告 造	to make, create, build, construct *jouh* *zào*
2815 *	逕	一 巛 巠 巠 巠 逕	directly; path *ging* *jìng*
2816 *	速	一 丆 冂 日 申 東 速	fast, swift, speedy; speed *chùk* *sù*

No.	Character	Strokes	Meaning / Pronunciation
2817 **	透	丿 亠 千 禾 秀 秀 透	to penetrate, disclose; thoroughly — tau — tòu
2818 *	逛	丿 犭 犭 犭 犷 狂 逛	to stroll — kwaang — guàng
2819 *	逢	丿 夕 夂 夆 夆 逢	to meet; whenever — fùhng — féng
2820 ***	進	丿 亻 仁 广 什 佳 進	to proceed, enter — jeun — jìn
2821 *	週	丨 刀 月 用 周 用 周 周 週	to revolve; week — jāu — zhōu
2822 *	逮	彐 ヨ 肀 聿 隶 逮	to seize — daih — dài
2823 *	逼	一 亠 产 百 畐 畐 畐 畐 逼	to compel; approaching — bīk — bī
2824 *	逸	丿 夕 夕 夕 兔 兔 逸	leisure; to run away — yaht — yì
2825 *	遁	丿 丿 厂 斤 斤 盾 盾 盾 遁	to escape, hide — deuhn — dùn
2826 *	遂	丷 丷 丷 芀 芀 遂	success; then — seuih — sùi
2827 *	遊	丶 亠 方 方 扩 扩 於 斿 遊	to travel, ramble, play — yàuh — yóu
2828 **	達	一 十 土 圥 幸 幸 達	to reach, arrive, attain — daaht — dá
2829 *	違	乛 乛 立 韦 韋 韋 違	to disobey, be apart — wàih — wéi

2830 *	遇		to meet *yuh* *yù*
2831 ***	道	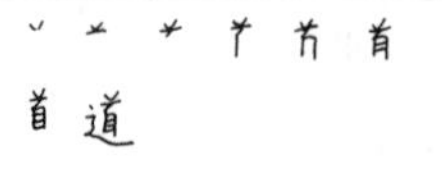	road, method; to say *douh* *dào*
2832 **	遍	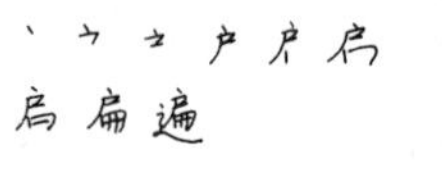	a time, round *pin* *biàn*
2833 ***	過		[1] to exceed, [1] pass; [1] fault; [2] past tense [1 2] *gwo* [1] *guò;* [2] *guo*
2834 **	運		to convey, transport, use; fate *wahn* *yùn*
2835 *	遙		far, distant, remote *yìuh* *yáo*
2836 *	遞		to deliver, send *daih* *dì*
2837 ***	遠		[1] far, [1] distant, [1] remote; [2] to avoid [1] *yúhn;* [2] *yuhn* [1] *yuǎn;* [2] *yuàn*
2838 *	遣	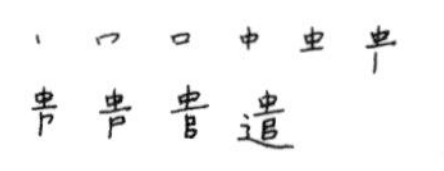	to dispatch, send, banish *hín* *qiǎn*
2839 *	遮		to cover, block *jè* *zhē*
2840 **	適		suitable, comfortable; just now; to go to *sìk* *shì*
2841 *	遭	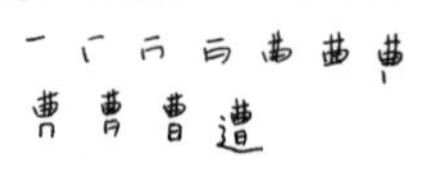	to meet; a time, turn *jòu* *zāo*
2842 *	遷	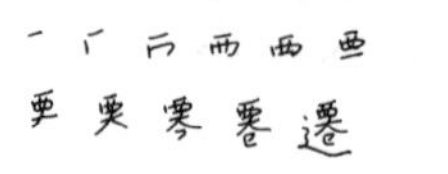	to move *chìn* *qiān*

No.	Character	Stroke order	Meaning / Readings
2843 *	遲	一コア尸尸尼尼 尼犀遲	late *chìh*　　　*chí*
2844 *	遼	一ナ大大夾夾 吞吞章尞遼	far, distant, remote *liùh*　　　*liáo*
2845 **	選	フコ己己己巳 弭弭巽選	to choose, elect *syún*　　　*xuǎn*
2846 *	遵	丷丷广并并尚 酋酋尊尊遵	to obey, follow *jeùn*　　　*zūn*
2847 *	遺	丶口口中虫虫虫 贵肯貴遺	to lose, leave behind *wàih*　　　*yí*
2848 *	邀	ノイ白白白臼 臭臭臭臭敫邀	to invite *yiù*　　　*yaō*
2849 *	避	フコアア尸启启 辟辟辟辟避	to avoid *beih*　　　*bì*
2850 ***	還	丶ロ四四罒罒 睘睘睘睘睘還	[1] to return; [2] still, [2] yet, [2] or, [2] more [1] [2] *wàahn*　　　[1] *huán;* [2] *hái*
2851 ***	邊	ノイ白白自臭臭 臭臭臭臭臭邊	edge, side *bìn*　　　*biān*

邑　Section

No.	Character	Stroke order	Meaning / Readings
2852 *	邑	丶口口吕吕 吕邑	city, district *yàp*　　　*yì*
2853 ***	那	フカ刃邢邓那 那	[1] that, [2] that one, [3] that (question), [4] then [1][2][3][4] *náh*　　　[1] *nà;* [2] *nèi;* [3] *nǎ;* [4] *nè*
2854 *	邪	一匚手牙牙邪	evil, vicious *chèh*　　　*xié*

2855 * 邦	三 丰 邦	state, country *bòng* *bāng*
2856 * 邱	ノ 亻 𠂉 斤 丘 邱	mound *yaù* *qiū*
2857 * 郊	丶 亠 六 亣 交 郊	countryside, suburbs *gaàu* *jiāo*
2858 * 耶	一 丅 丌 耳 耳 耶	ending article for question, Jesus *yèh* *yé*
2859 * 郎	丶 ㇇ ㇇ ㇇ 良 良 郎	young gentleman, bridegroom *lòhng* *láng*
2860 * 郡	㇇ ㇇ ㇇ 尹 尹 君 君 郡	district *gwahn* *jùn*
2861 *** 部	丶 亠 亠 立 立 音 音 部	section, department, measure word for books and vehicles *bouh* *bù*
2862 ** 郵	ノ 二 三 垂 垂 垂 垂 郵	mail, postal *yàuh* *yóu*
2863 *** 都	(都) 一 十 土 耂 耂 者 者 者 都	capital; also; all *doù* *dū*
2864 ** 鄉	乡 乡 乡 乡 乡 乡 乡 乡 乡 鄉	village *heùng* *xiāng*
2865 * 鄙	丨 口 口 口 口 咅 咅 啚 啚 啚 鄙	low, vile *péi* *bǐ*
2866 * 鄰	丶 丷 米 米 米 米 米 粦 粦 粦 鄰	neighbor; adjacent *leùhn* *lín*

酉 Section

2867 *	酋	ⸯ ⸯ 产 产 酋 酋 酋	a chief
			yàuh qiú
2868 **	配	酉 酉ⁿ 酉ᵀ 配	to match, unite; suitable
			pui pèi
2869 *	酌	酉 酉′ 酌 酌	to pour wine, consider; banquet, feast
			jeuk zhuó
2870 **	酒	氵 酒	wine, liquor
			jáu jiǔ
2871 *	酥	酉 酉′ 酔 酥 酥	crisp, flaky
			sòu sū
2872 *	酪	酉 酉′ 酌 酪 酪 酪 酪	cheese
			lok laò
2873 *	酬	酉 酉 酌 酬 酬	to repay, reward
			chàuh chóu
2874 *	酸	酉 酉′ 酔 酔 酸 酸 酸 酸	sour, distressed
			syùn suān
2875 *	酷	酉 酉′ 酔 酔 酷 酷 酷	cruel, oppressive, extreme
			huhk kù
2876 *	酵	酉 酉ᵀ 酉ᵗ 酔 酔 酔 酵 酵	to ferment; yeast
			haàu jiào
2877 *	醋	酉 酉′ 酔 酉ᵗ 酔 酔 醋 醋 醋	vinegar
			chou cù
2878 *	醇	酉 酉ˋ 酉 酉 酔 酔 醇 醇 醇	good wine; humble and earnest
			seùhn chún
2879 *	醉	酉 酉ˋ 酔 酔 酔 酔 醉 醉	drunk; to be infatuated with
			jeui zuì

2880 *	醃	酉 酉 酊 酡 酡 酯 酯 酯 醃	to salt
			yip　　　　　　　yān

2881 **	醒	酉 酊 酊 酊 酊 酊 酊 醒 醒	to wake up, be aware
			síng　　　　　　xǐng

2882 *	醞	(醖) 酉 酉 酊 酊 酊 酊 酊 酚 醞 醞	to brew
			wán　　　　　　yùn

2883 *	醜	酉 酉 酊 酊 酡 酡 酚 酚 醜 醜 醜	ugly, shameful
			cháu　　　　　　chǒu

2884 *	醬	㇄ ㇄ ㇄ ㇄ ㇄ ㇄ 牂 將 將 醬	sauce
			jeung　　　　　jiàng

2885 **	醫	一 匚 匸 匥 医 医 医 殹 殹 殹 醫	to cure, treat; doctor, physician
			yì　　　　　　　yī

2886 *	釀	酉 酡 酡 酡 酡 酡 酡 酡 釀 釀 釀 釀 釀	to brew; wine
			yeuhng　　　　niàng

米　Section

2887 *	采	㇒ ㇑ ㇜ 平 采	color, applause; brilliant
			choi　　　　　　cǎi

2888 *	釋	采 采 釆 釆 釆 釆 釋 釋 釋 釋 釋 釋	to explain, release
			sik　　　　　　shì

里　Section

2889 ***	里	㇑ 冂 冂 日 甲 甲 里	neighborhood, Chinese mile
			léih　　　　　　lǐ

2890 ***	重	㇒ ㇜ 重	[1] heavy, [2] important; [1] weight, [2] gravity; [3] again
			[1] chúhng; [2] juhng; [3] chùhng　　[1][2] zhòng; [3] chóng

2891 **	野	丶 冂 日 曰 甲 里 野 野 野 野	wilderness; wild
			yéh　　　　　　yě

2892 **	量	丶 冂 日 曰 旦 量	[1] to measure, [1] discuss; [2] capacity, [2] quantity
			[1] leùhng; [2] leuhng　　[1] liáng; [2] liàng

2893 *	釐	二 十 未 利 利 利 釐 釐 釐 釐 釐	to regulate; centimeter
			leìh　　　　　　lí

金　Section

2894 **	金	丿 人 今 全 金 金	gold, metal, money
			gàm　　　　　　jīn

2895 *	釜	八 少 父 釜	pot, pan, caldron
			fú　　　　　　fǔ

2896 **	針	金 釒 釒 針	needle, pin
			jàm　　　　　　zhēn

2897 *	釘	金 釒 釘	nail; to nail
			dèng　　　　　　dīng

2898 *	釦	金 釦 釦 釦	button, buckle
			kau　　　　　　kòu

2899 *	釣	金 釒 釣 釣	to fish
			diu　　　　　　diào

2900 *	鈔	金 釒 鈔 鈔 鈔	bank notes, money; to copy
			chàau　　　　　　chāo

2901 *	鈍	金 釒 鈍 鈍 鈍	dull, blunt
			duhn　　　　　　dùn

2902 *	鈕	金 釒 鈕 鈕 鈕	button, knob
			náu　　　　　　niǔ

2903 *	鉤	金 釒 釣 釣 鉤 鉤	hook
			ngàu　　　　　　gōu
2904 *	鈴	金 釒 釒 鈦 鈴 鈴	bell
			lìhng　　　　　　líng
2905 *	鉅	金 金 釒 鉅 鉅 鉅	steel, large, huge
			geuih　　　　　　jù
2906 *	鉗	金 釒 針 針 鉗 鉗	forceps, pincers
			kìhm　　　　　　qián
2907 *	鉋	金 釒 釟 鉤 鉤 鉋	plane; to plane
			pàauh　　　　　　bào
2908 *	鉛	金 釒 釞 釞 鉛 鉛	lead
			yùhn　　　　　　qiān
2909 **	銀	金 釒 釟 釟 銀 銀 銀	silver, money; silver color
			ngàhn　　　　　　yín
2910 **	銅	金 釒 釟 銅 銅 銅 銅	copper, bronze, brass
			tùhng　　　　　　tóng
2911 *	銜	彳 街 街 銜	title, rank; to hold in the mouth
			hàahm　　　　　　xián
2912 *	銑	金 釒 釟 釟 銑 銑	cast iron
			sín　　　　　　xiǎn
2913 *	銘	金 釒 釟 釛 銘 銘 銘	inscription; to remember forever
			mìhng　　　　　　míng
2914 *	銳	金 釒 釟 釟 銳 銳 銳	sharp, acute
			yeuih　　　　　　rùi
2915 *	鋁	金 金 釟 釟 釟 鋁	aluminium
			leúih　　　　　　lǚ

2916 *	銲	金 金 釒 釒 銅 銲 銲	to solder, weld	
			hohn	*hàn*
2917 *	銻	金 釒 釒 釒 銻 銻 銻	antimony	
			tài	*tī*
2918 *	鋒	金 釒 釒 釒 鋒 鋒	sharp edge of a tool or weapon; sharp	
			fùng	*fēng*
2919 **	鋪	金 金 釒 釒 鋪 鋪 鋪	[1] to spread, [1] pave; [2] store	
			[1] *pòu;* [2] *pou*	[1] *pū;* [2] *pù*
2920 *	銷	金 釒 釒 釒 銷 銷	to fuse, smelt, sell	
			siù	*xiāo*
2921 *	鋤	金 釒 釒 鋤 鋤 鋤 鋤	hoe, spade; to dig	
			chòh	*chú*
2922 *	銹	金 釒 釒 釒 銹 銹 銹	rust	
			sau	*xiù*
2923 ***	錄	金 金 釒 釒 釒 釒 錄	to copy, record, use; report, record	
			luhk	*lù*
2924 *	鋸	金 釒 釒 鋸 鋸 鋸 鋸 鋸	saw; to saw	
			geui	*jù*
2925 *	錦	金 釒 釒 釒 錦 錦 錦 錦	brocade; ornamental	
			gám	*jǐn*
2926 *	錐	金 釒 釒 釒 釒 錐 錐	drill	
			jeùi	*zhuī*
2927 *	錫	金 釒 釒 釒 錫 錫 錫	tin, pewter	
			sek	*xī*
2928 ***	錯	金 釒 釒 釒 釒 錯 錯 錯	mistake; wrong, incorrect, bad	
			cho	*cuò*

2929 ***	錢	金 釒 釤 錢 錢 錢	coin, money, cash
			chìhn	qián
2930 *	鋼	金 釒 釦 鈪 鋼 鋼 鋼 鋼	steel
			gong	gāng
2931 *	錶	金 釒 針 釬 鈝 錶 錶 錶	watch, meter
			bìu	bǐao
2932 *	錘	金 釒 釤 釒 鉌 鍂 錘 錘	weight
			chèuih	chúi
2933 *	鍋	金 釒 釦 鈪 鉭 鍋 鋦 鍋 鍋 鍋	sauce pan, cooking pot
			wò	guō
2934 *	鍵	金 釒 釓 釒 鍅 鍽 鍵 鍵 鍵	key; keyboard
			gihn	jiàn
2935 *	鍛	金 釒 釘 釫 鍒 鍛 鍛 鍛 鍛	to forge metal
			dyun	duàn
2936 *	鍘	金 釒 釦 鉬 鉬 鍘 鍘	lever-knife
			jaat	zhá
2937 *	鍊	金 釒 釒 鉬 鋼 鋼 鍊 鍊	to forge metal, refine; chain
			lihn	liàn
2938 *	鍬	金 釒 釩 釬 鉄 鍬 鍬 鍬 鍬	spade, hoe
			chìu	qiāo
2939 *	鍍	金 釒 釒 鉝 鈝 鈝 鍍 鍍 鍍 鍍	to gild, plate
			douh	dù
2940 *	錨	金 釒 釬 鉬 鉪 錨 錨 錨 錨	anchor
			naàuh	máo
2941 *	鎚	金 釒 釘 鈝 鈝 鋼 鎚 鎚 鎚	to hammer; hammer
			chèuih	chúi

2942 *	鎖	金 釒 釒' 釒" 鎖 鎖 鎖 鎖	lock; to lock	
			só	suǒ
2943 *	鎬	金 金' 金' 釒 釒 釒 釒 釒 釒 鎬	[1] bright; [2] mattock, [2] pick	
			[1] houh; [2] góu	[1] hào; [2] gǎo
2944 *	鎮	金 金 釒 釒 釒 釒 釒 鎮 鎮	to repress, calm; town	
			jan	zhèn
2945 *	鎗	金 釒 釒 釒 釒 釒 釒 釒 鎗 鎗 鎗	gun, pistol	
			chèung	qiāng
2946 *	鎊	金 金 金 釒 釒 釒 釒 釒 鎊 鎊	pound (currency)	
			bohng	bàng
2947 **	鏡	金 金 金 金 釒 釒 鏡 鏡 鏡 鏡 鏡 鏡	mirror, lens	
			geng	jìng
2948 *	鏇	金 釒 釕 釙 釙 釙 鏇 鏇 鏇 鏇 鏇	to whirl; lathe	
			syùhn	xuàn
2949 *	鏟	金 金 釒 釒 釒 釒 鏟 鏟 鏟 鏟	spade, shovel	
			cháan	chǎn
2950 ***	鐘	金 金 釒 釕 金 釒 鐘 鐘 鐘 鐘 鐘	bell, clock, hour	
			jùng	zhōng
2951 *	鐝	金 金 釬 釓 釓 鐝 鐝 鐝 鐝 鐝 鐝 鐝	pick, hoe	
			kyut	jué
2952 **	鐵	金 釒 釒 釒 鐵 鐵 鐵 鐵 鐵 鐵 鐵	iron; firm	
			tit	tiě
2953 *	鐮	金 釒 釒 釒 釒 釒 鐮 鐮 鐮 鐮 鐮	sickle, scythe	
			lìhm	lián
2954 *	鑑	金 金 釔 釕 釓 鑑 鑑 鑑 鑑 鑑 鑑 鑑	to examine, reflect; mirror	
			gaam	jiàn

2955 *	鑄	金 金' 釒' 釒 鈝 鈝 鈝 鈝 鑄 鑄 鑄 鑄 鑄 鑄	to cast; cast iron
			jyu *zhù*
2956 *	鑰	釒 釒 釒 釒 釒 釒 釒 釒 鑰 鑰 鑰 鑰 鑰 鑰	[1] key, [2] lock
			[1][2] *yeuhk* [1] *yào;* [2] *yuè*
2957 *	鑲	釒 釒 釒 釒 釒 釒 鈰 鈰 鑲 鑲 鑲 鑲 鑲 鑲	to inlay, border
			seùng *xiǎng*
2958 *	鑽	金 釒 釒 釒 鈝 鈝 鈝 鈝 鑽 鑽 鑽 鑽 鑽	[1] to drill, [1] go through, [1] go in; [2] drill
			[1][2] *jyun* [1] *zuān;* [2] *zuàn*
2959 *	鑼	金 釒 釒 釒 釒 釒 釒 釒 鑼 鑼 鑼 鑼 鑼 鑼	gong
			lòh *luó*

長 Section

| 2960 *** | 長 | 一 丁 F 王 乒 長 長 | [1] length, [1] strong point, [2] chief; [1] long, [2] older; [2] to grow |
| | | | [1] *cheùhng;* [2] *jeúng*   [1] *cháng;* [2] *zhǎng* |

門 Section

2961 ***	門	丨 丨 丨 丬 丬 丬 門	door, gate, entrance
			mùhn *mén*
2962 *	閃	門 閃 閃 閃	to flash, avoid
			sím *shǎn*
2963 *	閉	門 閇 閉 閉	to close, shut
			bai *bì*
2964 ***	開	門 開 開	to open, begin, drive
			hòi *kāi*
2965 ***	間	門 門 間 間 間	[1] between; [1] measure word for buildings; [2] space; [2] indirect
			[1] *gaàn;* [2] *gaan* [1] *jiān;* [2] *jiàn*

2966 **	閒	門 門 閈 閒	idle, leisure
			haàhn *xián*
2967 *	閘	門 門 閂 閘 閘 閘	floodgate
			jaahp *zhá*
2968 *	閣	門 門 閃 閃 閣 閣 閣 閣	mezzanine
			gok *gé*
2969 *	閨	門 閂 門 閂 閨 閨	boudoir
			gwài *gūi*
2970 *	閥	門 門 門 閅 閥 閥 閥	military, valve
			faht *fá*
2971 *	閱	門 閂 門 閱 閱 閱 閱	to inspect, read
			yuht *yuè*
2972 *	闊	門 閂 閅 閅 閅 閣 閣 闊	broad, wide, extravagant
			fut *kuò*
2973 *	闖	門 閂 閅 閅 閅 閣 闖	to rush in, enter abruptly
			chóng *chuǎng*
2974 **	關	門 閂 閆 閆 關 關 關 關 關	to close, arrest, turn off; gate, bolt
			gwàan *guān*
2975 *	闢	門 閂 閂 閂 閂 閣 閣 閣 閣 闢 闢 闢	to open, develop, deny (rumor)
			pìk *pì*

阜   Section

2976 *	阜	′ ′ ′ ′ 自 阜 阜	mound of earth; abundant
			fauh *fù*
2977 **	防	′ ′ ′ ′ ′ 阝 防 防	to defend, prevent
			fòhng *fáng*

2978 *	阱	阝 阼 阱	trap, pit
			jihng　　　　　　　jǐng
2979 *	阻	阝 阝丨 阽 阻 阻	to obstruct, hinder
			jó　　　　　　　　zǔ
2980 *	阿	阝 阝丶 阝一 阝可 阝可 阿	[1] to flatter; article for: a) [2] addressing some-one b) [3] exclamation point c) [4] ending phr. [1] ò; [2] a; [3] ǎ; [4] à　　[1] e; [2] á; [3] ǎ; [4] a
2981 *	附	阝 阝丶 阝丨 阝忄 附 附	to attach; appendix
			fuh　　　　　　　fù
2982 *	陋	阝 阝一 阝丆 阝丙 陋 陋 陋	vulgar, vile, narrow, humble
			lauh　　　　　　　loù
2983 **	限	阝 阝丶 阝彐 阝彐 阝艮 阝艮 限	boundary, limit; to restrict
			haahn　　　　　　xiàn
2984 *	降	阝 阝丶 阝夂 阝癶 阝夂 降 降	[1] to descend, [1] fall, [1] degrade, [2] surrender [1] gong; [2] hòhng　[1] jiàng; [2] xiáng
2985 *	陞	阝 阝丶 阝乀 阝丼 阝丼 阝丼 陞	to rise, raise
			sìng　　　　　　　shēng
2986 **	院	阝 阝丶 阝宀 阝宀 阝宀 陀 院	courtyard, hall
			yún　　　　　　　yuàn
2987 *	陝	阝 阝丶 阝忄 阝夾 陝 陝	Shanhsien in Hunan China
			sím　　　　　　　shǎn
2988 *	陣	阝 阝丆 阝一 阝丙 陌 陌 陣	line of troops, moment
			jahn　　　　　　　zhèn
2989 **	除	阝 阝丶 阝人 阝佘 阝佘 除	to get rid of, divide, deduct, exclude
			cheùih　　　　　　chú
2990 *	陪	阝 阝丶 阝亠 阝咅 阝咅 阝陪 陪 陪	to accompany
			pùih　　　　　　　peí

2991 *	陳	了 阝 阝 阡 阼 陌 陣 陳	to display, state; old (object)	
			chàhn	chén
2992 *	陶	了 阝 阝 阢 阺 陶 陶 陶	earthware, pottery; happy	
			tòuh	táo
2993 *	陷	了 阝 阝 阽 阽 阽 陷 陷 陷	to fall, sink, capture, betray	
			hahm	xiàn
2994 **	陸	了 阝 阝 阡 阹 陕 陸	land; six	
			luhk	lù
2995 **	陰	了 阝 阶 阶 阶 陰 陰 陰 陰	feminine; shade; gloomy, cloudy	
			yàm	yīn
2996 **	陽	了 阝 阝 阴 阳 阳 陽 陽 陽	masculine; sun	
			yeùhng	yáng
2997 **	隊	了 阝 阽 阹 陊 陊 隊 隊	group, team	
			deuih	duì
2998 **	階	了 阝 阶 阰 阰 陛 陛 階 階 階	stairs, grade	
			gàai	jiē
2999 *	隆	了 阝 阽 阹 降 降 隆 隆	prosperity; abundant, raised	
			luhng	lóng
3000 *	隔	了 丆 阝 阿 阿 阿 隔 隔 隔 隔 隔	to separate; every other (day, month, etc)	
			gaak	gé
3001 *	隙	了 阝 阝 阴 阳 陊 階 階 隆 隙	gap, opportunity, grudge	
			gwìk	xì
3002 **	際	了 阝 阽 陊 陊 陊 際 際 際	boundary; at the time, during	
			jai	jì
3003 *	障	了 阝 阷 阷 陪 陪 陪 陪 障	obstruction, barrier	
			jeung	zhàng

3004 *	隧	ⱀ ⱀ ⱀ ⱀ 阤 阬 陟 陟 隊 隊 隊 隧	subway, tunnel
			seuih　　　　　sùi
3005 **	隨	ⱀ ⱀ 阝 阽 阽 阽 阽 隋 隋 隋 隨 隨	to follow, accompany
			cheùih　　　　súi
3006 **	險	ⱀ 阝 阽 阽 阽 阽 阽 阽 險 險	danger; dangerous, malicious; almost
			hím　　　　　xiǎn
3007 *	隱	阝 阝 阽 阽 阽 阽 阽 阽 隱 隱 隱	indistinct; to hide, conceal
			yán　　　　　yǐn

<h3 align="center">隶　Section</h3>

| 3008 * | 隸 | 一 十 木 杢 李 杀 柰 𥝢 𣂑 𦎿 𣂑 𣂑 隸 隸 | slave, subordinate, a style of Chinese calligraphy |
| | | | daih　　　　　lì |

<h3 align="center">隹　Section</h3>

3009 *	隻	ノ イ イ 仁 什 隹 隹 隻	one, single; measure word for animals
			jek　　　　　zhī
3010 *	雀	⺊ 小 少 雀	small birds, sparrow
			jeuk　　　　　què
3011 *	雇	宀 宀 户 雇	to hire, rent
			gu　　　　　gù
3012 **	雄	一 ナ ナ 左 雄	masculine, male, strong; hero
			hùhng　　　　xióng
3013 *	雅	一 工 牙 牙 雅	elegant, refined
			ngáh　　　　　yǎ
3014 *	雁	一 厂 厂 厈 厓 雁	wild goose
			ngaahn　　　　yàn

3015 **	集	隹 隹 隹 集	to gather; collection of essays or poetry
			jaahp jí
3016 *	雌	㇒ ㇠ 止 此 此 雌	female, feminine
			chì cí
3017 *	雕	㇒ 冂 月 月 月 周 周 周 雕	to carve, engrave
			diù diāo
3018 ***	雖	㇒ 口 吕 吊 虽 虽 雖	although
			seùi suī
3019 **	雙	隹 雔 雔 雙	a pair; even, double
			seùng shuāng
3020 *	雛	㇒ 勹 匀 匀 匃 芻 雛	young bird
			chò chú
3021 **	雜	丶 亠 广 大 卒 卒 卒 杂 雜	mixed, confused, assorted; miscellaneous
			jaahp zá
3022 **	雞	㇒ 爫 爭 爭 奚 奚 奚 雞	chicken, hen, rooster
			gài jī
3023 ***	離	丶 亠 亣 产 卤 卤 离 离 离 離	to depart, separate; distance
			leìh lí
3024 ***	難	㇐ 艹 艹 世 芁 芺 芺 菓 菓 難	[1] difficult; [2] distress, [2] disaster
			[1] naàhn; [2] naahn [1][2] nàn

雨   Section

3025 **	雨	㇐ 冂 闩 雨 雨 雨	rain
			yúh yǔ
3026 *	雪	雨 雫 雪 雪	snow
			syut xuě

3027 **	雲	雪 雪 雪 雲 雲	clouds
			wàhn　　　　　　yún

3028 *	零	雷 雫 雫 雫 零 零	zero, fractional
			lìhng　　　　　　líng

3029 ***	電	雫 雫 雫 雫 雷 電	electricity, lightning; electrical
			dihn　　　　　　diàn

3030 *	雷	雫 雫 雫 雪 雷 雷	thunder, radar
			leùih　　　　　　léi

3031 *	需	雫 雫 雫 雫 雫 需	to need, require; necessity
			seùi　　　　　　xū

3032 *	震	雫 雪 雫 雫 雫 震	to tremble, shake
			jan　　　　　　zhèn

3033 *	霉	雫 雫 雫 雲 雫 霉 霉	mildew, mold
			mùih　　　　　　méi

3034 *	霍	雫 雫 雫 雫 雫 霍	quickly; cholera
			fok　　　　　　huò

3035 *	霜	雫 雫 雫 雫 霜 霜 霜 霜	frost
			seùng　　　　　　shuāng

3036 *	霞	雫 雫 雫 雫 雫 雫 雫 霞	vapor
			hàh　　　　　　xiá

3037 *	霧	雫 雫 雫 雲 雫 雫 雫 雫 雫 雫 霧 霧	fog, mist
			mouh　　　　　　wù

3038 *	露	雫 雫 雫 雫 雫 雫 雫 雫 霞 霞 露 露	[1] dew; [2] to expose, [2] disclose
			[1] [2] louh　　　　　　[1] lù; [2] lòu

3039 *	霸	雫 雫 雫 雫 雫 雫 雫 雫 雫 霸 霸 霸	tyrant
			ba　　　　　　bà

| 3040 * | 霹 | 雫 雫 雫 雫 雫 霄 霄 霹 霹 霹 霹 霹 | thunderclap |
| | | | *pik* ・ ・ ・ ・ *pī* |

| 3041 * | 靈 | 雫 雫 雫 雫 雫 雫 雫 雫 靁 靁 靈 靈 | soul, spirit |
| | | | *lìhng* ・ ・ ・ ・ *líng* |

青　Section

| 3042 ** | 青 | 一 十 主 丰 青 青 | green, young |
| | | | *chìng* ・ ・ ・ ・ *qīng* |

| 3043 ** | 靜 | 青 青 靑 靜 靜 靜 靜 | quiet, calm, peaceful |
| | | | *jihng* ・ ・ ・ ・ *jìng* |

非　Section

| 3044 ** | 非 | 丿 彐 乬 非 | no, not; mistake |
| | | | *fēi* ・ ・ ・ ・ *fēi* |

| 3045 ** | 靠 | 丿 亠 牛 生 牛 告 告 靠 | to rely on, be near, lean against |
| | | | *kaau* ・ ・ ・ ・ *kào* |

面　Section

| 3046 ** | 面 | 一 了 了 丙 而 而 面 | face, surface, side; measure word for mirrors and flags |
| | | | *mihn* ・ ・ ・ ・ *miàn* |

革　Section

| 3047 ** | 革 | 丶 十 艹 世 芇 苗 苗 苗 革 | leather; to change, remove, revolt |
| | | | *gaap* ・ ・ ・ ・ *gé* |

| 3048 * | 靶 | 革 革 靪 靶 靶 | target |
| | | | *bá* ・ ・ ・ ・ *bǎ* |

3049 *	靴	革 革′ 靪 靪′ 靴	boots
			heù　　　　　　　xuē
3050 **	鞋	革 革― 革十 鞋士 鞋	shoes
			haàih　　　　　　xié
3051 *	鞏	一 丅 工 刃 巩 巩 鞏	firm; to strengthen
			góng　　　　　　gǒng
3052 *	鞍	革 革′ 革 靴 靫 鞍 鞍	saddle
			òn　　　　　　　ān
3053 *	鞭	革 革 靪 靪′ 靪 靪 靪 靪 靪 鞭 鞭	whip; to whip
			bìn　　　　　　　biān

韋　Section

3054 *	韋	一 ユ 土 卉 吉 吉 声 壹 韋	soft leather
			wáih　　　　　　wéi
3055 *	韌	(靭) 丨 十 卄 艹 艹 苎 莒 革 靪 靭 靭	tenacious, tough
			yahn　　　　　　rèn
3056 *	韓	一 十 卉 古 古 吉 直 車 韓	Korea
			hòhn　　　　　　hán

音　Section

3057 ***	音	、 二 さ 立 产 音 音 音	sound, voice, tone, news
			yàm　　　　　　yīn
3058 *	韻	音 音′ 音阝 韵 韵 韻 韻 韻 韻	rhyme
			wáhn　　　　　　yùn
3059 **	響	く 乡 幺′ 乡 幺′ 乡幺 绊 绯 绯 绯 響	sound; loud
			héung　　　　　　xiǎng

	頁	Section	

3060 *	頁	一 ア 了 百 百 首 頁	page, sheet
			yihp yeh
3061 **	頂	一 丁 頂	the top; to support by the head, offend
			díng dǐng
3062 **	項	一 丁 工 項	item
			hohng xiàng
3063 **	順	ノ 川 順	smoothly, favorable, compliant; at one's convenience
			seuhn shùn
3064 **	須	彡 須	must, ought to
			seùi xū
3065 *	頌	八 公 公 頌	to praise
			juhng sòng
3066 **	預	ㄱ マ ヱ 予 預	pre-...; to prepare
			yuh yù
3067 *	頑	ニ テ 元 頑	obstinate, naughty
			waahn wán
3068 *	頒	八 分 分 頒	to award, proclaim
			baan bān
3069 **	頓	一 ㄷ ㅁ 屯 頓	to pause, stamp foot, bow head; suddenly
			deuhn dùn
3070 **	領	ノ 人 人 今 令 領	collar, talent and ability; to lead, receive, understand
			líhng lǐng
3071 *	頗	ㄱ 厂 广 広 皮 頗	very, somewhat
			pó pō

3072 ***	頭	一 厂 厂 百 丐 豆 頭	head, chief; measure word for animals; first
			taùh — toú
3073 *	頰	一 ナ ナ ヌ 夾 夾 頰	cheek
			gaap — jiá
3074 *	頸	一 丞 丞 巠 巠 頸	neck
			geńg — jǐng
3075 *	頷	ノ 人 人 今 今 合 合 頷	chin, jaw
			háhm — hàn
3076 *	頹	ノ 彡 千 禾 禾 秃 頹	depressed; to sink, collapse
			teùih — tuí
3077 *	頻	丨 ト 止 止 牛 步 步 頻	frequent, hurried
			pàhn — pín
3078 *	顆	丨 冂 曰 日 旦 果 果 顆	grain, measure word for small round things
			fó — kē
3079 *	額	丶 宀 宀 宀 宀 宊 宊 宊 客 客 額	forehead, fixed number
			ngaahk — é
3080 **	題	丨 冂 月 日 旦 早 是 是 題	subject, topic; to name
			taìh — tí
3081 *	顏	丶 亠 文 立 产 彦 顏	color, face
			ngàahn — yán
3082 **	願	一 厂 厂 厂 厎 厎 厡 厡 原 願	willing; to wish for; wish
			yuhn — yùan
3083 *	顛	一 匕 匕 匕 眞 眞 眞 顛	the highest place; to upset
			dìn — diān
3084 **	類	丷 丷 半 米 类 类 類	kind, sort
			leuih — lèi

3085 *	顧	丶亠广户户户户 雇 顧	to look back, look after, consider
			gu　　　　　　　gù
3086 *	顫	丶亠广肻肻肻肻 肻肻肻肻肻顫	to tremble, shiver
			jin　　　　　　zhàn
3087 **	顯	丶口曰四旦显显 显显顯	apparent; to show
			hín　　　　　　xiǎn
3088 *	顴	丶十艹艹莳莳莳 莳莳莳莳莳顴	cheekbones
			kyùhn　　　　　quán

風　Section

3089 **	風	丿几凡凡凤 凤凤風風	wind, breeze
			fùng　　　　　fēng
3090 *	颳	風風颳颳 颳颳颳	blowing of the wind
			gwaat　　　　guā
3091 *	颶	風風颶颶颶 颶	cyclone, hurricane
			geuih　　　　jù
3092 *	飄	一丶襾西西票票 票飄	to float
			piu　　　　　piāo

飛　Section

3093 ***	飛	㇟飞飞飞飞 飞飛飛	to fly
			fèi　　　　　fēi

食　Section

3094 **	食	丿人人今今 今食食食食	to eat, break a promise; food
			sihk　　　　shí

3095 *	飢	ノ 人 人 今 今 今 食 食 飠 飢	hunger; hungry gèi　　　　　jī
3096 **	飲	食 飠 飠 飩 飲	to drink; drink yám　　　　　yǐn
3097 ***	飯	食 食 飣 飣 飯	cooked rice, meal faahn　　　　fàn
3098 *	飾	食 飠 飠 飭 飾 飾	to decorate, act as; decoration sik　　　　　shì
3099 *	飼	食 飣 飼 飼 飼 飼	to feed, nourish jih　　　　　sì
3100 **	飽	食 食 飠 飽 飽 飽	to eat until full; satisfied baáu　　　　bǎo
3101 *	餃	食 食 飠 飠 飠 餃 餃	dumpling, ravioli gaáu　　　　jiǎo
3102 *	蝕	食 食 飠 飩 飩 蝕 蝕	to corrode, lose sihk　　　　shí
3103 **	養	丷 丷 羊 羔 養	to raise, bring up, maintain, nourish yeúhng　　　yǎng
3104 *	餅	食 食 飠 餅	biscuit, cookie béng　　　　bǐng
3105 *	餐	一 卜 ┌ 歺 歺 叔 叔 叔 叔 餐	meal chàan　　　　cān
3106 **	餓	食 食 飠 飠 餅 餅 餓 餓	hungry, starving ngoh　　　　è
3107 **	餘	食 飠 飠 飠 飠 餘	remainder, surplus yùh　　　　yú

3108 ***	館	食 食` 飠` 飠' 飭 飭 館 館	dwelling, restaurant *gwún*　　　　　*guǎn*
3109 *	饑	食 食` 飠` 飠 飠" 饑 饑 饑 饑 饑 饑	famine, hunger; hungry *gèi*　　　　　*jī*
3110 *	饒	食 食` 飠` 飠 飠 飠' 飠 飠 饒	to forgive; abundant *yìuh*　　　　　*raó*
	首　Section		
3111 **	首	` ` 丷 丷 ' 广 方 首 首	head, chief, leader; measure word for poems *saú*　　　　　*shoǔ*
	香　Section		
3112 **	香	ノ 一 千 禾 禾 香 香 香	smells good, fragrant; incense *heùng*　　　　　*xiāng*
3113 *	馨	一 十 士 声 吉 声 声 声 声 鼓 馨	fragrant *hìng*　　　　　*xīn*
	馬　Section		
3114 ***	馬	一 丆 F 丐 馬 馬	horse *máh*　　　　　*mǎ*
3115 *	馳	馬 馬' 馳' 馳	to gallop; fast *chìh*　　　　　*chí*
3116 *	馴	馬 馴	mild; to tame *sèuhn*　　　　　*xún*
3117 *	駁	馬 駁' 駁	to argue, reject *bok*　　　　　*bó*

3118 *	駐	馬 馬` 馬` 馰 駐	to stay, station jyu　　　　　　　zhù
3119 *	駕	宀 力 加 加 加 駕	to drive, manage ga　　　　　　　jià
3120 *	駛	馬 馬` 馬⁊ 馬口 駛 駛	to drive, sail sái　　　　　　　shǐ
3121 *	駝	馬 馬` 馬` 馬宀 駝 駝	camel; hunchbacked tòh　　　　　　tuó
3122 *	駭	馬 馬` 馰 駐 駭 駭 駭	terrified, startled hoih　　　　　　hài
3123 *	騎	馬 馬- 馬ナ 馬ナ 駐ナ 駐 騎 騎 騎	to ride kèh　　　　　　　qí
3124 **	騙	馬 馬` 馬ヶ 駇 駇 駝 騙 騙	to cheat, deceive pin　　　　　　piàn
3125 *	騷	馬 馬ヮ 駁 駁 馬ヌ 駁 騷 騷 騷 騷	to disturb, riot sòu　　　　　　sāo
3126 *	騰	ノ 刀 月 月ヽ 扩 胖 朕 騰	to run, leap, spare tàhng　　　　　téng
3127 *	驅	馬 馬ヮ 駈 駈 駈 駈 驅 驅	to expel, drive away kèui　　　　　　qū
3128 *	騾	馬 馬` 馬ヮ 駟 駟 駟 騾 騾 騾 騾 騾	mule leùih　　　　　luó
3129 *	驕	馬 馬` 馬ケ 駮 駮 騂 騂 騂 騂 騂 騂	to be proud; arrogant giù　　　　　　jiāo
3130 **	驗	馬 馬` 馬ヽ 駼 駼 駼 駼 駼 駼 駼	to examine, inspect; experience yihm　　　　　yàn

3131 *	驚	丶 一 艹 艹 芍 芍 苟 苟 苟 荷 敬 敬 驚	frightened ging	jīng
3132 *	驟	馬 馬 馬 馬 馬 馬 馬 馬 駿 駿 駿 驟	quickly, suddenly jaauh	zhòu
3133 *	驢	馬 馬 馬 馬 馬 馬 馬 馬 馬 驢 驢 驢	donkey lòuh	lǘ

骨   Section

3134 *	骨	丶 冂 冎 冎 骨 骨 骨 骨	bones gwat	gǔ
3135 *	骯	骨 骨 骨 骯 骯	dirty, filthy hòng	āng
3136 *	骼	骨 骨 骨 骼 骼 骼 骼	bones, skeleton gaak	gé
3137 *	髒	骨 骨 骨 骨 骨 骨 骨 骨 髒 髒 髒	dirty, filthy jòng	zāng
3138 **	體	骨 骨 骨 骨 骨 體 體 體 體 體 體 體	body, style; physical tái	tǐ

高   Section

3139 ***	高	丶 亠 亠 亠 高 高 高 高	tall, high, noble gòu	gāo

髟   Section

3140 *	髮	一 厂 F 三 長 長 髟 髟 髟 髟 髮 髮	hair faat	fǎ

3141 **	鬆	髟 髟 髟 髟 髟 鬆 鬆	loose, relaxing, disordered; to loosen
			sùng　　　　　sōng
3142 *	鬍	髟 髟 髟 髟 髟 髟 髟 鬍 鬍	mustache
			wùh　　　　　hú
3143 *	鬚	髟 髟 髟 髟 髟 髟 鬚 鬚 鬚	beard, whiskers
			soù　　　　　xū

鬥　Section

3144 **	鬥	一 丁 王 王 臣 臣 鬥 鬥 鬥 鬥	to fight, struggle
			dau　　　　　dòu
3145 **	鬧	鬥 鬥 鬧 鬧 鬧 鬧	to quarrel, make a disturbance, cause; noisy
			naauh　　　　nào
3146 *	鬨	鬥 鬥 鬥 鬨 鬨 鬨	lots of people making lots of noise
			hung　　　　hòng

鬯　Section

| 3147 * | 鬱 | 一 十 木 术 机 柈 椎 梅 樹 棩 槠 槠 磓 鬱 鬱 鬱 鬱 | grieved, sad |
| | | | wàt　　　　　yù |

鬼　Section

3148 **	鬼	丿 亻 竹 白 白 由 鬼 鬼 鬼 鬼	ghost, spirit of the dead
			gwái　　　　guǐ
3149 *	魁	鬼 魁 魁 魁	leader; great, highest
			fùi　　　　　kúi
3150 *	魂	二 云 云 魂	soul, spirit
			wàhn　　　　hún

3151 *	魄	ノ イ 竹 白 白 魄	soul, spirit	
			paak	po`
3152 *	魅	鬼 鬽 魅 魅	demon, charm, attraction	
			meih	mèi
3153 *	魔	、 一 广 广 疒 床 麻 魔	demon, devil; magical	
			mò	mó

魚　Section

3154 ***	魚	ノ ク ケ 角 角 角 角 魚	fish	
			yùh	yú
3155 *	鮑	魚 魚' 魚勹 魥 魥 鮑	abalone	
			baàu	bào
3156 **	鮮	魚 魚' 鮮 鮮	fresh, new	
			sìn	xiān
3157 *	鯉	魚 魚 魚口 魚口 魚旦 鯉 鯉	carp	
			léih	lǐ
3158 *	鯊	氵 氵丿 氵小 沙 沙 鯊	shark	
			sà	shā
3159 *	鯨	魚 魚 魚宀 魚宀 鯨 鯨 鯨 鯨	whale	
			kìhng	jīng
3160 *	鰓	魚 魚 魚勹 魚田 魚田 鰓 鰓 鰓 鰓	gills of a fish	
			sòi	sāi
3161 *	鰥	魚 魚 魚勹 魚罒 魚田 鰥 鰥 鰥 鰥	widower	
			gwàan	guān
3162 *	鰵	ノ 一 匕 与 每 每 鰵 鰵 鰵 鰵	cod	
			máhn	mǐn

3163 *	鱗	魚 魚 魚 魣 魣 鮴 鯦 鯗 鱗 鱗 鱗	scales of a fish
			leùhn lìn
3164 *	鱷	魚 魚 魛 魟 魛 魛 魟 鮃 鮃 鱷 鱷 鱷	crocodile, alligator
			ngohk e`

鳥 Section

3165 **	鳥	ノ イ ビ 户 户 島 鳥 鳥	bird
			liúh niǎo
3166 *	鳳	） 几 凡 凡 鳳	male phoenix
			fuhng fèng
3167 *	鳴	丶 丨 口 口 鳴	to chirp; cry of a bird, noise
			mìhng míng
3168 *	鴉	一 匚 牙 牙 鴉	crow
			ngà yā
3169 *	鴨	丶 口 口 日 甲 鴨	duck
			ngaap yā
3170 *	鴦	丶 口 冖 屮 央 鴦	drake Mandarin duck
			yeùng yāng
3171 *	鴛	’ ク タ タ 夗 鴛	female Mandarin duck
			yùn yuān
3172 *	鴿	ノ 人 𠆢 今 合 合 鴿	dove, pigeon
			gap, gaap gē
3173 *	鵑	丶 口 口 尸 𢎘 肙 鵑	cuckoo
			gyùn juān
3174 *	鵝	’ 二 千 毛 我 我 我 鵝	goose
			ngòh é

3175 *	鵲	⎟ 十 卄 廿 芉 芌 昔 昔 鵲	magpie	
			jeuk	*què*
3176 *	鶯	⎟ ⎞ 少 火 炏 炏 炏 鶯	nightingale	
			ngàng	*yīng*
3177 *	鶴	⎞ 宀 少 才 宇 宇 宇 寉 鶴	crane	
			hohk	*hè*
3178 *	鷗	一 匚 匚 匝 匹 匝 區 鷗	seagull	
			ngàu	*ōu*
3179 *	鷹	、 亠 广 广 疒 疒 府 府 疒 雁 鷹	eagle, hawk	
			yìng	*yīng*
3180 *	鸚	⎟ 冂 月 目 貝 貝 賏 賏 賏 嬰 鸚	parrot	
			yìng	*yīng*

| | 鹵 | Section | | |

3181 *	鹹 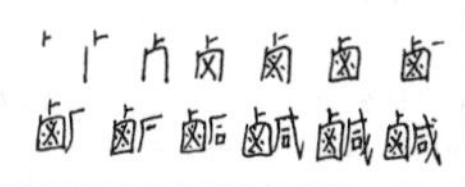	�⎟ 广 片 卤 卤 卤 卤 卤 卤 鹵 鹵 鹹 鹹 鹹	salty	
			haàhm	*xián*
3182 *	鹽	一 丁 丂 玉 玉 臣 臤 臨 臨 鹽 鹽 鹽 鹽	salt	
			yìhm	*yán*

| | 鹿 | Section | | |

3183 *	鹿	、 亠 广 庐 庐 庐 鹿 鹿 鹿 鹿	deer	
			luhk	*lù*
3184 *	麗	一 广 币 币 丽 麗	beautiful, graceful	
			laih	*lì*
3185 *	麟	鹿 鹿 鹿 鹿 鹿 麟 麟 麟 麟 麟 麟 麟	female unicorn	
			leùhn	*lín*

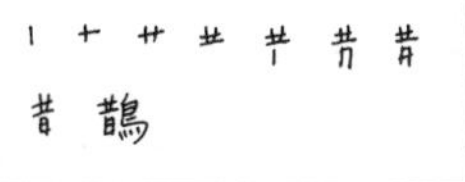

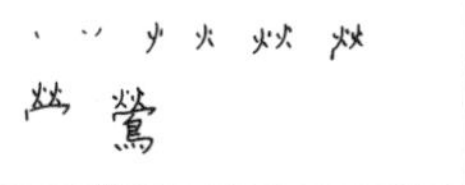

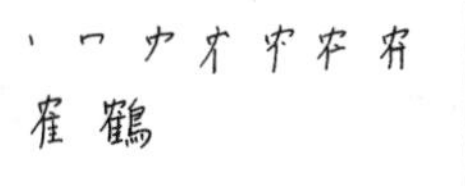

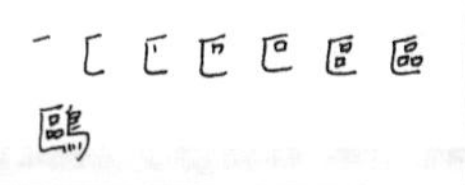

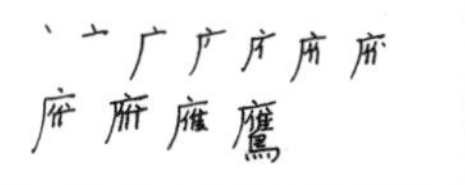

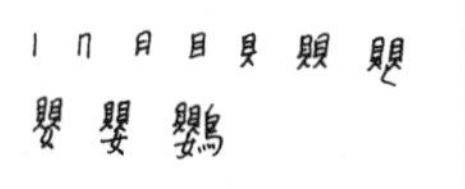

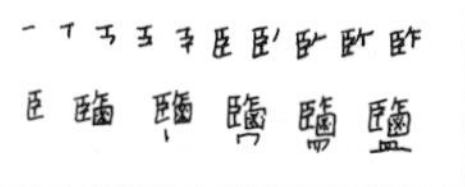

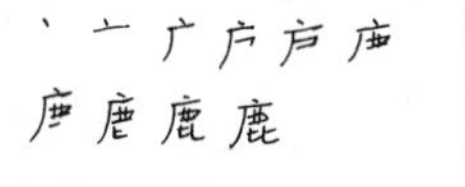

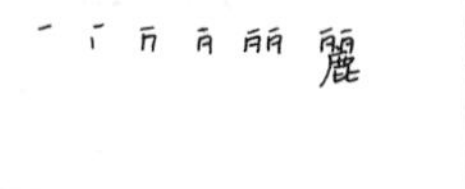

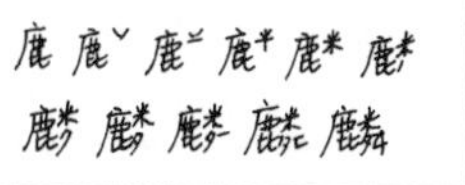

		麥 Section	

		麥 Section	
3186 **	麥	一 十 ォ ォ ぁ 未 夾 麥 麥 麥	wheat *mahk* *mài*
3187 *	麵	麥 麥 麵 麵 麵 麵 麵 麵	noodles *mihn* *miàn*

		麻 Section	
3188 **	麻	丶 宀 广 广 庁 床 麻	hemp, flax; numb *màh* *má*
3189 ***	麼	麻 麻 麼 麼	[1] [3] an interrogative particle; [2] what; [3] such [1] [2] *mà;* [3] *mò* [1] *ma;* [2] *má;* [3] *me*

		黃 Section	
3190 **	黃	丶 一 卄 艹 共 共 莆 莆 蕾 黃 黃	yellow *wòhng* *huáng*

		黍 Section	
3191 *	黍	丿 一 十 禾 禾 季 黍 黍	millet *syú* *shǔ*
3192 *	黎	禾 禾 利 勿 黎	people, dawn; black *làih* *lí*
3193 *	黏	黍 黍 黏 黏 黏 黏	adhesive; to glue; glutinous *nìm* *niàn*

		黑 Section	

3194 **	黑	丶 冖 四 四 里 黑	black, dark
			hàk　　　　　hēi
3195 *	默	里 黑 默 默 默 默	silent, quiet
			mahk　　　　mò
3196 ***	點	黑 黑 點 點 點 點	dot, point, drops, hour; to point, check, nod
			dím　　　　diǎn
3197 **	黨	丨 ⺌ ⺌ 兴 尚 尚 尚 黨	political party, league
			dóng　　　dǎng

	鼎 Section

3198 *	鼎	丨 冂 月 目 目 鼎 鼎 鼎 鼎 鼎 鼎 鼎	caldron, firm
			díng　　　dǐng

	鼓 Section

3199 *	鼓	一 十 士 吉 吉 吉 壴 壴 壴 鼓 鼓 鼓	drum; to clap, rouse
			gú　　　　gǔ

	鼠 Section

3200 *	鼠	丶 亻 亻 亻 臼 臼 臼 鼠 鼠	rat, squirrel
			syú　　　shǔ

	鼻 Section

3201 *	鼻	丶 丿 白 自 自 鳥 鳥 鳥 鼻 鼻 鼻	nose
			beih　　　bí
3202 *	鼾	鼻 鼻 鼾	snore
			hòhn　　　hān

		齊 Section
3203 **	齊	` ⺀ 亠 亣 亣 亣 亦 亦 亦 亦 亦 齊 齊` even, together, complete; orderly *chàih* — *qí*
3204 *	齋	齊 齋 齋 vegetarian *jàai* — *zhāi*

		齒 Section
3205 *	齒	`丨 卜 止 止 尘 步 步 齿 齿 齿 歯 齒 齒` teeth *chí* — *chǐ*
3206 *	齡	齒 齒 齒人 齒令 齒令 齡 age *lìhng* — *líng*
3207 *	齣	齒 齒 齣 齣 齣 齣 a scene in a play *chèut* — *chū*

		龍 Section
3208 *	龍	` ⺀ 亠 ⺊ 立 产 产 育 育 育 龍 龍 龍` dragon *lùhng* — *lóng*

		龜 Section
3209 *	龜	`丿 勹 勹 ⺈ ⺈ 虍 色 色 龟 龟 龟 龟 龟 龜 龜 龜` tortoise *gwài* — *gūi*

		侖 Section
3210 *	侖	`丿 人 入 个 合 合 侖 侖 侖 侖 侖 侖` flute *yeuhk* — *yuè*

INDEX

*** Character Index

修 133	紙 2179	帳 831	責 2678	硬 2018	損 1203	疑 1921
倍 139	缺 2235	強 892	貨 2680	程 2069	搶 1204	盡 1973
倒 141	臭 2356	惜 989	軟 2765	童 2102	敬 1286	睡 1992
准 236	般 2371	推 1147	野 2891	答 2112	新 1307	種 2071
剛 280	茶 2399	掛 1148	陸 2994	統 2189	暗 1358	稱 2073
哥 443	荒 2400	掃 1150	陰 2995	絕 2191	暖 1359	管 2122
哭 444	草 2406	掉 1163	頂 3061	結 2192	極 1500	算 2123
夏 593	被 2525	排 1164	鳥 3165	絲 2194	歲 1562	節 2126
套 616	記 2572	接 1170	麥 3186	腦 2332	滅 1698	精 2154
娘 655	討 2573	救 1276	麻 3188	菜 2417	照 1789	緊 2206
孫 695	訓 2576	敗 1278	備 168	補 2536	煤 1793	線 2207
害 721	財 2676	族 1314	剩 285	費 2687	碎 2020	聞 2281
展 771	起 2722	既 1318	創 286	越 2724	碰 2022	與 2361
師 827	通 2807	望 1388	勝 306	達 2828	福 2047	蓋 2437
席 828	造 2814	殺 1575	勞 307	遍 2832	禍 2048	認 2604
弱 890	透 2817	深 1663	啊 461	運 2834	罪 2238	誤 2610
恩 957	酒 2870	清 1665	善 463	郵 2862	羣 2250	趕 2726
息 959	針 2896	混 1667	喊 470	鄉 2864	義 2251	輕 2769
恐 963	院 2986	淨 1668	圍 518	量 2892	落 2421	適 2840
捉 1135	除 2989	淺 1673	場 553	閒 2966	葉 2427	銀 2909
採 1146	門 3144	涼 1674	富 728	陽 2996	裝 2532	銅 2910
效 1275	鬼 3148	球 1880	寒 729	隊 2997	解 2566	領 3070
料 1298	假 152	理 1881	帽 835	階 2998	誠 2603	齊 3203
旁 1312	偉 155	產 1898	復 925	雄 3012	資 2693	增 574
旅 1313	停 160	略 1912	惡 980	集 3015	跳 2738	墨 577
柴 1441	動 303	盛 1968	換 1174	雲 3027	較 2767	察 733
格 1443	務 305	眼 1986	提 1176	項 3062	農 2790	寬 737
根 1456	區 329	窗 2089	插 1181	順 3063	預 3066	層 779
桌 1457	參 360	竟 2100	散 1281	須 3064	頓 3069	廠 870
流 1650	唱 455	章 2101	敢 1282	飲 3096	飽 3100	廣 871
消 1651	商 457	粗 2149	普 1349	黃 3190	催 178	彈 893
烟 1774	啦 460	組 2183	晴 1352	黑 3194	像 184	影 905
烈 1780	堂 543	細 2184	替 1380	亂 36	劃 287	德 931
特 1841	堅 547	終 2187	棉 1491	傳 172	奪 619	慶 1013
班 1878	基 548	習 2258	游 1686	傷 174	獎 620	敵 1288
留 1908	夠 598	脫 2322	減 1694	勢 310	態 1008	數 1290
益 1966	婚 659	脚 2323	溫 1695	勤 311	旗 1317	暫 1364
砲 2015	婦 660	處 2468	無 1785	園 520	槍 1502	模 1512
破 2016	婆 661	蛋 2481	痛 1932	媽 675	榮 1506	樓 1514
租 2061	寄 722	術 2515	登 1950	幹 845	歌 1551	樣 1518
笑 2107	密 724	規 2558	發 1951	感 991	演 1710	樂 1519
粉 2146	將 746	設 2577	眾 1988	愁 1004	滿 1721	熱 1801
級 2174	專 747	許 2579	着 1989	搖 1195	漢 1722	熱 1802

確 2025	險 3006	辭 2786
窮 2092	靜 3043	鏡 2947
篇 2130	壓 582	關 2974
編 2208	幫 839	願 3082
練 2213	戲 1061	類 3084
罵 2243	檢 1533	騙 3124
衝 2517	濟 1749	勸 314
調 2619	營 1813	嚴 503
論 2621	禮 2050	寶 741
趣 2728	總 2219	覺 2562
輪 2771	績 2222	警 2651
選 2845	聲 2283	黨 3197
鋪 2919	臨 2354	爛 1818
際 3002	舉 2363	續 2232
隨 3005	薄 2447	護 2653
靠 3045	虧 2472	鐵 2952
鞋 3050	謝 2636	響 3059
養 3103	講 2637	權 1541
餓 3106	賽 2712	聽 2286
餘 3107	鮮 3156	讀 2654
鬧 3145	斷 1308	變 2655
嘴 493	歸 1564	顯 3087
器 494	糧 2163	驗 3130
奮 621	織 2225	體 3138
戰 1060	翻 2261	讓 2656
擔 1243	職 2285	觀 2564
據 1247	舊 2364	
橋 1523	藏 2452	
樹 1527	蟲 2503	
橫 1529	豐 2663	
歷 1563	轉 2778	
燒 1806	醫 2885	
燈 1810	雙 3019	
獨 1864	雜 3021	
磨 2029	雞 3022	
積 2078	題 3080	
糖 2159	鬆 3141	
興 2362	壞 584	
衛 2518	懶 1045	
親 2561	礙 2032	
豬 2667	藥 2459	
辦 2785	識 2647	
醒 2881	贊 2714	

Complete Character Index

吉 390	旬 1324	伯 85	吠 403	弄 878	每 1582	貝 2672
合 391	曳 1373	估 86	吹 404	弟 887	求 1598	赤 2717
同 392	曲 1374	伴 87	吼 405	形 898	汞 1606	走 2719
后 393	有 1384	伶 88	呀 406	役 906	汽 1607	足 2731
向 394	朽 1396	伸 89	君 407	彷 907	沙 1608	身 2756
吏 395	朱 1397	何 90	否 408	忍 936	沖 1609	車 2762
吐 396	杂 1398	似 91	吞 409	忌 937	汹 1610	辛 2782
回 511	次 1543	但 92	吧 410	忘 938	沃 1611	辰 2788
因 512	此 1557	佈 93	吾 411	志 939	沒 1612	返 2794
在 524	死 1566	位 94	吸 412	快 944	決 1613	近 2795
地 525	汝 1601	低 95	呈 413	我 1055	沐 1614	迎 2796
多 596	污 1602	住 96	吻 414	戒 1056	汪 1615	邑 2852
夷 608	汗 1603	佐 97	呆 415	抓 1079	汰 1616	那 2853
妄 626	江 1604	佔 98	囹 513	投 1080	沉 1617	邪 2854
奸 627	池 1605	你 99	困 514	把 1081	灾 1761	邦 2855
她 628	灰 1760	伺 100	址 526	折 1082	灼 1762	里 2889
好 629	百 1953	佃 101	均 527	技 1083	灶 1763	防 2977
如 630	竹 2105	佛 102	坐 528	批 1084	灸 1764	阱 2978
字 688	米 2145	作 103	坑 529	找 1085	牢 1837	
存 689	羊 2246	佣 104	坊 530	扭 1087	狂 1849	**8**
宅 702	羽 2254	克 205	壯 588	扮 1088	男 1905	並 16
守 703	老 2263	兑 206	夾 609	抄 1089	皂 1954	乖 28
安 704	考 2264	兵 219	妙 631	抗 1090	矣 2006	乳 34
宇 705	而 2266	冶 234	妖 632	扶 1091	祁 2035	事 39
寺 743	耳 2274	冷 235	妨 633	抒 1092	社 2036	些 45
尖 755	肉 2291	删 260	妥 634	扯 1093	秃 2054	亞 46
州 803	肌 2292	初 261	妗 635	抑 1094	私 2055	享 50
帆 819	臣 2352	判 262	妒 636	抖 1095	秀 2056	京 51
年 843	自 2355	别 263	妓 637	抛 1098	究 2083	佩 105
式 881	至 2357	利 264	孝 690	改 1270	糸 2165	佳 106
弛 886	舌 2365	刨 265	宋 706	攻 1271	罕 2237	佻 107
忙 940	舟 2369	助 296	完 707	旱 1325	肘 2293	使 108
戍 1051	色 2380	努 297	宏 708	更 1375	肛 2294	來 109
戎 1052	血 2512	劫 298	尾 762	杜 1399	肝 2295	侈 110
成 1053	行 2513	匣 325	局 763	李 1400	肚 2296	例 111
戌 1054	衣 2520	却 349	尿 764	村 1401	良 2378	侍 112
扦 1076	西 2554	卵 350	岔 783	材 1402	芋 2381	侏 113
扛 1077	迅 2791	含 397	巫 809	杉 1403	芒 2382	供 114
扣 1078	迄 2792	呎 398	希 820	杆 1404	見 2557	依 115
收 1269	巡 2793	吵 399	序 850	构 1405	角 2565	免 207
旭 1321		吟 400	庇 851	杏 1406	言 2568	兒 208
早 1322	**7**	告 401	床 852	束 1407	谷 2658	兩 214
旨 1323	串 18	吝 402	廷 875	杖 1408	豆 2659	其 220

字	號	字	號	字	號	字	號	字	號	字	號	字	號
具	221	奔	613	忽	943	服	1386	爬	1820	述	2798	勇	301
典	222	妻	638	性	945	枕	1409	爭	1821	邱	2856	卑	340
函	250	妾	639	怪	950	枉	1410	爸	1825	采	2887	南	341
刮	266	妹	640	怕	952	杳	1411	沐	1830	金	2894	即	352
到	267	姊	641	怯	953	杷	1412	牧	1838	長	2960	卸	353
制	268	姐	642	怖	955	東	1413	物	1839	門	2961	厚	354
刷	269	姑	643	或	1057	枇	1414	狀	1848	阜	2976	叛	369
券	270	始	644	房	1065	板	1415	狗	1850	阻	2979	咱	428
刻	271	姓	645	所	1066	杪	1416	狐	1851	阿	2980	哈	429
刺	272	委	646	承	1086	枝	1417	玫	1873	附	2981	品	430
剎	273	姆	647	拒	1097	林	1418	玩	1874	雨	3025	咳	431
卒	337	孤	691	拖	1099	枚	1419	疙	1922	青	3042	咬	432
卓	338	季	692	拘	1100	松	1420	的	1955	非	3044	哄	433
協	339	孟	693	押	1101	析	1421	盂	1962			哇	434
卦	346	定	709	拔	1102	果	1422	盲	1976	**9**		咸	435
卷	351	宙	710	抬	1103	杯	1423	直	1977	亭	52	哉	436
參	359	官	711	抵	1104	欣	1544	知	2007	亮	53	哀	437
取	366	宗	712	招	1105	步	1558	祈	2037	侮	116	咽	438
叔	367	宜	713	抽	1106	歧	1559	空	2084	侯	117	垣	537
受	368	尚	756	拌	1107	武	1560	糾	2166	侵	118	垮	538
呵	416	居	765	披	1108	氛	1591	耍	2268	侶	119	城	539
咐	417	屆	766	拐	1109	沫	1618	股	2297	侷	120	型	540
呪	418	屈	767	抱	1110	沸	1620	肴	2298	便	121	奏	614
周	419	岳	784	拍	1111	泛	1621	肥	2299	係	122	契	615
呢	420	岸	785	拙	1112	油	1622	肯	2300	促	123	姨	648
味	421	岩	786	拉	1113	波	1623	育	2301	俊	124	姻	649
命	422	巷	815	拇	1114	法	1624	肪	2302	俏	125	姿	650
和	423	帕	821	拂	1115	沿	1625	肢	2303	俗	126	威	651
呻	424	帚	822	拆	1116	治	1626	肺	2304	俘	127	姦	652
咎	425	帛	823	抹	1117	注	1627	肩	2305	保	128	娃	653
咀	426	帖	824	放	1272	沾	1628	臥	2353	俟	129	姪	654
呼	427	幸	844	斧	1303	泳	1629	舍	2366	俠	130	孩	694
固	515	底	853	於	1310	河	1630	花	2383	信	131	室	714
坦	531	店	854	明	1326	泡	1631	芬	2384	俄	132	宣	715
垂	532	府	855	昂	1327	況	1632	芳	2385	兔	209	客	716
垃	533	延	876	易	1328	泥	1633	芙	2386	冒	227	封	744
坡	534	弧	888	昆	1329	沫	1635	芥	2387	冠	230	屋	768
坪	535	弦	889	昔	1330	泣	1636	芽	2388	剃	274	屎	769
坤	536	往	908	昏	1331	沽	1637	虎	2465	則	275	屍	770
夜	597	征	909	旺	1332	炊	1765	虱	2473	削	276	帝	825
奇	610	彼	910	昌	1333	炒	1766	表	2521	前	277	帥	826
奈	611	忠	941	昇	1334	炎	1767	衫	2522	勁	299	幽	848
奉	612	念	942	朋	1385	炕	1768	迫	2797	勃	300	度	856

建 877	柔 1426	甚 1895	苗 2392	風 3089	哮 445	恥 966
彦 899	查 1427	界 1906	苔 2393	飛 3093	唉 446	悔 968
後 911	柏 1428	畏 1907	茅 2394	食 3094	唇 447	悟 969
很 912	柑 1429	疫 1923	苦 2395	首 3111	哲 448	悅 973
待 913	枯 1430	皆 1956	苟 2396	香 3112	哪 449	悄 975
律 914	柚 1431	皇 1957	若 2397		埋 541	扇 1068
徊 915	某 1432	盅 1963	苛 2398		夏 593	拿 1129
急 946	東 1433	盆 1964	虐 2466	**10**	套 616	拳 1130
怒 947	枴 1434	相 1978	虹 2474	乘 29	娘 655	挈 1131
思 948	柳 1435	盾 1979	衍 2514	修 133	娟 656	挪 1132
息 949	柱 1436	盼 1980	要 2555	俯 134	娛 657	挫 1133
怎 951	架 1437	省 1981	訂 2569	俱 135	孫 695	振 1134
怨 954	染 1438	看 1982	計 2570	倆 136	容 717	捉 1135
恒 956	柄 1439	眉 1983	訃 2571	併 137	家 718	捕 1136
恨 958	柵 1440	砌 2013	貞 2673	倉 138	宮 719	捆 1137
恢 962	歪 1561	砍 2014	負 2674	倍 139	宴 720	挾 1138
恰 965	殆 1567	祖 2038	赴 2720	們 140	害 721	捍 1139
恤 967	段 1573	神 2039	赳 2721	倒 141	射 745	捎 1140
扁 1067	毒 1583	祕 2040	躬 2757	候 142	展 771	挨 1141
拜 1096	泉 1619	祝 2041	軌 2763	倚 143	屑 772	捐 1142
拼 1118	洞 1638	秋 2057	軍 2764	借 144	屐 773	挺 1143
挑 1119	活 1639	秒 2058	逃 2799	倡 145	島 787	捌 1144
按 1120	洒 1640	科 2059	迴 2800	倫 146	峭 788	採 1146
挖 1121	洗 1641	穿 2085	退 2801	值 147	峯 789	效 1275
拷 1122	洋 1642	突 2086	迷 2802	倘 148	峽 790	料 1298
拾 1123	洣 1643	竿 2106	遞 2803	倔 149	峻 791	旁 1312
括 1124	洽 1644	紅 2167	追 2804	個 150	差 810	旅 1313
持 1125	津 1645	紀 2168	迹 2805	兼 223	師 827	晏 1341
拭 1126	洩 1646	約 2169	送 2806	准 236	席 828	時 1342
指 1127	洲 1647	紉 2170	郊 2857	凋 237	庭 857	晉 1343
拴 1128	洪 1648	缸 2234	耶 2858	凍 238	座 858	書 1376
政 1273	派 1649	美 2247	郎 2859	剗 278	庫 859	朗 1387
故 1274	炳 1769	者 2265	酋 2867	剖 279	弱 890	柴 1441
斫 1304	炬 1770	耐 2267	配 2868	剛 280	彩 900	校 1442
施 1311	炮 1771	胡 2306	重 2890	剝 281	徐 916	格 1443
昨 1335	炸 1772	胎 2307	陋 2982	勉 302	徒 917	桅 1444
映 1336	炭 1773	胞 2308	限 2983	匪 326	徑 918	桃 1445
昧 1337	版 1833	背 2309	降 2984	原 355	恩 957	核 1446
星 1338	牲 1840	胖 2310	面 3046	哨 439	息 959	框 1447
春 1339	狠 1852	胃 2311	革 3047	哺 440	恕 960	栽 1448
是 1340	狡 1853	茄 2389	章 3054	員 441	恙 961	桑 1449
柿 1424	玻 1875	英 2390	音 3057	唐 442	恐 963	桐 1450
枢 1425	珍 1876	茂 2391	頁 3060	哥 443	恭 964	株 1451
				哭 444		

案 1452　疾 1926　脆 2315　逝 2812　偷 163　娶 666　情 979
粟 1453　病 1927　胳 2316　逗 2813　兜 210　娼 667　悼 981
桔 1454　疼 1928　胸 2317　造 2814　鳳 243　執 696　悴 982
桂 1455　疲 1929　脂 2318　逞 2815　副 282　寄 722　惕 984
根 1456　盈 1965　脅 2319　速 2816　剪 283　宿 723　恬 986
桌 1457　益 1966　臭 2356　透 2817　動 303　密 724　惆 987
栩 1458　眠 1984　致 2358　逛 2818　勒 304　寂 725　惜 989
梁 1459　眞 1985　航 2370　逢 2819　務 305　寇 726　戚 1058
殊 1568　矩 2008　般 2371　郡 2860　匙 323　將 746　挽 1145
殷 1574　砲 2015　茶 2399　酌 2869　匿 328　專 747　推 1147
氧 1592　破 2016　荒 2400　酒 2870　區 329　尉 748　掛 1148
氣 1593　祥 2043　茫 2401　釜 2895　參 360　屏 774　捨 1149
泰 1634　秧 2060　茲 2402　針 2896　啥 450　屜 775　掃 1150
流 1650　租 2061　荊 2403　釘 2897　唬 451　崩 792　措 1151
消 1651　秤 2062　茸 2404　閃 2962　問 452　崗 793　掌 1152
涉 1652　秩 2063　荔 2405　陸 2985　售 453　崖 794　掀 1153
海 1653　窄 2087　草 2406　院 2986　唯 454　崇 795　掂 1154
浪 1654　站 2099　虔 2467　陜 2987　唱 455　崎 796　掘 1155
浮 1655　笑 2107　蚜 2475　陣 2988　唾 456　巢 804　授 1156
浦 1656　粉 2146　蚊 2476　除 2989　商 457　帷 829　捧 1157
涕 1657　紐 2171　蚌 2477　雙 3009　啓 458　帶 830　掖 1158
浸 1658　納 2172　蚤 2478　靭 3055　啞 459　帳 831　捐 1159
浩 1659　紋 2173　衷 2523　飢 3095　啦 460　常 832　捲 1160
浴 1660　級 2174　袁 2524　馬 3114　圈 516　庶 860　掠 1161
烟 1774　紗 2175　被 2525　骨 3134　國 517　庸 861　捶 1162
烘 1775　紡 2176　袖 2526　高 3139　堆 542　康 862　掉 1163
烤 1776　紛 2177　袍 2527　鬥 3144　堂 543　張 891　排 1164
烝 1777　素 2178　記 2572　鬼 3148　培 544　強 892　掙 1165
烙 1778　紙 2179　討 2573　　　　執 545　彗 896　掏 1166
烏 1779　純 2180　訊 2574　**11**　域 546　彫 901　探 1167
烈 1780　索 2181　託 2575　乾 35　堅 547　彪 902　控 1168
爹 1826　紫 2182　訓 2576　偉 151　基 548　彬 903　捫 1169
特 1841　缺 2235　豈 2660　假 152　埠 549　徘 919　接 1170
狼 1854　羔 2248　豹 2668　倦 153　夠 598　從 920　捷 1171
狹 1855　翁 2255　貢 2675　偏 154　奢 617　徙 921　掩 1172
珠 1877　翅 2256　財 2676　偉 155　娩 658　得 922　救 1276
班 1878　耙 2269　起 2722　偕 156　婚 659　悠 970　教 1277
瓷 1892　耕 2270　辱 2789　做 157　婦 660　您 971　敗 1278
留 1908　耗 2271　通 2807　健 158　婆 661　惠 972　敏 1279
畝 1909　耿 2275　逐 2808　側 159　婢 662　悉 974　敘 1280
畜 1910　脊 2312　連 2809　停 160　婊 663　惟 976　斜 1299
症 1924　能 2313　這 2810　偵 161　娶 664　悅 977　斬 1305
疹 1925　脈 2314　途 2811　偶 162　婉 665　悽 978　族 1314

旌 1315	添 1677	終 2187	軌 2758	喜 465	復 925	斑 1294
旋 1316	淑 1678	羞 2249	軟 2765	喉 466	徨 926	斐 1295
旣 1318	淚 1679	翌 2257	進 2820	喻 467	循 927	斌 1296
晤 1344	港 1680	習 2258	週 2821	喲 468	惡 980	斯 1306
晦 1345	焉 1781	聆 2276	逮 2822	喘 469	悲 983	晚 1348
晝 1346	烹 1782	聊 2277	部 2861	喊 470	悶 985	普 1349
農 1347	焊 1783	脖 2320	野 2891	喪 471	惠 988	景 1350
曼 1377	爽 1828	脛 2321	釦 2898	啼 472	惑 990	智 1351
曹 1378	牽 1842	脫 2322	釣 2899	喂 473	惰 994	晴 1352
望 1388	猛 1856	腳 2323	閉 2963	喧 474	惶 996	晰 1353
梳 1460	猜 1857	船 2372	陪 2990	喝 475	愉 997	晾 1354
條 1461	率 1870	航 2373	陳 2991	圍 518	復 998	晶 1355
梛 1462	現 1879	舶 2374	陶 2992	堵 550	惻 1000	最 1379
梅 1463	球 1880	莊 2407	陷 2993	報 551	惱 1002	替 1380
梭 1464	理 1881	莫 2408	陸 2994	堪 552	愕 1003	曾 1381
桶 1465	甜 1896	莖 2409	陰 2995	場 553	扉 1069	期 1389
梗 1466	產 1898	荷 2410	雀 3010	堡 554	掣 1173	朝 1390
械 1467	略 1912	處 2468	雪 3026	堤 555	換 1174	棕 1473
桿 1468	痕 1930	蚯 2479	頂 3061	堰 556	揚 1175	椅 1474
梓 1469	痊 1931	蛇 2480	魚 3154	壹 589	提 1176	棧 1475
梯 1470	盒 1967	蛋 2481	鳥 3165	壺 590	描 1177	棟 1476
梢 1471	盛 1968	術 2515	鹿 3183	堵 591	揸 1178	棋 1477
梨 1472	眼 1986	袋 2528	麥 3186	媒 668	揶 1179	棵 1478
欲 1545	眷 1987	袱 2531	麻 3188	婿 669	揮 1180	植 1479
殺 1575	研 2017	規 2558		嫂 670	插 1181	椒 1480
毫 1586	票 2042	覓 2559	**12**	寬 727	揀 1182	棒 1481
氫 1594	祭 2044	視 2560	傢 164	富 728	握 1183	森 1482
涎 1661	移 2064	設 2577	傅 165	寒 729	揹 1184	棗 1483
凄 1662	窒 2088	訝 2578	傑 166	尊 749	捏 1185	棱 1484
深 1663	窗 2089	許 2579	傘 167	尋 750	掇 1186	棘 1485
淡 1664	竟 2100	訛 2580	備 168	就 758	揉 1187	棚 1486
清 1665	章 2101	訟 2581	晃 228	屠 776	揍 1188	棠 1487
淘 1666	第 2108	訣 2582	凱 244	嵌 797	揩 1189	棍 1488
混 1667	笛 2109	訪 2583	割 284	幀 833	揖 1190	棲 1489
淨 1668	符 2110	跂 2661	剩 285	幅 834	揭 1191	棺 1490
淮 1669	笨 2111	貧 2677	創 286	帽 835	揪 1192	棉 1491
淹 1670	粒 2147	責 2678	勝 306	幾 849	搜 1193	棄 1492
淫 1671	粘 2148	貪 2679	勞 307	厢 863	掁 1194	款 1546
液 1672	粗 2149	貨 2680	博 342	廁 864	散 1281	欺 1547
淺 1673	組 2183	販 2681	啊 461	廊 865	敢 1282	欽 1548
涼 1674	細 2184	貫 2682	喚 462	弒 882	敦 1283	殘 1569
淋 1675	累 2185	赦 2718	善 463	御 923	敝 1284	殖 1570
涯 1676	紹 2186	趾 2732	單 464	徧 924	敞 1285	殼 1576

毬 1587	着 1989	菊 2414	跛 2737	黑 3194	彙 897	極 1500
氯 1595	短 2009	菌 2415	軸 2766		徬 928	槌 1501
渾 1681	硬 2018	菩 2416	遍 2823	**13**	微 929	歇 1549
湊 1682	禽 2052	菜 2417	逸 2824	亂 36	感 991	歲 1562
渠 1683	稀 2065	菱 2418	遁 2825	傲 169	愛 992	毀 1577
渺 1684	稍 2066	萍 2419	遂 2826	催 170	想 993	殿 1578
渡 1685	稅 2067	虛 2469	遊 2827	傭 171	愚 995	滙 1696
游 1686	稈 2068	蛛 2482	達 2828	傳 172	意 999	滋 1697
湖 1687	程 2069	蛙 2483	違 2829	債 173	愈 1001	滅 1698
渣 1688	童 2102	街 2516	遇 2830	傷 174	愁 1004	溺 1699
渦 1689	答 2112	裁 2529	道 2831	傾 175	惹 1005	滑 1700
湧 1690	筆 2113	裂 2530	遍 2832	僅 176	愧 1006	溶 1701
測 1691	等 2114	裙 2535	過 2833	募 308	慌 1009	溜 1702
渴 1692	筐 2115	補 2536	運 2834	勤 309	愴 1010	源 1703
湯 1693	筋 2116	裕 2537	郵 2862	勢 310	慎 1012	溝 1704
減 1694	筒 2117	詞 2584	都 2863	勤 311	慨 1014	溢 1705
溫 1695	筍 2118	評 2585	鄉 2864	嗜 476	搖 1195	溪 1706
焦 1784	策 2119	詆 2586	酥 2871	嗓 477	搗 1196	準 1707
無 1785	粟 2150	訴 2587	量 2892	嗟 478	搓 1197	滓 1708
然 1786	粧 2151	註 2588	鈔 2900	嗅 479	搞 1198	照 1789
焰 1787	粥 2152	詐 2589	鈍 2901	嗚 480	搧 1199	煮 1790
焚 1788	粵 2153	詠 2590	鈕 2902	嗆 481	搾 1200	煲 1791
爲 1822	紫 2188	診 2591	開 2964	嗦 482	搬 1201	煎 1792
犂 1843	統 2189	詛 2592	間 2965	嗎 483	搭 1202	煤 1793
猴 1858	給 2190	象 2665	閒 2966	圓 519	損 1203	煩 1794
猶 1859	絕 2191	貂 2669	陽 2996	園 520	搶 1204	煉 1795
琴 1882	結 2192	賀 2683	隊 2997	塗 557	搏 1205	爺 1827
瓶 1893	絡 2193	貴 2684	階 2998	塘 558	搽 1206	猿 1860
甥 1899	絲 2194	貼 2685	隆 2999	塞 559	敬 1286	獅 1861
畢 1911	絨 2195	買 2686	雇 3011	填 560	斟 1300	猾 1862
番 1913	羨 2252	費 2687	雄 3012	塌 561	新 1307	瑞 1883
異 1914	翔 2259	貿 2688	雅 3013	塢 562	暑 1356	當 1916
畫 1915	脾 2324	貸 2689	雁 3014	塊 563	暈 1357	痰 1936
疏 1920	腑 2325	貳 2690	集 3015	塔 564	暗 1358	麻 1937
痛 1932	腎 2326	販 2691	雲 3027	奧 618	暖 1359	痺 1938
痘 1933	腕 2328	貯 2692	項 3062	嫁 671	會 1382	盟 1970
痣 1934	脹 2329	超 2723	順 3063	媳 672	業 1493	盞 1971
痢 1935	腔 2330	越 2724	須 3064	嫉 673	楷 1494	晴 1990
登 1950	腦 2332	趁 2725	飲 3096	嫌 674	楊 1495	睁 1991
發 1951	舒 2367	跋 2733	飯 3097	媽 675	椰 1496	督 1993
皓 1958	華 2411	跌 2734	魁 3149	幹 845	楣 1497	矮 2010
盜 1969	菇 2412	距 2735	黃 3190	廈 866	楓 1498	碗 2019
衆 1988	萃 2413	跑 2736	黍 3191	廉 867	楚 1499	碎 2020

碉 2021	蛾 2485	鉅 2905	嘗 488	摔 1210	熊 1798	腐 2327
碰 2022	蜂 2486	鉗 2906	嘆 489	摟 1211	熏 1799	腑 2338
碑 2023	蛻 2487	鉋 2907	圖 521	摒 1212	爾 1829	膀 2339
禁 2045	裝 2532	鉛 2908	團 522	摻 1213	牌 1834	膏 2340
祿 2046	裔 2533	閘 2967	境 565	摑 1215	獄 1863	臺 2359
福 2047	裏 2534	隔 3000	墊 566	摘 1216	瑰 1884	與 2361
禍 2048	裘 2538	陳 3001	墓 567	摺 1217	瑣 1885	舞 2368
稚 2070	裸 2539	零 3028	塾 568	敲 1287	璃 1886	蒜 2430
筷 2120	褂 2541	電 3029	墅 569	旗 1317	疑 1921	蒙 2431
綏 2196	裨 2542	雷 3030	塵 570	暢 1360	瘋 1939	蒞 2432
綁 2197	解 2566	靶 3048	摘 571	槍 1502	瘦 1940	蓄 2433
經 2198	詩 2593	靴 3049	壽 592	榨 1503	監 1972	蒸 2434
罪 2238	試 2594	頌 3065	夢 599	榛 1504	盡 1973	蒼 2435
罩 2239	詳 2595	預 3066	夥 600	榜 1505	睡 1992	蓉 2436
置 2240	詫 2596	頑 3067	奪 619	榮 1506	瞄 1994	蓋 2437
羣 2250	誇 2597	頒 3068	獎 620	構 1507	碟 2024	蓮 2438
義 2251	詭 2598	頓 3069	嫡 676	槐 1508	種 2071	蜢 2488
聖 2278	話 2599	飾 3098	嫩 677	榴 1509	稱 2073	蜜 2489
聘 2279	該 2600	飼 3099	孵 697	榻 1510	窩 2090	裹 2540
肆 2288	詢 2601	飽 3100	寧 731	榡 1511	窪 2091	製 2543
肄 2289	詣 2602	馳 3115	寥 732	歉 1550	端 2103	裳 2544
肅 2290	誠 2603	馴 3116	寢 734	歌 1551	筵 2121	複 2545
腰 2331	資 2693	魅 3152	寨 735	殞 1571	管 2122	裾 2546
腹 2333	賈 2694	鳳 3166	寞 736	漑 1709	算 2123	認 2604
腫 2334	賊 2695	鼓 3199	對 751	演 1710	箋 2124	說 2605
腸 2335	賄 2696	鼠 3200	屢 777	漠 1711	筝 2125	語 2606
腥 2336	跳 2738		嶇 798	滯 1712	節 2126	誓 2607
腿 2337	路 2739	**14**	幕 836	漬 1713	精 2154	誣 2608
舅 2360	跟 2740	僕 177	彰 904	漂 1714	粽 2155	誡 2609
艇 2375	跨 2741	催 178	微 930	漲 1715	粹 2156	誤 2610
萬 2420	跪 2742	傻 179	愍 1007	漁 1716	綿 2199	誦 2611
落 2421	躲 2759	傀 180	態 1008	滲 1717	網 2200	誨 2612
著 2422	較 2767	僧 181	慈 1011	漸 1718	維 2201	誌 2613
董 2423	載 2768	僑 182	慷 1017	滴 1719	綱 2202	誘 2614
葬 2424	農 2790	偽 183	慢 1018	漆 1720	綢 2203	豪 2666
蔥 2425	遙 2835	像 184	慟 1021	滿 1721	綽 2204	貌 2670
葛 2426	遮 2836	凳 245	慣 1022	漢 1722	綠 2205	賓 2697
葉 2427	遠 2837	劃 287	慘 1023	漏 1723	緊 2206	賒 2698
葡 2428	遣 2838	厭 356	慚 1025	漱 1724	綫 2207	趕 2726
葦 2429	酪 2872	嘔 484	截 1059	漫 1725	罰 2241	趙 2727
虜 2470	酬 2873	嘉 485	搔 1207	滾 1727	署 2242	輕 2769
號 2471	鉤 2903	嘍 486	摸 1208	熄 1796	聚 2280	輔 2770
蜆 2484	鈴 2904	嗷 487	摧 1209	熔 1797	聞 2281	辣 2783

遮 2839	劈 290	憐 1029	歎 1553	編 2208	賬 2705	養 3103
適 2840	劍 291	憫 1030	毆 1579	緒 2209	質 2706	餓 3106
遭 2841	厲 357	憮 1031	殼 1580	締 2210	賤 2707	餘 3107
邊 2842	嘿 490	憤 1033	漿 1726	緩 2211	趣 2728	駐 3118
鄙 2865	噴 491	摩 1214	潑 1728	緝 2212	趟 2729	駕 3119
酸 2874	墜 572	摹 1218	潛 1729	練 2213	踢 2743	駛 3120
酷 2875	墮 573	撥 1219	潤 1730	緣 2214	踐 2744	駝 3121
醉 2876	增 574	撕 1220	澎 1731	罵 2243	踏 2745	髮 3140
銀 2909	墟 575	撚 1221	潵 1732	罷 2244	躺 2760	鬧 3145
銅 2910	墳 576	撤 1222	潔 1733	羹 2253	輪 2771	魄 3151
銜 2911	墨 577	撮 1223	澇 1734	膠 2341	輞 2772	鴉 3168
銑 2912	嬌 678	撲 1224	潦 1735	膝 2342	輝 2773	黎 3192
銘 2913	嫻 679	撓 1225	潰 1736	膚 2343	輦 2774	齒 3205
閣 2968	嬉 680	撞 1226	澆 1737	蔓 2439	遲 2843	
閨 2969	實 730	撈 1227	澄 1738	蔭 2440	遼 2844	
閥 2970	察 733	撩 1228	潮 1739	蔣 2441	選 2845	**16**
障 3003	寬 737	撬 1229	熱 1800	蝠 2490	遵 2846	儒 191
雌 3016	審 738	播 1230	熱 1801	蝸 2491	遺 2847	儘 192
需 3031	寫 739	撐 1231	熱 1802	蝶 2492	鄰 2866	冀 224
領 3070	導 752	撒 1232	熨 1803	蝟 2493	醋 2877	凝 240
頡 3071	屨 778	撒 1233	瘡 1941	蝗 2494	醇 2878	勳 312
餃 3101	層 779	撫 1234	瘤 1942	蝦 2495	醉 2879	噪 492
蝕 3102	幣 837	撐 1235	瘡 1943	衝 2517	醃 2880	嘴 493
餅 3104	幟 838	撑 1236	瘟 1944	褲 2547	銳 2914	器 494
駁 3117	廟 868	撻 1237	皺 1960	褥 2548	鋁 2915	噸 495
骯 3135	廢 869	敵 1288	盤 1974	誕 2615	銲 2916	噬 496
魂 3150	廠 870	數 1289	瞎 1995	誰 2616	錦 2917	噱 497
鳴 3167	廣 871	數 1290	瞌 1996	請 2617	鋒 2918	壁 578
麾 3189	廚 872	暱 1361	確 2025	諒 2618	鋪 2919	墾 579
鼎 3198	弊 879	暮 1362	碼 2026	調 2619	銷 2920	壇 580
鼻 3201	彈 893	暴 1363	磁 2027	課 2620	鋤 2921	奮 621
齊 3203	影 905	暫 1364	磅 2028	論 2621	銹 2922	學 698
	德 931	模 1512	穀 2072	談 2622	閱 2971	憑 1032
15	徹 932	標 1513	稿 2074	誹 2623	際 3002	憲 1034
傻 185	慶 1013	樓 1514	稽 2075	誼 2624	隧 3004	憶 1036
價 186	慰 1015	槽 1515	稻 2076	諂 2625	隨 3005	懂 1037
億 187	慫 1016	椿 1516	窮 2092	豎 2662	震 3032	懊 1038
儉 188	憂 1019	概 1517	窖 2093	賦 2699	霉 3033	憾 1040
儀 189	慮 1020	樣 1518	箭 2127	賣 2700	靠 3045	懈 1041
僻 190	慾 1024	樂 1519	箱 2128	賠 2701	鞋 3050	戰 1060
凜 239	慧 1026	樞 1520	範 2129	賜 2702	鞏 3051	撼 1238
劉 288	憔 1027	槳 1521	篇 2130	賞 2703	鞍 3052	操 1239
劇 289	憎 1028	歐 1552	糊 2157	賢 2704	颱 3090	擋 1240
						擅 1241

擔 1243	蓬 2133	邀 2848	嬰 681	瞥 1999	賺 2711	擾 1256
擁 1244	糕 2158	避 2849	孺 699	瞧 2000	賽 2712	擲 1257
擂 1245	糖 2159	還 2850	尷 759	瞭 2001	趨 2730	擺 1258
擇 1246	縛 2215	醒 2881	嶺 799	瞪 2002	蹈 2750	斃 1292
據 1247	縫 2216	錄 2923	嶼 800	矯 2011	輾 2777	斷 1308
擄 1248	縣 2217	鋸 2924	幫 839	禮 2050	醞 2882	曙 1367
整 1291	緻 2218	錦 2925	懷 840	穗 2079	醜 2883	朦 1391
曆 1365	髣 2272	錐 2926	彌 894	糟 2160	鍋 2933	檸 1535
曉 1366	構 2273	錫 2927	徽 933	糠 2161	鍵 2934	檬 1536
機 1522	膩 2344	錯 2928	應 1035	糞 2162	鍛 2935	櫃 1537
橋 1523	膨 2345	錢 2929	懇 1039	總 2219	鍘 2936	櫈 1538
樽 1524	興 2362	鋼 2930	懦 1042	縱 2220	鍊 2937	檯 1539
橙 1525	艙 2376	錶 2931	戲 1061	縮 2221	鍬 2938	歸 1564
橡 1526	蔬 2442	錘 2932	戴 1062	績 2222	鍍 2939	瀉 1751
樹 1527	蔽 2443	險 3006	擎 1242	繁 2223	錨 2940	瀑 1752
樵 1528	蕉 2444	雕 3017	擊 1249	翼 2260	鎚 2941	瀋 1753
橫 1529	蕩 2445	霍 3034	擠 1250	聯 2282	闊 2972	濾 1754
樸 1530	螢 2496	靜 3043	攔 1251	聲 2283	隱 3007	獵 1866
橘 1531	融 2497	頭 3072	擦 1252	聰 2284	隸 3008	璧 1888
歷 1563	衞 2518	頰 3073	撐 1253	膽 2346	雖 3018	瞻 2003
濁 1740	衡 2519	頸 3074	擬 1254	臂 2347	霜 3035	礎 2031
激 1741	親 2561	領 3075	檀 1532	臉 2348	霞 3036	禱 2051
濃 1742	諾 2626	頹 3076	檢 1533	臨 2354	韓 3056	竅 2095
澳 1743	謀 2627	頻 3077	檔 1534	舉 2363	顆 3078	竄 2096
澡 1744	謂 2628	餐 3105	氈 1588	艱 2379	颱 3091	簡 2134
澤 1745	諧 2629	館 3108	濕 1746	薑 2446	騎 3123	簧 2135
燙 1804	謀 2630	駭 3122	濯 1747	薄 2447	鮮 3156	糧 2163
燃 1805	諸 2631	駱 3136	濫 1748	薪 2448	鴿 3172	繞 2224
燒 1806	諷 2632	閹 3146	濟 1749	蕭 2449	黏 3193	織 2225
燐 1807	諺 2633	鮑 3155	濱 1750	薦 2450	點 3196	繩 2226
燉 1808	謎 2634	鴨 3169	燦 1811	虧 2472	舁 3202	翻 2261
燕 1809	豬 2667	鴦 3170	燭 1812	螺 2498	齋 3204	職 2285
燈 1810	貓 2671	鴛 3171	營 1813	蟀 2499	龍 3208	臍 2349
獨 1864	賭 2708	黔 3195	燬 1814	蟄 2500	龠 3210	舊 2364
瞞 1997	賴 2709		燥 1815	蟑 2501		藍 2451
磨 2029	踹 2746	**17**	爵 1823	謙 2635	**18**	藏 2452
磚 2030	踴 2747	償 193	牆 1831	謝 2636	叢 370	薯 2453
禦 2049	踱 2748	優 194	獲 1865	講 2637	鬱 499	薩 2454
穎 2077	蹄 2749	儲 195	環 1887	謠 2638	壘 583	藐 2455
積 2078	輸 2775	勵 313	療 1945	膳 2639	嬸 682	藉 2456
窺 2094	輻 2776	嚇 498	癌 1946	謗 2640	懲 1043	蟬 2502
築 2131	辦 2784	壕 581	癆 1947	謊 2641	戳 1063	蟲 2503
篤 2132	辨 2785	壓 582	瞬 1998	購 2710	擴 1255	襪 2549

覆 2556　　辦 1890　　騙 3124　　譯 2648　　躍 2754　　**23**　　　　**27**
謬 2642　　疆 1917　　鬍 3142　　議 2649　　轟 2781　　戀 1049　　鑽 2958
謹 2643　　礙 2032　　鯨 3159　　譬 2650　　辯 2787　　攣 1265　　鑼 2959
豐 2663　　穩 2080　　鵲 3175　　警 2651　　鐵 2952　　攬 1266　　顴 3088
蹤 2751　　穫 2081　　麗 3184　　瞻 2715　　鐮 2953　　曬 1371　　鼺 3164
軀 2761　　簫 2136　　　　　　　躁 2753　　闢 2975　　籠 2144
轉 2778　　簿 2137　　**20**　　釋 2888　　露 3038　　聾 2287　　**28**
邊 2851　　簽 2138　　勸 314　　鐘 2950　　霸 3039　　襲 2553　　豔 2664
醬 2884　　簾 2139　　嚨 501　　鍬 2951　　霹 3040　　變 2655　　鸚 3180
醫 2885　　籃 2140　　嚼 502　　飄 3092　　響 3059　　顯 3087
釐 2893　　繡 2227　　嚴 503　　饑 3109　　顧 3085　　驗 3130　　**29**
鎖 2942　　繫 2228　　嚷 504　　饒 3110　　驅 3127　　驚 3131　　鬱 3147
鎬 2943　　繳 2229　　蘗 585　　馨 3113　　驃 3128　　髒 3137
鎮 2944　　繪 2230　　壤 586　　騷 3125　　魔 3153　　體 3138
鎗 2945　　羅 2245　　孀 683　　騰 3126　　鰥 3161　　鱗 3163
鎊 2946　　臘 2350　　寵 740　　鰓 3160　　鶯 3176　　麟 3185
闖 2973　　藝 2457　　寶 741　　鹹 3181　　鶴 3177
雙 3019　　藤 2458　　龐 873　　麵 3187　　　　　　　**24**
雛 3020　　藥 2459　　懸 1044　　黨 3197　　**22**　　囑 508
雜 3021　　藕 2460　　懺 1047　　齡 3206　　囊 506　　攪 1267
雞 3022　　蟹 2504　　攏 1259　　齣 3207　　囉 507　　纏 2233
離 3023　　蠅 2505　　攔 1260　　龜 3209　　孿 700　　罐 2236
霧 3037　　蟻 2506　　曦 1370　　　　　　　巔 801　　蠱 2510
鞭 3053　　襤 2550　　爐 1817　　**21**　　攣 895　　讓 2656
額 3079　　證 2644　　穰 1845　　儷 196　　攤 1263　　釀 2886
題 3080　　譜 2645　　獻 1868　　羆 505　　攢 1264　　靂 3041
顏 3081　　譏 2646　　疊 1918　　屬 780　　權 1541　　驟 3132
鬆 3141　　識 2647　　癢 1948　　懼 1048　　歡 1554　　鷹 3179
鯉 3157　　贈 2713　　礦 2033　　攝 1261　　灘 1756　　鹽 3182
鯊 3158　　贊 2714　　競 2104　　攜 1262　　灑 1757
鵑 3173　　蹲 2752　　籌 2141　　欄 1540　　癮 1949　　**25**
鵝 3174　　轍 2779　　籍 2142　　殲 1572　　竊 2097　　廳 874
　　　　　　轎 2780　　糯 2164　　灌 1755　　聽 2286　　灣 1758
19　　辭 2786　　繼 2231　　爛 1818　　臟 2351　　螢 2511
嚙 500　　鏡 2947　　耀 2262　　籤 2143　　讀 2654　　觀 2564
壙 584　　鏃 2948　　艦 2377　　續 2232　　贖 2716　　躡 2755
懶 1045　　鏈 2949　　蘇 2461　　蘭 2464　　鑑 2954　　鑰 2956
懷 1046　　關 2974　　藹 2462　　蠣 2508　　鑄 2955　　鑲 2957
曠 1368　　難 3024　　蘋 2463　　蠢 2509　　顫 3086
曝 1369　　韻 3058　　蠔 2507　　襯 2552　　驕 3129　　**26**
爆 1816　　願 3082　　襪 2551　　覽 2563　　鬚 3143　　讚 2657
犢 1844　　顛 3083　　覺 2562　　譽 2652　　鷩 3162　　驢 3133
獸 1867　　類 3084　　觸 2567　　護 2653　　鷗 3178

Mandarin Index

Cantonese Index

bottle, 191
bottom, 107
bottom of shoes, 131
boudoir, 279
boundary, 83, 192, 193, 280, 281
bountiful, 120
bow, 110, 134, 262
bow head, 287
bowels, 227
bowl, 201
box, 64, 197, 210
boxing, 129
boxing ring, 138
boy, 93
brag, 71
brain, 227
bramble, 157, 233
bran, 213
branch, 140, 152
brand, 181
brass, 274
brave, 62, 187, 254, 259
break, 126, 128, 135, 201
break a promise, 289
break into pieces, 136, 201
break off, 215
break up, 141
breast, 40, 88, 226
breath, 116
breeze, 289
brew, 272
bribe, 257
brick, 202
brick oven, 180
bridegroom, 270
bridge, 160
bridle, 62
brief, 200
briefly, 192
bright, 42, 54, 145, 147, 180, 196, 222, 277
brightness, 263
brilliant, 145, 183, 221, 234, 272
bring, 105, 129, 139
bring together, 136
bring up, 290
broad, 97, 108, 279
broadcast, 137
brocade, 275
broccoli, 232
broken, 184
bronze, 274
broom, 104, 111, 131
brother, 54, 74, 110, 145
brush, 60, 139, 209
bubbles, 168, 169
bucket, 156
buckle, 273
bud, 232

Buddha, 46
Buddhist monastery, 60, 98
Buddhist monk, 52
build, 109, 135, 159, 201, 236, 266
building, 108, 160
bulky, 212
bullet, 110
bunch, 151
bundle, 130
bundle up, 244
bureau, 99
burn, 180, 182, 183
burst, 184
bury, 82, 235
bushy, 157
business, 158
busy, 114
but, 45, 66, 69, 117, 181
butcher, 100
butter up, 251
butterfly, 240
button, 214, 273
buy, 170, 219, 256, 258
buy or sell on credit, 257
by, 44, 144, 192, 243
bypass, 218
cabin on a ship, 231
cage, 211
cake, 213
calculate, 210, 247
caldron, 273, 299
calendar, 148
calf, 186
call, 69, 73, 75, 251
calm, 277, 285
camel, 292
camp, 183
can, 113, 219
Canada, 62
canal, 169
cancel, 63
cancer, 195
candle, 183
candy, 213
cane, 151, 153
cannon, 180, 201
Canton, 212
canvas, 104
cap, 105
capable, 82
capacity, 273
capital, 42, 256, 270
captive, 48
capture, 138, 238, 281
car, 262
card, 66, 185
careful, 120, 252
careless, 193, 232, 233
carelessly, 199

carp, 295
carpet, 166
carry, 105, 123, 129, 130, 139, 255
carry between 2 people, 127
carry in the arms, 128
carry in the elbow, 260
carry on shoulders, 125, 128, 131, 138
carry on the back, 133, 225
carry out, 101
carry with both hands, 125
cart, 262
carve, 60, 111, 283
case, 197
cash, 276
cassia, 155
cast, 127, 137, 278
cast iron, 274, 278
casual, 225
cat, 255
catch, 130, 188, 217
cattle, 186
catty, 143
caught between, 66
cause, 43, 46, 109, 119, 127, 229, 253, 256, 294
caution, 123, 253
cautious, 118, 120
cave, 170, 206
cavity, 227
cease, 219
cedar, 151
celebrate, 120
celebration, 120
cent, 43, 58
center, 39, 87
centimeter, 273
central, 160
ceremony, 53, 55, 204
certain, 95, 143, 153, 196
certainly, 114, 168, 202
chaff, 213
chain, 39, 276
chair, 157
chance, 52, 149
change, 133, 140, 145, 149, 253, 285
chant, 248
chapter, 208, 210
character, 93
charcoal, 180, 182
charm, 295
charming, 92, 170, 254
chase, 259, 266
chat, 222, 251
cheat, 73, 162, 248, 292
check, 299
cheekbones, 289
cheeks, 228, 288

cheer, 76
cheerful, 115, 162
cheese, 271
cherish, 121
chess, 157
chest, 161, 210, 226
chestnut, 155
chew, 73, 78
chicken, 283
chickenpox, 194
chief, 53, 217, 271, 278, 288, 291
child, 43, 54, 94, 208
childish, 205
chilly, 97
chin, 288
China, 39, 190, 234
chinaware, 202
Chinese, 39, 74, 176, 234
Chinese coat, 244
Chinese ink, 84
Chinese jacket, 245
Chinese script writing, 158
chirp, 296
chlorine, 167
choked, 77
cholera, 284
choose, 133, 138, 269
chop, 44, 61, 143, 201
chop firewood, 161
chopsticks, 210
chrysanthemum, 234
cicada, 241
cigarette, 180
cinnamon, 155
circle, 80, 190
circular, 265
circumstances, 99
citizens, 166
city, 81, 104, 269
claim, 245
clam, 239
clamor, 76, 79
clan, 95, 144
clap, 128, 299
clarify, 178
class, 171, 189, 205, 209
classics, 216
clause, 68
claws, 184
clean, 168, 172, 177, 236
cleanse, 170
clear, 145, 146, 147, 158, 172,
    177, 178, 180, 196
clear away, 128
clear sky, 147
clear the throat, 77
clearly, 164
clever, 45, 141, 206, 223
cliff, 102
climb, 184

clip, 87
clock, 277
clogs, 100
close, 70, 98, 132, 140, 215, 265,
    278, 279
closet, 161
cloth, 104
clothes, 150, 242, 244
clothing, 243
clouds, 284
cloudy, 281
clown, 38
club, 157, 158
clue, 217
clumsy, 128, 209
coach, 51
coagulate, 57
coal, 182
coarse, 212
coconut, 158
cod, 295
coerce, 226, 265
coffin, 158
coffin with a corpse inside, 153
coin, 276
coincide, 209
cold, 57, 97, 172
collapse, 81, 83, 102, 288
collar, 287
colleague, 52
collect, 101, 114, 129, 139, 140,
    173, 223
collection, 234
college major, 213
collide, 137, 202
collude, 63
color, 231, 272, 288
column, 154
comb, 155
combine, 49, 70, 128
come, 47
comfortable, 120, 170, 185, 230,
    268
command, 43, 46
commander, 98
commander in chief, 105
commandment, 250
commission, 46
commit, 90
common, 48, 57, 108, 147
communicate, 266
companion, 45, 47, 68, 86, 150
company of soldiers, 44
compare, 98, 154, 165, 242, 262
compel, 265, 267
compensate, 257
compete, 208
compile, 216, 263
complain, 115
complete, 55, 72, 80, 95, 142,

    210, 300
completed, 95
completely, 117
complex, 244
complexion, 255
compliant, 287
complicated, 218
compose, 46, 97, 159, 216
compound, 244
compound word, 248
comprehend, 117, 122
conceal, 64, 235, 237, 282
conceal the truth, 199
conceive, 93
concentrate, 98, 169
concept, 160
concerned, 121
conch, 240
concubine, 88, 89
condition, 83, 117, 147, 169
condolences, 110
confer, 131
confess, 47, 127, 249
confide, 52
confidence, 48
confiscate, 126
confused, 113, 283
congratulate, 203, 256
conjecture, 107
connect, 132, 215, 266
connection, 213
conquer, 62
conscience, 243
consent, 224, 247
consider, 118, 271, 289
console, 120, 137
conspicuous, 234
constant, 116
constipation, 203
constitution, 122, 169
construct, 210, 266
consult, 75, 253
consume, 171
contact, 169
contain, 96, 197, 263
continent, 171
continue, 215, 218
continuing, 256
continuous, 266
contract, 88
contradictory, 101
contribute, 130
control, 132, 138, 210
convenience, 287
convenient, 47
conversation, 249, 251
converse, 141
convex, 58
convey, 268

desert, 176
desire, 120, 162
desk, 155, 162
desolate, 148, 172
destiny, 72
destroy, 128, 135, 164, 165, 175, 201
destroy by fire, 184
detain, 176
detect, 46
detective, 51
determination, 114
determine, 168
devalue, 256
develop, 279
develop photographs, 148
devil, 295
devise, 211
dew, 284
dexterous, 103
diagnose, 248
diarrhea, 179
dictionary, 55
die, 42, 65, 142, 164, 215, 266
die young, 87
difference, 103
different, 122, 164, 192
difficult, 79, 231, 283
dig, 59, 129, 131, 275
digest, 171
dignity, 90
dilemma, 113
diligent, 63
dim, 145, 146, 150
dime, 166, 246
diplomatic, 91
direct, 72, 79, 98, 141, 235
direction, 70, 143
directly, 266
director, 235
dirt, 84
dirty, 167, 293
disappear, 152
disappointed, 118, 121
disaster, 179, 204, 283
discard, 158
discharge, 67
disciple, 113
disclose, 141, 267, 284
discontinue, 143
discount, 126
discover, 246
discuss, 170, 250, 253, 273
discussion, 251
disease, 193
disgrace, 264
disguise, 126
disgust, 67
disgusting, 117
dish, 202

dislike, 67, 92, 121
dismiss, 136
disobey, 267
disorder, 41, 67
disordered, 294
disorderly, 214
dispatch, 268
display, 59, 139, 281
disposition, 115
dispute, 247, 264
dissect, 60
disseminate, 137
dissolve, 171, 175, 240
distance, 193, 283
distance from, 260
distant, 268-269
distinct, 180
distinguish, 59, 264
distinguished, 51, 53, 65, 164
distress, 117, 120, 283
distressed, 119, 271
distressing, 231, 264
distribute, 137, 144
district, 65, 82, 217, 269, 270
disturb, 70, 134, 137, 139, 140, 292
disturbance, 294
ditch, 81, 173, 175
dive, 177
diverging, 163
divide, 58, 61, 193, 280
divulge, 171
dizzy, 145
do, 46, 50, 106, 134, 184, 242
do not, 59, 63, 233
do one's best, 128
dock, 83, 178
doctor, 86, 272
document, 44, 149
dog, 187
dollar, 53, 80
donkey, 293
door, 124, 278
dormitory, 96
dot, 299
double, 49, 244, 283
doubt, 92, 118, 187, 193
dove, 296
down, 38
doze, 199
dozen, 125
draft, 139, 206
drag, 126, 127, 135, 149, 186
dragon, 300
drain, 173
draw, 127, 133, 149, 193, 218
draw back, 217
draw out, 132
drawer, 100
dread, 192

dream, 86
dredge, 137
dregs, 174, 175, 213
dress, 150, 244
dress up, 126, 212
dried meat, 228
drift, 171, 176
drifting, 234
drill, 138, 275, 278
drink, 76, 290
drip, 176
drive, 113, 242, 278, 292
drive away, 292
drop, 81, 132, 234
drops, 176, 299
drought, 145
drown, 168, 172, 175
drug, 165, 237
drum, 138, 299
drunk, 271
dry, 41, 180, 184
dry by the fire, 181
dry in the air, 147
dry in the sun, 148
dry weather, 145
duck, 296
duckweed, 234
dull, 72, 146, 152, 273
dumb, 75
dumpling, 290
duplicate, 244
durable, 82, 215
during, 281
dusk, 145, 148
dust, 84
duty, 44, 62, 205, 223
dwarf, 47, 53
dwelling, 291
dye, 154
dynasty, 43
dysentery, 194
each, 69, 165
each other, 41
eagle, 297
ear, 222
earlier, 60
early, 145
early age, 107
earn, 258
earnest, 165, 210, 271
earth, 80, 81, 85
earthen vessel, 219
earthenware, 190, 281
easily, 75
east, 152
easy, 145, 173
eat, 69, 289
eat until full, 290
eccentric, 53
economize, 137

edge, 217, 269
edge of a sword, 58
edition, 185
educated, 111
effect, 141, 191
egg, 66, 239
eggplant, 232
eight, 55, 130
eject, 78
elbow, 224
elect, 269
electrical, 284
electricity, 284
elegant, 48, 91, 111, 142, 204, 206, 217, 234, 282
elephant, 254
elevate, 229
elevated, 145
eliminate, 59, 171
embankment, 83
embarrassing, 99
embrace, 123, 128, 135, 138
embroider, 218
embryo, 225
emigrant, 52
emigrate, 52
eminent, 206
emotion, 118
emperor, 105, 196
empire, 80
employ, 52, 223
empty, 54, 97, 207, 238
enable, 50
enclosure, 80
encourage, 62, 63
end, 99, 152, 156, 159, 208, 215
end of a period, 148
end of a tree, 156
endure, 82, 96, 114, 182, 221
enemy, 43, 142, 204
energy, 61, 203, 225
engage, 223, 246
England, 232
English, 232
engrave, 60, 111, 283
enjoy, 42, 257
enlarge, 108, 139
enlist, 63
enormous, 103
enough, 86, 260
enrich, 177
enter, 55, 146, 267
enter abruptly, 279
entertain, 96, 162
enthusiastic, 120, 261
entice, 63
entire, 55, 192, 215
entirely, 49
entrance, 278
entrust, 79, 90, 125, 247

entwine, 218
environment, 72
envy, 89, 92
epidemic, 195
equal, 80, 209
equalize, 80
equally, 63
equip, 243
erect, 254
escape, 208, 265, 267
especially, 99
essay, 142, 208
establish, 109, 208, 219, 247
esteem, 99
estimate, 45, 107, 142, 174
eternal, 167
eulogize, 131, 253
Europe, 163
even, 87, 106, 283, 300
evening, 86, 147, 148
evenly, 63
event, 112
everlasting, 167
every, 57, 69, 165, 251
everywhere, 113
evidence, 252
evil, 58, 269
exactly, 116
exaggerate, 249
examination paper, 66
examine, 97, 153, 154, 161, 206, 221, 248, 277, 292
example, 47, 159
excavate, 129, 131
exceed, 259, 268
exceedingly, 149
excel, 259
excellent, 53
excessive, 168, 175, 197
exchange, 54, 133, 145
excite, 178
exclamation of surprise, 72
exclude, 280
excrement, 100
excuse, 116, 237, 250
exercise, 138
exhale, 72, 73
exhaust, 197
exhausted, 79, 194
exhibit, 100
exist, 80, 93
expand, 100, 139, 176
expanded, 228
expect, 150
expel, 136, 266, 292
expense, 140, 191, 256
expensive, 256
experience, 164, 292
experienced, 221
explain, 246, 272

explanation, 248
explode, 180, 184
expose, 148, 284
expose in the sun, 148
express, 126, 192
extend, 45, 192, 242
extensive, 148
exterior, 86
exterminate, 164, 175
extinguish, 175, 182
extravagant, 47, 88, 279
extreme, 53, 87, 197, 229, 271
extremely, 61, 149, 159, 194, 207, 215
exuberant, 232
eye, 198, 199
eyebrows, 198
fabric, 104, 105
face, 228, 229, 285, 288
faction, 171
factory, 108
fade, 57, 244
fading, 243
faint, 145, 147
fair, 55
faithful, 114
fake, 50, 52
fall, 84, 132, 204, 234, 260, 280, 281
fall down, 135
fall forward, 43
fall over, 49
false, 50, 247, 248, 252
fame, 70
familiar, 75, 183
family, 96, 144, 199
family surname, 166
famine, 291
famous, 223, 234
fan, 124, 135
fantasize, 106
fantasy, 106
far, 268, 269
farm, 46
fashion, 160
fast, 266, 291
fasten, 129, 214, 217, 218
fat, 224, 226, 227
fate, 72, 217, 268
father, 184, 185, 220
father-in-law, 55, 220
fatigued, 79
fault, 72, 99, 268
favor, 97, 116, 118
favorable, 287
fear, 115, 116, 120, 123, 124, 192
fearful, 119
feast, 96, 105, 210, 271
feather, 166, 220

hedgehog, 240
heel, 260
heifer, 186
hello, 76
helm, 230
help, 106, 134, 178
hemp, 298
hen, 283
her, 89
herd, 220
hero, 48, 51, 282
heroic, 232
hesitating, 113
hibernate, 241
hibiscus, 232, 236
hide, 44, 64, 82, 177, 199, 237, 262, 267, 282
high, 102, 293
highest, 288, 294
hill, 39, 101
hinder, 89, 202, 262, 280
hinge, 160
hire, 52, 282
historical, 69
history, 69, 164
hit, 125, 128
hoard, 79
hobby, 76
hoe, 275, 277
hold, 70, 82, 125, 129, 133, 136, 208
hold by both hands, 131
hold in the mouth, 70, 274
hold under the arm, 130
hold up, 140
hold with two fingers, 133
hole, 93, 170, 199, 206, 207
holiday, 50
hollow, 207
holy, 222
home, 96
honest, 108, 141, 210, 249
honey, 240
Hong Kong, 173
honor, 98, 159
honorable, 141
hoof, 261
hook, 63, 274
hope, 56, 104, 150, 198
horizontal, 161
horn, 246
horse, 291
host, 39
hot, 180, 183
hot weather, 147
hotel, 157
hour, 277, 299
house, 95, 100, 108, 124
house in the country, 84
household, 96, 124

hover, 221
how, 69, 115, 181, 191, 254
however, 45, 117, 181
howl, 74
hug, 138
huge, 103, 109, 274
hum, 248
humble, 65, 238, 252, 271, 280
humiliate, 47
hunchbacked, 292
hundred, 196
hundred million, 53
hunger, 290, 291
hunt, 46, 188
hurricane, 289
hurried, 48, 64, 114, 288
hurry, 259
hurt, 52, 96, 135
husband, 38, 85, 87, 92
hydrogen, 166
hypocritical, 52
I, 71, 73, 123
ice, 57
icy, 56
idea, 119
identical, 70
identification, 252
identify, 264
idle, 115, 119, 122, 172, 279
idol, 51
if, 50, 89, 232, 233, 245
illness, 116
illustration, 80
image, 52, 112
imaginary, 106
imitate, 44, 136, 141
imitate writing, 229
immature, 205
immediate, 208
immediately, 67
immerse, 171, 172
imminent, 265
immortal, 43
impart, 131
impeach, 71, 132
imperial, 162
imperial court, 150
implore, 203
important, 245, 272
important point, 160
impulse, 242
in, 80, 144
in addition, 56
in comparison, 262
in detail, 248
in front of, 60
in general, 160
in progress, 163
in style, 229
in touch, 218

incense, 291
inch, 70, 98
incite, 119
inclined, 50, 52
include, 63, 70, 129
income, 140
incorrect, 275
increase, 49, 62, 84, 173
indent, 58
indicate, 129
indifferent, 57, 172, 176
indignant, 122
indirect, 278
indistinct, 282
induce, 250
indulge, 175, 217
inexpensive, 47
infant, 93
infatuated, 271
infect, 51, 154
inferior, 62, 65, 162
inflate, 227
influence, 118
inform, 45, 82, 248
infuse, 168
inhale, 71
injure, 52, 135
injustice, 96
inlay, 102, 278
inn, 157
inner, 243
inquire, 75, 167, 248, 249
insane, 195
inscription, 274
insect, 241
insects, 145
insert, 133
inside, 55, 243
inspect, 97, 279, 292
instant, 199
instigate, 121
instruct, 247
instructor, 105
instrument, 53
insult, 47, 264
intelligence, 121
intelligent, 121
intend, 139
intention, 114
intercept, 124
interest, 59, 116, 229, 259
interesting, 259
interfere, 106
interpret, 253
interrogate, 249
interrupt, 133
intersection, 101
intestines, 227
intimate, 96, 148
intimidate, 74, 130

monkey, 188
monopolize, 85, 140
month, 149
monument, 202
mood, 114
moon, 149
morality, 114
more, 119, 149, 269
moreover, 38, 39, 149, 221
morning, 145, 147, 150
mortgage, 127
mosquito, 239
moss, 232
most, 149, 159
moth, 239
moth-eaten, 239
mother, 91, 92, 165
mother-in-law, 91
motherly, 120
motion, 62, 229
motive, 114
mound, 102, 270
mound of earth, 279
mountain, 101
mountain pass, 102
mountain range, 102
mountain top, 103
mourn, 77
mourning, 76
mouth, 68, 73, 78
move, 62, 113, 129, 135, 136,
    205, 236, 250, 268
moved, 138
movie, 112, 185
Mr., 71
Mrs., 87
much, 86, 247
mucous, 171
mud, 170
muddy, 170, 172, 173, 178
mulberry tree, 155
mule, 292
multiply, 40
murder a superior, 110
muscle, 224, 289
mushroom, 234
music, 160
must, 113, 114, 287
mustache, 294
mustard greens, 232
mute, 75
mutual, 198
my, 71
mysterious, 88, 203
nag, 79
nail, 273
naked, 244, 258
name, 69, 70, 72, 90, 238, 288
nap, 199, 242, 246
napkin, 104

narrow, 187, 207, 280
native town, 211
natural, 229
nature, 115
naughty, 287
navel, 228
navigate, 230
near, 130, 256, 265, 285
neat, 142
necessity, 284
neck, 226, 288
nectar, 240
need, 245, 284
needle, 273
needy, 255
negative, 255
neglect, 114, 115
neglectful, 177
negligent, 120
negotiate, 253
neighbor, 270
neighborhood, 272
nephew, 91, 191
nervous, 120
nest, 103, 207
net, 216, 219
net amount, 172
net weight, 172
network, 216
nevertheless, 66
new, 143, 295
news, 116, 222, 223, 286
newspaper, 82
next, 162, 221
nickname, 216
niece, 91, 191
night, 86
nightingale, 297
nine, 40
no, 38, 285
nobility, 184
noble, 120, 256, 293
nod, 299
node, 210
noise, 296
noisy, 70, 76, 294
none, 181
noodles, 298
noon, 65
north, 64
nose, 299
not, 38, 71, 233, 285
not yet, 150, 168
note, 58, 210
note-paper, 210
notice, 159
notify, 266
nourish, 82, 224, 290
now, 189, 233
nuclear, 154

numb, 298
number, 142, 202, 238
numbness, 194
numerous, 196, 218, 234
nun, 99
nurture, 137
nutrition, 183
o'clock, 146
oak tree, 161
oar, 160
oath, 197, 249
obedient, 40, 150
obey, 47, 113, 223, 269
object, 126, 186
obscene, 172
obscure, 146
observe, 97, 246
obstinate, 287
obstruct, 82, 133, 138, 139, 202,
    280
obstruction, 129, 281
obtain, 188
occupation, 158, 223, 242
occupied, 114
occupy, 138
ocean, 170
odd, 87
of, 40
offend, 56, 137, 187, 219, 287
offer, 47, 72, 87, 188
office, 95, 238
officer, 85, 95
official, 95, 149
offspring, 243
often, 101
oil, 169
oily, 228
ointment, 227
old, 68, 221, 230, 281
old lady, 91·
old man, 55, 220
older, 86, 278
oldest, 94
omen, 54, 190
on, 80, 144
on duty, 49
one, 38, 85, 282
one by one, 266
oneself, 104
onion, 235
only, 52, 69, 75, 99, 117, 188
only if, 125
open, 75, 110, 141, 278, 279
open the eyes, 199
opening, 68, 170, 207
opera, 61
opinion, 119, 245
opportunity, 63, 160, 281
oppose, 68, 98, 126, 265
opposite, 68

race, 144, 206, 258
radar, 284
ragged, 245
rail, 262
railing, 162
rain, 283
rain falling heavily, 177
rainbow, 239
raise, 127, 131, 133, 134, 138, 280, 290
raise funds, 63
raise head, 44
raise or feed animals, 192
raised, 281
rake, 152, 222
ramble, 267
rampart, 85
random, 225
rank, 73, 132, 209, 214, 274
rape, 90
rapid, 115
rare, 219
rash, 193
rat, 222, 299
rate, 189
rather, 97
ratio, 189
ration, 59
ravine, 253
ravioli, 290
raw, 191
reach, 68, 100, 229, 249, 267
reaching, 81
read, 253, 279
real, 97, 198
reason, 79, 140, 189, 192, 208, 217
rebel, 68, 265
recall, 122
receipt, 138
receive, 68, 126, 132, 140, 214, 265, 287
recently, 60
reciprocal, 198
reciprocate, 82
recite, 250
recite a poem, 71
recognize, 249, 252
recommend, 237
record, 155, 161, 185, 195, 213, 247, 250, 263, 275
recover, 113, 116
recovered, 194
red, 39, 151, 213, 258
redeem, 258
reduce, 174, 217
reed, 211, 235
reeds, 232
refine, 182, 276
refined, 93, 107, 111, 212, 282

reflect, 146, 277
refrain from speaking, 78
refreshed, 185
refuse, 66, 127, 131, 264
region, 82, 83, 103
register, 131, 195, 248
regret, 117, 118, 122, 123
regretful, 122, 162
regular, 105
regulate, 59, 137, 273
regulation, 47, 245
reiterate, 69
reject, 127, 291
relation, 48
relationship, 49
relative, 124
relatives, 199, 246
relax, 110
relaxing, 294
release, 140, 246, 272
religion, 141
rely on, 43, 47, 49, 237, 258, 285
remain, 192, 266
remainder, 290
remark, 248
remarkable, 87
remember, 122, 247
remember forever, 274
remit, 174
remote, 268, 269
remove, 136, 285
rent, 205, 282
repair, 48, 244
repay, 53, 271
repent, 117, 123
replace, 149
reply, 79, 122, 209, 245
report, 275
represent, 43
repress, 85, 126, 277
reputation, 150, 223, 253
request, 167
require, 284
rescue, 130, 134, 141
research, 201
resemble, 45, 52
resembling, 112
resentment, 116, 120
reserve, 192
reside, 46, 100
residence, 94, 100, 107, 230
resign, 264
resist, 126, 127, 138, 204
respect, 44, 46, 98, 102, 116, 124, 141, 162
respectful, 252
responsibility, 62, 255
rest, 44, 116, 162
restaurant, 291
restore, 116

restrain, 59, 126, 151, 213
restraint, 127
restrict, 127, 280
results, 153
retreat, 265
return, 79, 113, 144, 164, 265, 269
return something, 259
reverential, 223
reverse, 221
review, 174, 244
revive, 237
revolt, 68, 285
revolve, 267
revolving, 265
reward, 88, 257, 271
rhyme, 286
rhythm, 128
rib, 226
rice, 206, 212, 290
rice dumpling wrapped in leaves, 212
rice gruel, 212
rice shoot, 205
rich, 96, 178
riddle, 251
ride, 81, 135, 292
ride in a vehicle, 40
ridge, 155, 159, 225
ridge of a hill, 102
ridicule, 133, 251, 252
rifle, 159
right, 162
right side, 69
righteousness, 220
ring, 190
rinse, 177
riot, 292
ripe, 183
rise, 65, 145, 146, 176, 259, 280
rising sun, 145
risk, 56
river, 167, 169
river bank, 171
road, 260, 266, 268
roar, 71, 74
roast, 180, 181, 183
rob, 62, 132, 135, 197
robber, 64, 96, 197
robe, 243
rock, 101, 201, 236
rod, 156, 208
roll, 66, 105, 132, 263
roll about, 177
roll around, 144
roll between hands, 134
roll over, 263
roll up, 132
room, 95, 100, 108, 124
roost, 158

rooster, 283
root, 150, 155
rope, 214, 218
rose, 189, 190
rotate, 263
rotten, 151, 184, 226
rough, 102, 110, 178, 212
round, 79, 80, 259, 268
round up, 54
rouse, 299
row, 39, 59, 132, 242
row a boat, 59
rub, 128, 129, 134, 136, 139
rub on, 135
rub the hands, 134
rubber, 161, 227
rudder, 230
rude, 50
rug, 166
rugged, 102
ruin, 85, 141, 164, 165, 261
ruined, 71, 85, 108
ruined place, 84
rule, 60, 200, 208, 215, 245
ruler, 99, 189, 200
rules, 112
rumor, 252
run, 87, 259, 260, 292
run away, 267
run into, 202
rush against, 242
rush at, 168
rush in, 279
Russia, 48
rust, 275
sable, 254
sack, 54, 79
sacrifice, 186, 203
sad, 117, 118, 119, 120, 121,
   124, 294
saddle, 286
safe, 95
sage, 222
sail, 104, 211, 230, 292
salary, 112, 236
saliva, 75, 170, 172
salt, 272, 297
salted beans, 254
salty, 297
salute, 134
sample, 76
sand, 168
sandalwood, 161
satire, 251
satirize, 252
satisfied, 176, 260, 290
sauce, 272
sauce pan, 276
saucer, 202
save, 53, 93, 130, 140, 141, 198,

235, 256
saw, 275
say, 41, 149, 249, 251, 252, 268
scab, 195
scale, 205
scales of a fish, 296
scar, 194
scarce, 104, 219
scatter, 137, 141
scattered, 205
scene in a play, 300
scenery, 147
scheme, 209, 251
scholar, 43, 53, 85
school, 84, 154
science, 189, 205
scissors, 61
scold, 72, 143, 219
scoop, 129
scope, 210
scorched, 181
scrape, 59
scratch, 125, 135
scratch lightly, 137
screen, 100, 105, 211
scrub, 60
scythe, 277
sea, 171
seagull, 297
seal, 66, 98, 124, 208
search, 98, 132, 134
season, 94, 146
seat, 45, 107
secluded, 53
second, 42, 61, 162
second of time, 205
secret, 96, 147, 203
secretary, 203
secretly, 177, 204
section, 164, 215, 270
secure, 89, 95, 206
sedan chair, 263
sediment, 174, 175, 213
see, 150, 198, 245, 246
seed, 206
seedling, 205
seek, 126
seize, 46, 88, 125, 138, 267
select, 128, 130, 133
self, 229
self-discipline, 138
selfish, 204
sell, 75, 170, 255, 257, 275
sell wholesale, 126
semen, 212
send, 96, 103, 130, 266, 268
send back, 164
send out, 196
senior, 94
sentence, 68

separate, 59, 281, 283
sequence, 205, 209
series, 88
serpent, 239
servant, 38, 51, 52, 112
serve, 47
serve as, 54
service, 112
set, 88
set free, 140
set time, 150
set up, 247
seven, 38, 170
sever, 143
several, 107, 142
severe, 67, 78, 102
sew, 214, 217
sew by machine, 262
sex, 115
shade, 219, 236, 281
shadow, 112
shady, 236
shake, 127, 130, 133, 134, 284
shake off, 128
shall, 98
shallow, 173
shame, 116
shameful, 116, 272
shape, 111, 160, 187
share, 45, 139
share of stock, 224
shark, 295
sharp, 59, 99, 274, 275
sharp edge, 275
sharp point of grass, 231
sharpen, 60
shave, 59, 60
she, 44, 89, 112
shed, 157
shed skin, 240
sheep, 220
sheet, 110, 287
shelf, 154
shell, 165, 255
shelter, 100, 107
shepherd, 186
shield, 198
shift, 113, 129
shin, 226
shine, 146
shine at, 182
shine on, 221
ship, 230, 231
shirt, 243
shiver, 77, 78, 289
shivering, 57
shoes, 101, 286
shoot, 98, 232
shoot out, 168
shop, 107

shore, 101, 173, 179
short, 200, 201
short of, 162, 219
short time, 148
short-tempered, 261
shortcoming, 200
should, 122, 193, 245, 249
shoulder, 227
shoulders, 225
shout, 69, 70, 76, 79
shovel, 277
show, 111, 139, 144, 203, 229,
242, 250, 289
show a movie, 146
shower, 173
shrewd, 212
shrimp, 240
shrink, 217
shut, 132, 278
shuttle, 156
shy, 220
sick, 194
sickle, 277
sickness, 116, 193, 194
side, 144, 269, 285
side by side, 39
side of, 50
sigh, 77, 163
sight, 246
sign, 160, 185, 211, 219, 238
silent, 96, 299
silk, 105, 215, 216
silkworm, 241
sill, 154
silly, 52
silver, 274
silver color, 274
similar, 45
simple, 161, 173, 211, 214
simply, 69
since, 144, 229
sincere, 97, 114, 122, 198, 210,
214, 238, 249
sincerity, 243
sing, 75, 163, 248
single, 75, 93, 188, 282
sink, 84, 168, 281, 288
sir, 71
sister, 90
sister-in-law, 89, 92
sit, 81
situation, 63
six, 55, 281
size, 238
skate, 175
skeleton, 293
sketch, 133
ski, 175
skill, 126, 237, 242
skillful, 75, 103

skin, 196, 228
skirt, 244
sky, 87, 207
slack season, 172
slander, 165, 248, 251, 252
slanting, 143, 163
slap, 136
slap on and spread, 128
slaughter, 61, 100
slave, 88, 282
slave girl, 91
sleep, 97, 198, 199, 228, 246
sleeve, 243
slice, 185
slide, 175
slightly, 205
slip, 175
slip away, 226
slippery, 175
slope, 81
slow, 112, 120, 217
sluggish, 119
small, 99, 113, 142, 166, 173,
215, 241
small birds, 282
small clam, 239
small cup, 197
small island, 102
small light, 170
small table, 57
smallpox, 194
smear, 83
smell, 72, 77, 223
smells good, 291
smelt, 57, 182, 275
smile, 209
smoke, 180, 182
smooth, 175
smoothly, 287
smother, 207
snail, 240
snake, 239
snatch, 135
sneaky, 58, 187, 188
sneeze, 78
snore, 299
snow, 283
soak, 171, 176
soak through, 176
soap, 196
soar, 221
society, 203
socks, 245
soft, 153, 216, 262
soft leather, 286
soil, 80, 85, 170
solder, 275
soldier, 55, 65, 85
sole, 75
solemn, 90, 223, 233

solicit, 54
solid, 97
somber, 157
some, 107, 153
somewhat, 287
son, 43, 54, 93, 192
son-in-law, 85, 92
song, 149, 163
soon, 98
sorrow, 73, 120, 124
sorrowful, 117, 120, 121, 172
sorry, 162
sort, 165, 288
soul, 285, 294, 295
sound, 89, 223, 286
soup, 174, 220
sour, 271
source, 175
south, 66
space, 207, 278
spacious, 141, 216
spade, 60, 275, 276, 277
spare, 198, 292
sparrow, 282
sparse, 193, 205
speak, 149, 246, 249, 252
spear, 159, 200
special, 98, 164, 186, 192
specify, 160
speech, 246, 249
speed, 266
speedy, 266
spell, 128
spend, 191, 222, 256
sphere, 189
spicy hot, 264
spider, 239
spike, 206
spin, 139
spin cloth, 214
spirit, 203, 212, 285, 294, 295
spit, 70, 75
spittoon, 197
splash, 177
spleen, 226
splendid, 89, 263
split, 243
split open, 61
spoil, 97
spoiled, 184, 226
spoon, 64
spot, 142
spout, 174
spray, 78
spread, 45, 51, 100, 128, 133,
137, 139, 141, 230, 242, 275
spread out, 128
spread seed and fertilizer, 222
spring, 168, 211
spring season, 146

sprinkle, 170, 179
sprout, 174, 196, 232
spy, 51, 207, 251
square, 143
squash, 190
squat down, 261
squeeze, 133, 135, 138, 159
squirrel, 299
squirt, 78, 98
stab, 60, 124
stable, 206
stage, 69, 162, 229
stain, 167, 176
stairs, 156, 281
stake, 160
stalk, 156, 205
stall, 139
stamp, 124, 236
stamp foot, 287
stand, 44, 107, 208
standard, 175, 205
star, 146
stare, 200
start, 61, 75, 90, 196, 259
startled, 119, 292
starving, 290
state, 103, 265, 270, 281
state freely, 126
statement, 264
statesman, 228
station, 208, 292
statistics, 215
stay, 192, 292
stay at, 96, 158, 214
steal, 51, 208
steam, 168, 235
steel, 274, 276
steelyard, 205
steep, 102
stem of a flower, 156
stem of a plant, 233
step, 214
step upon, 261
stern, 157
stew, 183
stick, 156, 158, 208, 256
stick for fortune telling, 66
stiff, 201
stiffen, 130
still, 40, 43, 99, 188, 269
stimulate, 130, 178
sting, 60, 69
stir, 127, 140
stir up, 131, 137
stockings, 245
stomach, 224, 225
stone, 201
stone house, 201
stool, 58, 161
stoop, 100

stop, 44, 46, 50, 97, 128, 116, 151, 162, 163, 203, 207
stopped, 104
storage bin, 79
store, 53, 107, 140, 223, 237, 275
store up, 101, 206, 256
storehouse, 108, 157
story, 101
stove, 180, 184
straight, 198, 208
straighten, 130, 201
straightforward, 115, 185, 189, 198, 222
strain, 179
strange, 87, 115, 192
straw, 205, 233
stream, 103, 175
street, 81, 242
street song, 252
strength, 61, 62, 63
strengthen, 85, 286
stretch, 45, 110, 139
strict, 67, 78
strike, 125, 132, 134, 136, 138, 165
string, 39, 218
string of a bow, 110
string of a musical instrument, 110
strip, 60, 156
stripe, 142, 214
strive, 62, 88, 184, 208
stroke, 193
stroll, 261, 267
strong, 50, 60, 79, 82, 85, 110, 201, 215, 282
strong point, 278
struggle, 88, 132, 294
stubborn, 50, 79, 119, 139
studies, 205
study, 48, 94, 201, 207, 253
stuff, 83
stumble, 260
stupid, 119, 209, 241
style, 109, 160, 162, 183, 293
stylish, 146
subject, 288
subject to, 101
subordinate, 282
subscribe, 246
substance, 186, 257
substitute, 43, 149
subtract, 174
suburbs, 270
subway, 282
succeed, 123, 218
success, 99, 267
successful, 123
such, 143, 298
suck, 71, 77

sudden, 148
suddenly, 40, 62, 115, 207, 287, 293
suds, 168, 169
suffering, 158
suffocating, 118
sugar, 213
suggest, 109, 133
suit of clothes, 245
suitable, 95, 193, 206, 268, 271
sultry, 118
sum up, 160
summary, 192
summer, 86, 147
summon, 69
sun, 144, 281
sunset, 86
superficial, 228
superior, 254
superstitious, 265
supervise, 197, 199
supply, 47, 215
support, 126, 129, 131, 137, 140, 258
support by the head, 287
support with the hand, 125
suppose, 50
suppress, 63, 85
surprised, 247, 249
surely, 114
surface, 242, 285
surging, 168
surname, 90
surpass, 259
surplus, 290
surrender, 280
surround, 80, 190, 218
surrounded, 79
suspect, 92, 193
suspend, 122
suspicion, 118
swallow, 71, 78, 183
swamp, 207
swear, 72, 197, 249
sweat, 167
sweep, 131
sweet, 191
sweet potato, 237
swell, 176, 227
swift, 141, 265, 266
swim, 169, 174
swimming, 169
swindle, 128
swing, 134, 139
switch, 133, 250
swollen, 228
sword, 58, 61
symbol, 114, 209
sympathize, 116, 117, 121
system, 213

Now Available ...

Audio Tapes
for

Read And Write Chinese
A Guide to the Chinese Characters

- Guide to Pronunciation
- Tone Chart
- Pronunciation for 3,210 Characters
- 3 Tape Set - 210 minutes

$25 - Please specify Cantonese or Mandarin

Understanding Chinese
A Guide to the Usage of Chinese Characters

- Guide to Pronunciation and Tone Chart
- Everyday Short Phrases
- Character Combinations by Subject with Definitions
- 2 Tape Set - 144 minutes

$17 - Please specify Cantonese or Mandarin

Companion audio cassette tapes for the books **Read And Write Chinese** and **Understanding Chinese** are now available. Recorded by native speakers, these tapes demonstrate proper pronunciation of the characters and phrases found in the books.

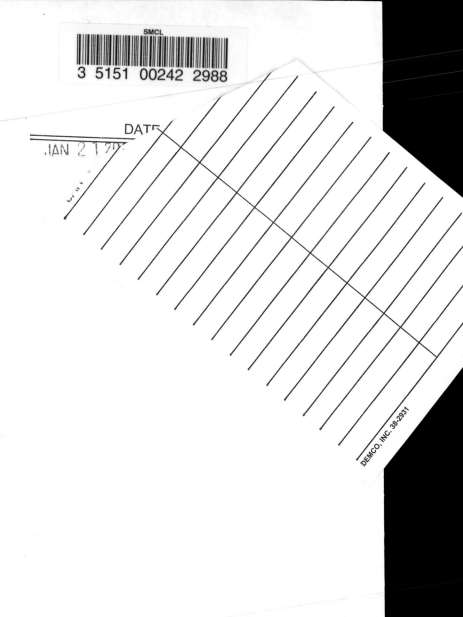

DATE

JAN 2 1

DEMCO, INC. 38-2931